D0835055

Longing for Belonging:

Pilgrimage of Transformation

Diane Zimberoff, M.A.

WELLNESS PRESS ISSAQUAH, WA

Published by

Wellness Press
The Wellness Institute
Issaquah, WA
1-800-326-4418

ISBN 978-0-9622728-6-8

Table of Contents

FOREWORD

This book is the story of one woman's yearning for God, and at the same time it illuminates the universal relentless longing of all human beings for connection with their Source. I am reminded of three poetic statements of that yearning, one from the Muslim tradition, one from Judaic, and one from Christian.

Eight hundred years ago, the Sufi mystic Rumi wrote the poem *Love Dogs*[1]:

One night a man was crying,
>   *Allah*! *Allah*!
His lips grew sweet with the praising,
Until a cynic said,
>   "So! I have heard you
calling out, but have you ever
gotten a response?"

The man had no answer to that.
He quit praying and fell into a confused sleep.

He dreamed he saw Khidr, the guide of souls,
In a thick, green foliage.
>   "Why did you stop praising?"
"Because I've never heard anything back."
>   "This longing
you express *is* the return message."

The grief you cry out from
Draws you toward union.

Your pure sadness
That wants help
Is the secret cup.

Listen to the moan of a dog for its master.
That whining is the connection.

There are love dogs
No one knows the names of.

Give your life
To be one of them.

Ultimately, we all give our lives to be something, and we all cry out from grief. To what end? Union, or exile? Another approach to exploring and understanding this human dilemma is presented by Rabbi DovBer, Maggid of Mezritch (?-1772), in the following well-known analogy.[2]

> The human experience of exile is comparable to a father who conceals himself from his son. Not that the father does not want to be together with his son, but rather the purpose of the concealment is to awaken within the son a desire and yearning to find his father. After all, when the son is constantly in the presence of his father, his desire to be with his father is not revealed, for "continuous pleasure is not pleasure."
>
> There arises a situation, however, when the son ceases searching for the Father. He claims that "the signs of our redemption we have not seen, and there is none among us who know how long" (Psalms 74:9). He, therefore, concludes that G-d must have forsaken us and he loses hope and discontinues his search for G-d. When the Father sees that the son is no longer seeking him, *then* the exile truly begins. As long as the son is searching for the Father, this constitutes a preparation, a beginning, and a spark of the redemption -- for the search for Redemption is what is occupying the son.
>
> Therefore we must increase in light, and not just any light, but specifically the light of *simcha* (joyousness). Since *simcha* "breaks all boundaries and limitations," it breaks through the person's limitations, the limitations of this world, and the limitations imposed by this dreadful darkness.

Union, or exile? We live on the verge of eternity, and every moment brings a new opportunity to choose. Jesus captured the universal law in this way: "Blessed are they which do hunger and thirst after righteousness: for they shall be filled" (Matthew 5:6). Those who yearn for spiritual unfoldment and growth in their connection with God will attain it, *as long as* they continue to be focused on satisfying this compelling hunger rather than squandering the opportunity by falling into distractions. Emmet Fox[3] (1886-1951) summarizes this beatitude:

> provided we are truly wholehearted in our efforts, provided, that is to say, that we really are *hungering and thirsting for righteousness*, then, at last, we shall surely be filled. It could not happen that a wholehearted search for truth and righteousness, if persevered in, should not be crowned with success. God is not mocked, nor does He mock his children.

David Hartman
Spring Equinox, March 20, 2008

Chapter 1
Waking Up to Personal Transformation

We've all come to this earth for two reasons. One is to experience certain lessons that our souls need to develop. To accomplish this, we take on a personality and choose a family and life experiences that will provide those lessons for us. But it's only through awareness, consciousness, and constant vigilance that we can perceive what these soul lessons are. We must be able to see beyond the personality and the drama that it creates to fully understand what all the pain is about.

The second reason is to address any "unfinished business." The universe doesn't make social promotions like some schools do, where students are passed to the next level even though they're not ready to move on. We need to digest our experiences fully or the undigested remnants remain, usually giving us a kind of soul heartburn. That means that any experience we have ever had that is not yet fully integrated requires attention sooner or later. Ignoring or denying or repressing it only delays an ultimate resolution.

We experience these lessons whether we're conscious of our reasons for being here or not. In our day, however, many people are beginning to awaken to their reasons for being here, and you can see this when they begin really seeking out God and trying to connect with their souls in order to correct their mode of living. This is when they understand that, the sooner they grasp the lesson, the sooner they are truly free.

My own longing for God and a spiritual connection began when I was very young. I remember asking my parents to take me to temple and Sunday school, but when they did, I was disappointed. Today, I know why. I was searching for a spiritual connection, and I just couldn't find that there. I soon became disillusioned with all the hypocrisy that I saw. Going to temple seemed more like a social experience than a spiritual one. My father tried to convey as much as he could to me of his love and connection with the Jewish faith. But it just didn't seem to touch my spirit.

There was something else, though, that did.

Note to the reader: throughout the book I have adopted the convention of using the pronouns "he" and "she" arbitrarily, approximately equally. And I have substituted pseudo names for all the real people I have discussed to illustrate my points in order to protect their privacy.

I have included at the conclusion of each chapter a personal questionnaire that will, hopefully, help you to apply the lessons I am sharing to your own life.

I always had a penchant for listening to people's problems, and my heart longed for the connection I felt when my friends shared their deepest feelings with me. I remember my mother commenting to me in junior high school about how much time I spent listening to the problems of my friends. It seems as though I was always the person that others came to with their stories of being mistreated by their parents or secretly fondled by their fathers or brothers. I never tired of giving advice and attempting to find solutions to help them ease their pain. Of course during this time, I had no idea how my life would unfold and what an important indication this was regarding my life's purpose.

When we look back on our lives, though, we can see that the things we're inexorably attracted to give us clues about who we really are and what our life is all about. As my place in this world involves therapeutic counseling, those early days could have been a substantial clue if I knew then how to reflect on them. And for those who are raising children today, it is in fact a critical part of that role to observe their children so as to help them find clarity about their life purposes as early as possible. Actually, many children *do* have this clarity, and part of observing is simply to listen and hear what our children are telling us about who they are. Unfortunately, many parents before the 1980s did not really know how to listen and acknowledge children for who they are. Thank God things are changing.

I continued to be an "amateur therapist" for my friends all through high school and college. But while I was counseling others, I still had no clue about what to major in until one day, as I looked through the college catalogue, I came across "criminology" in the sociology department. The classes were about prisons and prison systems. I had no idea why that caught my attention, but I was fascinated by it. From that day on, I was totally motivated in my studies and took all the abnormal psychology and sociology classes I could.

My first job was in a correctional facility for young women, and I immediately connected with the prisoners and with the correctional staff. I was fascinated with the relationships between the prisoners and the guards. I spent a good deal of off-duty time studying those relationships.

While on duty, I was a counselor and learned more from the young women about gangs, abuse, violence, abandonment, and courage than I could ever have learned elsewhere. I learned about life from them and about the incredible struggle for survival that my middle class Jewish upbringing never taught me. They showed me what it was like to live on the streets at the age of twelve or to have stepfathers who sexually abused them. They showed me why many of them turned to each other to meet their sexual and emotional needs. Later, it would become clear to me how these experiences were important to me in terms of my existential issues, and I would see the purpose for attracting them into my life.

While in this job, I felt very connected to the black people that I met at the prison and remembered that, in high school, I was attracted to a black basketball player who sat behind me in geometry. He introduced me to jazz and folk music and we spent a lot of time together. I was also attracted to African drumming and all the music that he listened to. We eventually became lovers, which was definitely unacceptable in 1958 in the white suburbs of Chicago. It was another one of those experiences that would later help me to better understand myself and my purpose.

After college, I married the man my parents liked and lived a life of quiet desperation for several years. During this time — the early 1960s — I was drawn to helping blacks in their struggle and persuaded my husband to move to Mississippi so that I could engage in civil rights work there. I became very active in that movement and again connected with the black people in their struggle for real freedom. I was literally risking my life every day there to teach people about their rights and to teach them how to take their power. I never understood why I was so driven to "fight" for the underdog, but it felt like a deep calling. This desire to help the underdog later turned to helping the women's movement. I began to feel that same driving passion to educate and "free" women from their oppression. For a while, men became the enemy and women were the focus of my world. I even began to have romantic relationships with women, and had the strange experience of feeling that I knew the competition and lust and protective instinct that men felt inside toward women. When I later began to experience past life regressions, this experience came into focus in relation to my past life as a man on a ship.

Eventually, I left my secure but lifeless marriage and began traveling around the world. I knew that there was something out there that was much more fulfilling, but I had no idea what it was or where I should look. I was on a search so deep that I could not even put it into words yet. I found myself drawn to many things, though I didn't know why. It felt as if my life was a great mystery that was being revealed to me day by day.

For some reason, I found myself reading many books about meditation and felt that I should study yoga. One day, a friend of mine began telling me about a spiritual master from India who had come to this country. She brought me to meet Baba Muktananda, and suddenly I felt like I had "come home." The music, the people, and the spirituality really touched my heart and soul. I didn't want to ever leave. Meditation became a part of my everyday life, and chanting took me to states of ecstasy that I had never before experienced. Through meditation, I began to see things more clearly. I gave up both alcohol and marijuana, which had clouded my thinking for years. The "high" that I was experiencing spiritually was much better than anything that had been chemically induced. And a line that Ram Dass (Dr. Richard Alpert) wrote seemed to wake me up. He said it is much better to "be high" than to "get high." I finally got what he meant.

Mid-Life Transformation

It seemed that I was moving out of the arena of politics and moving into the world of spiritual seeking. I was searching for the meaning of life. Of *my* life. This was the beginning of what many people refer to as the mid-life crisis, but which I call "mid-life transformation." It is a time when people traditionally begin questioning their lives up to that point and looking for new meaning.

For my own search, I found myself leaving a successful, private psychotherapy practice, allowing my ex-husband to have temporary custody of my daughter, and giving up most of my worldly possessions to begin traveling around the world. As I look back on that time, it is one of the most courageous and exciting times of my life. I can't imagine doing anything like that now, but at that time it was exactly what I needed to do.

Inside, I was discovering a fine line between excitement and fear. I was terrified to leave my secure life in order to go out into the world in search of adventure and meaning. I wasn't even sure what I was looking for … but I knew it must be out there somewhere. The undeniable force that drove me would take many years, many experiences, and a greatly expanded consciousness to understand.

As I followed my inner guidance, I found myself attracted to ocean liners and traveling on the sea. This was a little strange, since I had never been on an ocean liner and wasn't aware of any reason to be drawn to this. But as I began traveling this way, I found that each day I was more and more driven to get my seaman's papers so that I could work on a ship — a rather bizarre shift from a career in psychotherapy. It wasn't an easy thing to pursue. It was the old catch-22 of job seekers everywhere: you couldn't get your seaman's papers unless you had a job, and you couldn't get a job on a ship unless you first had your papers. I spent months trying to overcome what seemed to be a closed industry.

After much perseverance and some amazing connections with people, I finally got my seaman's papers and landed a job on a large ocean liner.

Again, this was an experience that would take me time to understand. Why would I be attracted to working on ships and traveling on the sea? To my surprise, though, I found that I was immediately comfortable on the ship. It felt familiar to me. I had what they called "sea legs," and was able to carry large trays of food with complete balance even during storms. The old-time waitresses on board the ship were amazed that I caught on so quickly.

While on the ship, I met many people who felt familiar to me, as if I had known them before. They felt the same way about me, which seemed strange since they had been at sea most of their lives. Many aspects of life on the ship felt so familiar to me that I began to marvel at the whole experience.

One night I was out on the deck just watching the stars when I had a strange experience. It was as if another lifetime was flashing before my eyes. I began to relive an experience of being a seaman who ended up on a sinking ship. I had been very much in love with a young woman on board, who became separated from me during the frenzy of the event. I ran around trying to find her and I finally did connect with her just when we realized that we were going to drown. That night, I experienced the sinking of the ship, the water coming in, and the exact feeling of drowning. I knew that she and I went down together totally connected by our love. I came out of what I would later recognize as a past-life memory as a man, feeling very curious about the meaning of it all.

It was not until twenty years later when I saw the movie *Titanic* with my daughter that I fully understood my strong pull to complete the "unfinished business" I had with the sea and why my daughter and I always felt so connected to each other, more like old friends. We both had very strong reactions to the movie, and for the first time she told me that she knew she had been on the *Titanic* when it sank. I was shocked, because she and I had never talked about that connection before. I know that humans often come back into lifetimes with people with whom they have past-life connections, but this was the first time we acknowledged this link between us.

I have spent many other nights — as well as several hypnotherapy sessions — where I would again experience the sinking ship and more pieces of this "past life" puzzle would come to me. I felt connected with the seaman who was so obsessed with the relationship that was lost through the disaster. Could this woman I lost through drowning have come back as my daughter in this lifetime? Through these reflections and this hypnotherapy work, the drive to get my seaman's papers and work on a ship made more sense to me. My time in the women's movement also became clearer to me since, in that life, I had been in the body of a man and had felt all the feelings of protectiveness so normal to most men.

The Spiritual Search Continues

During this time, I spent years reading spiritual books concerning meditation practices. I was fascinated by several of the masters living in India who were becoming known to Westerners. I had connected with Muktananda and had been living with him in his Oakland ashram before shipping out from San Francisco. After making my peace with the sea, I found myself returning to land and seeking to reconnect with Baba Muktananda. I also wanted to meet some of the other spiritual Masters that I had read about, like Sai Baba and a female saint name Anandamayi Ma. In the months that followed, I started wanting to travel to India and to learn more about the connection I felt to that culture. Before long, I was on my way.

While in India, I felt as though I had come home to a land, a culture, and a people that I knew. And while there, I must have had a sign tattooed across my forehead that said, "spiritual seeker." Everywhere I went, I was attracting people who would invite me to come and have the *darshan* (spiritual blessing) of a saint that just "happened" to be in the area. Each one of these meetings with saints and spiritual masters was amazing. I have a high regard for the teachings and blessings that they gave me, though it would be twenty years before I fully realized the meaning of all these serendipitous meetings.

That meaning became clear, in fact, through past life work later on. I had the experience of being born in India to some very poor but very spiritual parents. One of my uncles began to realize that I had some natural spiritual gifts and thus asked my parents if he could take me to visit some saints. We spent many months traveling from village to village receiving blessings and teachings from saints and spiritual masters. They told my uncle to continue my training because of the gift of healing. One day we were attempting to cross the Ganges River on a flat boat when a storm came up. We were tossed into the Ganges and thus my mission in that life was interrupted, again by a drowning.

In any case, after several months in India, I finally realized that I was on a spiritual quest. It felt as though I were making a pilgrimage to the Holy Land, that I was metaphysically in search of Mecca or the Promised Land. Actually, I was in search of the meaning of God and the meaning of life. Each day, I became more aware of the depth of my search. I am the kind of person who needs to experience things in order to believe in them.

I cannot just read a book or listen to a sermon and fully accept a concept as powerful as God. I needed a personal *experience*.

One day, my friends and I were on a large raft on our way to meet a 200-year-old man named Dwaria Baba. I met an Indian family on this trip that immediately began talking to me. We felt some kind of connection and spent the whole time together conversing. When we returned to Delhi, they invited me back to their home for dinner. After that, we connected and made plans together every day. They told me they felt drawn to me and wanted to introduce me to their "family Guru." They said he did not have a name, since he didn't want people following him, but that I could call him Maharaji. They said that he did not have one home, but rather he lived everywhere. I didn't understand this at first, but I was happy enough to have a chance to meet with him. So we went out in the streets of Delhi and soon encountered this six-foot tall man with a white beard who was dressed in orange robes. A six-foot tall Indian is very rare and stands out among the other Indian people. His eyes twinkled and he laughed as he greeted me. It was as if he had been waiting for me to find him, and I finally had.

Receiving the blessing of oranges from Dwaria Baba

Since Maharaji spoke no English and I spoke no Hindi, we had to learn how to communicate in other ways. He would signal me to sit next to him as he sat in the meditation position. I did so and went into a deep state of meditation almost immediately. Soon, I began to receive meditation instruction internally and I knew it was from him. He instructed me to bring my attention to my third eye and breathe light into it. I was amazed that he could communicate with me internally. My conscious mind was going crazy trying to figure out how he could communicate thoughts to me and especially how they could be in a language I understood. My spiritual mind knew that this was no problem for an enlightened being. It was as if his spirit was connecting with mine. Through that connection, I started knowing exactly when our meditations were over and my eyes would open at the same time as his. For a while, this astonished me and I would look to him. He would simply laugh. Things that were so unusual to my small, uninitiated mind were perfectly normal to him and his expanded consciousness.

On the river trip with my adopted Indian family

The day after my first meeting with Maharaji, my new "adopted" family asked if I would like to see him again, and of course I said that I did. We began walking the streets of Delhi, but didn't see him for several days. They said that they never knew where or if they would find him. But when the time was right, he always appeared. Sometimes it felt as if he suddenly manifested right there before our eyes. We were walking along and suddenly he was in front of us. And he always greeted us with a great deal of love, which made me feel more and more drawn to being with him. We would always find some place where we would go to meditate, and he would continue his instructions for us.

One particular day — when I was in meditation and his instructions came into my thoughts — he began teaching me to breathe out through the top of my head. This was a strange idea for me, but I followed his instructions. I soon felt myself lifting out of my body and I was a little frightened. After the meditation, he was trying to tell me something in Hindi, but I couldn't understand. Finally, the words, "I body no" came out of his mouth. I wasn't sure what he was talking about. He spent the next several months teaching me the meaning of these simple yet profound words.

Meditating with Maharaji

"I Body No"

One day my new family told me they wanted to take me to a beautiful lake that was way up in the mountains. They said it would take two days by car to get there and that we would drive. I arrived at their house in the morning and was immediately greeted by Maharaji. The family and the servants began to pile into two cars, but Maharaji did not enter either one. I asked about this, and they said, "He doesn't ride in cars."

I thought about this and asked, "Well, is he coming to the mountains with us? And if so, how will he get there?" They just looked at me and moved their heads from side to side, as Indians often do. The meaning seemed to be, "We'll see."

So we left him there and he smiled and laughed as he waved goodbye to us. We spent the next two days looking at the magnificent scenery in the mountains. On the way up, we camped one night in a beautiful spot near a creek. The servants prepared delicious Indian food and always remembered to cook some food not quite so spicy for me. On the third morning, we pulled up to the mountain lake where we would stay, and I was shocked to see Maharaji waiting there, waving and laughing as he greeted us.

I am sure my mouth must have fallen open as I looked to the other family members for some sort of explanation. I started asking rapid-fire questions. "How did he get here? Did he take a train, a bus, a plane?" They smiled and said there was no way to get here except by private car, and they reiterated that Maharaji did not ride in cars. "Well, how did he get here?" I asked again, a little more loudly than before. The family began to shake their heads from side to side again, Indian style, as if to say they did not know or were not going to say. Then, Maharaji just looked me straight in the eye and said once more, "I body no," which I interpreted as meaning, I am not my body.

I spent the next few days pondering this whole situation. Could he have "transported" himself in some way that my conscious mind didn't really understand? It was the only solution I could fathom, even though it made no sense. But when we later sat in meditation, the teaching became clearer. Through teachings given to me in my meditation I learned that, when you're not attached to the body, it has more capabilities than when you are. One of these capabilities is called *bilocation* — the ability to be in two places at once. Apparently this was something Maharaji could accomplish. He was letting me know that we — as Westerners — are too attached to the body and to the limited ideas that we have of it. I was excited by the possibilities in what he said, although they still made little sense to my logical mind.

The Indian family told me that it was quite a blessing to have such a wonderful saint such as Maharaji as my personal guru. They said that he usually avoids students — especially Westerners. Apparently, I had a past-life connection with him and them and that was why we had met. This was also the reason that I had been drawn into my spiritual search and why it brought me into India. They said that I was "remembering" on a subconscious level what my other lives had been, and I was trying to rediscover who I was.

As I thought about this, I began to remember the nights on the ship when I had tuned into another lifetime as a seaman. The puzzle pieces began fitting together and making sense. I realized that, as we become more conscious, we begin searching for the meaning of our lives. That involves finding out who we are, and the reality of who we are is incredibly vast — much more so than recognizing the roles we play from day to day in the world.

In fact, each person is a complex organism made up of a vast amount of energy with millions of years of experiences, lessons, and abilities to rediscover. When Maharaji said, "I body no," he was telling me that this body is just a very small vehicle in which this huge energy of the soul is temporarily housed. The existence of this body is just one of millions of bodies which are all so limited, temporary, and insignificant. Every day, the words that he kept repeating for me took on more and more meaning.

Eventually, we drove back to the family home — again, without Maharaji in our car. He waved goodbye as we left, just as he had before. He smiled and laughed, and I was sad to be apart from him. I was growing very fond of him and felt so much love in his presence. When we returned to Delhi and pulled into the driveway, however, there he was to greet us, just where we had left him nearly a week before. I caught myself feeling amazed again, and then remembered, "I body no." He didn't even have to say the words, because I had finally gotten it. Or so I thought.

More Lessons

After being in India for a while, I started getting sick. I had difficulty breathing and it seemed to get worse everyday. It felt like some kind of bronchitis or asthma. The smoke-filled air, the pollution, and the dust from all the unpaved roads felt like they were adding to the problem.

I visited several Ayurvedic doctors, but nothing they gave me helped. I then found some homeopathic doctors and received treatment from them, again with no results. I tried some Western antibiotics and that didn't help either. Slowly, desperation began sinking in and I was unable to rest at night. I grew exhausted.

One night, I was sitting up and Maharaji entered the home. He motioned for me to come and sit next to him for meditation. I did so. As we sat, I was coughing and could hardly breathe. My feelings of despair were certainly prevalent, and I began thinking that, if I was not better by morning, I would have to make arrangements to fly back to the U.S. As I had this thought, Maharaji motioned for me to come and sit on his lap. It was strange, because I had never been that physically close to him before. But I did curl up in his lap and he rocked me all through the night. I felt like a baby in the arms of her mother. I received so much love from him. I was going in and out between different states of consciousness all night. This was my first awareness of soul travel, but back in those days I didn't even have a name for it. I felt like our souls were merging and dancing together.

When I woke in the morning, I looked into the clear eyes of Maharaji. I knew that, somehow, he and I had been spiritually traveling together all night. He was smiling and looked lovingly at me. I sat up and soon noticed that I could breathe perfectly. I couldn't believe it! I was better! I looked at him incredulously, and of course he just said, "I body no" and laughed. So now this little phrase took on a whole new meaning. This time the phrase "I body no" was not about bilocation or attachment to the body. It was about healing the body as well.

Limited thinking has taught us to believe that doctors and medicine are our healers. But this message was that some people have powers to heal others on subconscious levels. In some way, he was able to contact my soul and bring healing to my body. I am not my body, but I am my soul. That soul is in charge of the body's health to a greater degree than we realize. I liked that and was excited to know more about how it all worked.

I began talking to my Indian family about all of this, and they were very helpful in explaining much of what was happening to me. They explained that what we, as ordinary humans, think of as *miracles* are just normal everyday occurrences to spiritual masters like Maharaji. He was trying to teach me that we are so much more than our bodies and our conscious minds, and that vast powers are available to us through meditation and spiritual practice. If we begin to meditate daily, we open up channels in our brains that connect us to higher and higher sources of energy.

They explained all of this, and then they looked at me more seriously. "You understand," they said, "that it *really is unusual* for someone like Maharaji to take on a Westerner as such a close student." I nodded, to show that I understood, but they shook their head back and forth once more. "*Really unusual,*" they repeated, emphasizing that I *didn't* get it. "He is teaching you because he knows that you are meant to be a spiritual teacher in your own country, and that you will bring this knowledge into the hearts and minds of thousands of people he could never reach." They reiterated that my past life connection to him attracted me here to India and lead me directly to him to be instructed for this purpose.

I knew that the time had come for me to move on. Something was pulling me forward like a powerful magnet, toward what I did not know.

After leaving Maharaji and my Indian family, I decided to visit a few other saints before returning to America. I visited Varanasi (Benares) and learned how people came there to die. They were lined up along the edge of the Ganges River with exactly the amount of money they needed to purchase the wood. I asked, what wood do they need to purchase? It was explained that the expired bodies would be set on fire on a cross made of wood and then set afloat on the river of Mother Ganga. I looked out on the river and saw the floating fires/bodies. I sat there in amazement, never having seen anything in the world like that before. I went to the biggest Shiva temple there on the river and meditated on how the Indian people accepted death and life and rebirth in such a different way than we did. Perhaps it was because they knew they would be coming back that they did not fear death as much as we did.

I started asking myself if I was complete with India or if there was something more I needed. I was filled with all that I had learned from Maharaji and my Indian family. As I meditated there on the Ganges River, I got in touch with the deep longing that I had felt much of my life. I still had many questions about this. I could meditate and feel Mahariji's presence with me, but there still seemed to be more that I needed to learn.

"Divine Homesickness"[4] is a big spiritual issue for many people. It is the longing to go back to a time when we were one with God. Some people refer to it as "going home." We have discovered this existential issue through the thousands of hypnotherapy sessions and regressions we have witnessed over the years. It is an experience of deep angst, the profound anguish of separation from God. This is what I also refer to as "the longing for belonging." It is the place in all of us that we may or may not be aware of, a longing to be one with Spirit, with the Divine Mother, with the Christ energy, with the Creator or whatever tradition attracts you. Most substance addictions, eating disorders and other compulsive behaviors are used unconsciously to numb the pain of the unfulfilled longing for spiritual connection. So much of what plagues us is behavior used to cover up the pain of feeling the angst, the pain of separation.

Krishna Das, one of the greatest *kirtan wallas* (singer of chants), tells his story of going to India and the incredible longing for God that drove him to travel to such a foreign land in the Sixties. I felt that same driving force which wouldn't leave me alone. Somehow I just couldn't be content in my life. I left my marriage, my home, my work, even my beloved daughter (which was the most heart-wrenching) to search for the Holy Grail. It is this longing, this deep emptiness that screams to be filled up. This inner turmoil is very familiar to every junkie, every alcoholic and every sex and relationship addict. People use food, drugs, spending and sex to try to numb the pain of this separation. It may be called "mid-life crisis" in which people behave very out of character: devoted wives and mothers have affairs, loving husbands and fathers desert their families, and thousands of young women and men flee to India to meditate in the Himalayas in search of "The Truth." Millions of people are seeking gurus and spiritual teachers, megachurches and televangelism because of this same longing. People are flocking to fundamentalist churches where they can have a heart-warming and ecstatic spiritual experience rather than just a dry intellectual one. The dry, empty and rigid religions of the past have now opened up the new generations of people seeking a spiritual experience of God in so many different ways and from one corner of the planet to the other.

When I left for my spiritual pilgrimage, I never had any idea that I was looking for God. As children, we learn to fear God, that He is going to punish us. All the baggage that is put onto God from our families, churches/synagogues and teachers are crowding our unconscious minds and preventing us from opening up to who we really are. Many of us never found the love and the connection in the religious institutions from our childhood that we were seeking. In order to find God, we need to recognize and surrender to the longing for belonging which is our separation from God, begging and crying to return to the arms of the Divine Mother.

When I left on my spiritual pilgrimage in the early 1970s, I had no idea I was seeking God or that I was experiencing divine homesickness. I just kept listening to my inner knowing and following my inner guidance. I stopped participating with drugs and alcohol which allowed me to be able to hear those clear voices. I filled my days with spiritual books, chanting and daily meditation. I learned that praying is asking God for what we want and meditation is listening for the answers. It was at this time, when my mind and body were clear that I knew I was being clearly guided to go to India.

It took me a full year to prepare for the Pilgrimage. I released all of my material possessions and made clear plans for my daughter to live with her father. I wasn't able to leave until I knew for sure that she was safe and was with someone who loved her very much. I then carefully sorted through my belongings and was very clear to only take what was essential for survival. I knew I'd be carrying everything in my backpack and it would be heavy. Trying to decide what I actually needed was a huge process in itself.

Once in India, I had the names of several spiritual families to visit who could help me. I still was not clear why I was in such a foreign land. Each town or village that I came to, I was led to different temples and was blessed to have the *darshan* (spiritual blessing) of several Masters. One of these was Sai Baba, a highly enlightened spiritual master on the planet at this time. I was able to sit up very close to him and my heart was opened by all the incredible love exuding from him. The more I sat in front of him, the more love I felt. And that powerful love lasted for a while, but just like the drugs I used to do, I noticed that I kept wanting another dose when I was not in his presence. That longing was getting even stronger now that I knew what I was seeking. I could see that others felt the same way. People would push and shove to get up close to him, even though his love definitely radiated throughout any space he was in. And as I sat in front of him, I could also watch the ego trying to get approval. Does he see me? Is he looking at me? And all that stuff that I needed to let go of in order to experience the Oneness of just being there in the moment of bliss with him, and then in the next moment of bliss, and then in the next. Each day we could go to be with Sai Baba and sit in bliss. As I look back, I now realize that we all took his presence for granted. Then one day they announced he was leaving to go on a trip and some people went with him and most did not.

At first, I could still feel the love just sitting in front of his picture and being in the temple. But after a while the ego/mind came in and starting questioning the whole experience. Is he really my guru? Is he really enlightened? And just on and on as only the ego/mind can. I became restless and felt like I needed to leave and keep searching. What am I searching for? I couldn't seem to answer my own question. Soon I came to another town and someone told me about Anandamayi Ma. She was the most important female saint on the planet, and I was told that she would give me darshan. My ego/mind knew immediately that is just what I needed: a female saint! The Divine Mother herself, incarnated, was inviting me for a blessing! Wow! I was thrilled!

I took my backpack and my picture of Sai Baba, and went to meet the Divine Mother. The experience was amazing. I sat in the bliss of Oneness again everyday. Her smile opened my heart, her voice touched my soul, and she exuded a love that I had never felt before. This must be it, my ego/mind told me! What I've needed all along was the Divine feminine as a teacher, as a guru! We sat with her every minute that we could and then meditated with her picture until we fell asleep into deep bliss. Then the next day we would awake to ask where Ma was and when we could see her. Just as with Sai Baba, my existence depended on hers. I waited in line to get up close to her and stayed all day in the temple as long as she was there. We looked for her, followed her around, and spoke about her every movement. We were totally consumed with her presence. I felt so happy. I finally belonged in this beautiful spiritual community where people were on a spiritual path. Ma taught us everyday how to love God and one another.

Suddenly one day, Ma (as we called her) had to leave to travel to visit some of her devotees in another part of India. They didn't know how long she would be gone and only a few of her close devotees got to go with her. I was crushed. There I was again, sitting in front of her picture and back in the feeling of emptiness. The longing for belonging was even stronger than ever before. I realized that this whole community of people meant nothing to me when Ma was gone. They said that her presence was always there in the temple. But I began to notice that when the guru was gone, the devotees all had personalities. And those personalities were not quite as loving or joyful as they were when Ma was there. I meditated and tried to bring her back, but it seemed impossible. I struggled and eventually felt that it was time to leave.

I decided to go up North to begin hiking in the Himalayas. I tried to use my mantra to quiet my thoughts, but with every step I was feeling more and more pain. It felt like I had left all the bliss and love down with my gurus and I was getting more and more empty with every step. Why couldn't I hold it? I kept feeling that I needed to find another guru, one that wouldn't leave me. But that seemed impossible. I was in a hopeless quandary. What was I craving? What was I longing for?

The divine homesickness, was getting intense, but I didn't have a label for the intensity at that time. I just put one foot in front of the other as if I was on a specific path to get somewhere. In reality, I had no clear idea of where I was going or what I was about to experience. I just kept walking and feeling the angst on a very deep level. Eventually, I found a cave that seemed somewhat protected. It seemed as though I could stay for a while and meditate and try to get clear. One of the chai wallas (chai tea vendors) saw me going up into the caves and followed me there. I think he was worried about an American woman being up there alone. He brought me some chai tea and biscuits and then left me to my misery. I began to cry rivers and rivers of tears which seemed never-ending. I never knew I had so much pain inside. It actually felt kind of good to feel so free to let it all out. I felt so alone up in those magnificent mountains. And then I realized that the isolation was part of what felt so good.

When the tears seemed to be all cried out, I began to realize that it was just me and God up here. I lit a candle and some incense in front of my pictures of Sai Baba and Anandamayi Ma and began to pray and meditate. I was in a deep trance state that lasted for a long time. I seemed to be asking for God to come to me and to let me experience him or her. My mind became more and more confused as I cried for, prayed to, and pleaded with God to give me a sign that he was real. I didn't even know who I was praying to. Was I asking Baba or Ma or just God? I was begging for just one sign or a clue that would lead me in the right direction.

After what seemed like several days and nights had passed, I began to sense a lightening of my heart and a quieting of my spirit. As the time passed I began to feel the love envelop my heart, just as I had in the presence of Sai Baba and Anandamayi Ma. I was extremely aware of my breath and felt like with every breath, the light was getting brighter. I could notice the ego/mind trying to come in, and I noticed that if I kept breathing, my breath prevented the thoughts from interrupting the experience. I have no idea how long the most intense part lasted, but it was definitely all of the night and much of the next day.

Soon I began to see and feel Jesus and he was smiling. I felt the most intense love coming from him and at the same time emanating from my heart. That love was just like the love I had felt in the presence of Sai Baba and Anandamayi Ma. But it was now within me in the form of Jesus. I kept trying to quiet the thoughts but suddenly my conscious mind popped out and shouted, "Jesus?" "What are you doing here? I'm Jewish and looking for my Indian guru. How did Jesus get here?"

Then I heard him gently reply that he was Jewish also, that in fact he was every religion and no religion. He had many amazing teachings for me. One of them was that "God does not want us to be divided in His name. God wants us to be united in his name. We are all One." So I sat with that for a long time and continued to focus on my breath. In those moments and hours and days, I knew exactly what he meant and my very being embraced the amazing truth of those simple words. I knew what came from him was pure truth and what came from my mind was ego. I was able to quiet the ego/mind simply by breathing! How amazing!

The next teaching he gave me was that we should not get caught up in the form of God. We need to let go of our expectations of what we think God *looks like* or what God *should be*. I sat with that for quite a while. I finally realized that is why God brought himself to me in the form of Jesus. Raised Jewish, Jesus was a *bad word* in my childhood home. Jesus would be *the last* being in the world that a Jewish woman could accept as God. Any one of the Hindu Gods or Goddesses would have been much easier for me to receive than Jesus. And yet in those highly enlightened weeks and months, Jesus touched my heart like no one else ever had. And he kept saying, "Don't get attached to my form or to any form of God. God is formless. God is the love that you are feeling. God is the inner peace and the Oneness with every living being that you feel. God is everywhere and in everyone. You are not special."

I sat with that for a long time. *I am not special.* Everyone is enlightened. Everyone is God and the Divine Mother and Jesus and Baba.. Confused, I asked why was I given this incredible awakening experience. Jesus replied, "Just because you asked." Those words kept ringing in my ears, "just because you asked." All the crying and begging and praying flashed before my eyes. Yes, I certainly had asked!

I then began hearing what I later on discovered to be Bible verses. I had read some of the Old Testament but I had never read the New Testament, so I was not familiar with them. "Ask and you shall receive, knock and the door will be opened." That came a lot anytime the ego/mind tried to minimize or maximize my experience.

The *chai walla* would come to the cave from time to time and bring me fresh chai and biscuits. He never disturbed me and instinctively, culturally and spiritually knew exactly what was happening and what I needed. His beautiful *seva* (selfless service) has always been an amazing teaching for me. He never wanted anything in return and I could sense his spiritual connectedness. He was very quiet inside of himself and very humble. I learned by his coming everyday, without being asked, or praised or paid, what true devotion to God meant. It was all so simple, and I saw how complicated I had made everything.

One day as I continued to sit in the cave, feeling the Christ energy and the Divine Mother at the same time inside my heart, I began laughing and laughing for what seemed like hours. It was the most amazing cosmic joke that had been played on me. Or actually that I had played on myself! I was seeing this whole spiritual quest that I had been on as an amazing pilgrimage to fill up that deep inner longing and to find God. I had prepared for a year, released all my personal belongings, left my daughter, husband and job to travel half way around the world. I searched in all these little Indian villages and huge overwhelmingly crowded cities. I sought teachings from many different teachers and gurus and trekked into a wild and dangerous area of the Himalayan Mountains. And the huge cosmic joke was that God was within me all the time! I was looking outside of myself for what was as close as my heart! I just kept laughing and laughing and it felt that Jesus was laughing with me.

Now I knew that he couldn't leave me the way that my other teachers had, or more accurately the way that I had experienced their loss. God is inside all of us all the time. We are God, we are the Divine Mother, we are the Christ energy, we are all One. Sai Baba and Anandamayi Ma and Jesus and Diane and the chai walla are all the same! Divine homesickness, the longing for belonging, the anguishing angst, is healed not by food, drugs or alcohol to numb the pain but by conscious awareness through the breath! Wow! The healing is about being superconscious rather than in shock, dissociated and unconscious.

The next time the chai walla came to refresh my tea, I made eye contact with him and we both smiled and then we began laughing and laughing. He was able to share my joy and no words were necessary at all. He could see right into my soul and I into his. We exchanged a *namaste* bow, and he quietly left.

As the days passed by, I began to ask what I was supposed to do with all of this. Jesus came to me and said I had been blessed to have many teachers. I began to reflect on all my teachers both in India and in the U.S. Fritz Pearls, Eric Berne, Freud, Jung and Yogananda all passed before my eyes. Jesus said it was time for me to return home and share what I had been given. I realized that was my seva, but I had no idea how it would all look. I trusted that more would be revealed.

As I walked down the mountain, I came upon the chai stand and my friend who had served me so humbly. I stopped to have some tea with him. Sitting nearby were some Indians that spoke a little English, and they translated something he had wanted to tell me. It was basically that he had been worried at first because the caves had dangerous animals like tigers in them. He could soon see that I was protected by the big light of the Divine Mother, and knowing that allowed him to be able to leave me there alone. I had no idea of the danger in the mountains as I had felt so safe and protected there. The mountains felt like home to me. Little did I know then that I would end up living my life in the beautiful Cascade Mountains of Washington.

I continued down the mountain and began to feel that I needed to see Sai Baba once more before I left India. I went into his ashram and smelled the familiar aroma of incense and the excitement around Sai Baba. Remarkably, I was easily able to get a seat up close. As I sat there I was aware of feeling very different than the last time I had been there. I didn't feel attached as though I *had* to have a seat right in front of him. The inner longing was filled up. The desperateness and longing were gone. I was at peace and I felt the Divine within me. Wow! The difference was so overpowering, that I began to realize something major had happened. I didn't want the ego/mind to run with analysis of my gift, so I just sat there in front of Baba's seat and breathed in the love.

I noticed the ego/mind jumping back and forth between wanting to say, "Wow, I think I've just received enlightenment" to the other part trying to deny the whole experience. "You're just making this all up. Why in the world would Jesus come to you? You've been up in the mountains too long and you must have gone crazy up there!" and then back to the other side, "Wow! You're enlightened." I had to stop this inner dialogue and so I went back to my breathing, which was helpful in diminishing the ego's incessant dialogue.

Sai Baba entered and then just smiled for a long time looking around the room. As he began to speak, our eyes met and I could feel our souls dancing together with Jesus and Divine Mother and all the Masters of love and light that have ever been on this planet and some who have not lived here. In that moment, I realized that God is formless and yet is also in every form. Sai Baba began to speak and at the same time his words seemed to be coming from Jesus. He pronounced very clearly, "It is good for all Westerners to know Jesus." His eyes laughed as he confirmed the presence of Jesus which was so overpowering to me in that moment. He seemed to be looking right at me and right through me and I experienced the full presence of his Divine being. There really are no words to describe the transformation that took place for me there. If I had ever tried to doubt my experience, there was now no longer any way I could do that. I knew now that I had been called here to see this living Saint before leaving India so he could set my ego/mind at rest.

During that last meeting with Sai Baba, he confirmed many of the things that Jesus had taught me and was continuing to teach me in every quiet moment. He talked about the importance of doing *pranayama* breathing. This message confirmed what I had been experiencing about the breath and how it brought me closer to spirit and further away from confused thinking. The breathing has been done for thousands of years by saints all over India for God Realization. God realization…I pondered that concept for a while. So that must be what I came here for and that is what I am bringing back with me. I wonder what I will do with that in America. At that time, I had no idea what the future held for me.

* * * * *

This was a wake-up call for me. I was a therapist for many years and I approached that therapy along the traditional lines. But something stirred in me and drove me to begin searching for something more. In India I had my eyes opened to wholly new ways of thinking. And it made me realize something that would change my approach to therapy forever after.

The word *psychology* actually means the study of the soul. But it has come to mean the study of the mind, of perception, and of cognition. In much of Western psychology, the soul has been purposely omitted in an attempt to be more "scientific." Psychologists have continuously worked to become more accepted by the medical community, which was Freud's domain.

While there is a lot of use in dealing with the mind, this has left a gap in people's holistic healing. We are not just body, emotions, and mind. There is a spiritual element as well, and many of us in the field of emotional and mental therapy have recognized that fact — consciously or unconsciously — and have headed on a spiritual search, wanting to bring this last element into healing. Transformational therapy is the result, using various techniques to understand the spiritual healing a person needs to experience and to take them through that healing.

This doesn't keep therapists from working with people's emotions and minds. Instead, it fills out that work. When you start to see the cause of many emotional and mental challenges, you know how to work with them and how to heal them. If you never look into these causes, then you are dealing with symptoms only, and you can only really do patch work. I believe this is why I've taught so many therapists in the last 25 years who are more and more drawn to spiritual aspects of their healing work.

I think what it comes down to is that we've grown tired of using bandages to heal ourselves over and over when the real problem is that we keep tripping and cutting ourselves. If we can learn to stop tripping, we don't need the bandages any more.

Unfortunately, HMOs and insurance companies have limited the number of therapy visits they will cover, and have come up with terms like "Solution Focused Therapy" to suggest that people can be fixed up and sent on their way within six visits. In fact, though, most therapists know the truth: this is really "bandage therapy." It does *not* usually find a solution to the *problem*, but only to the *symptom*.

In transformational therapy, though, we see the symptom as a clue to the underlying spiritual issue that a person is dealing with. And if you want to go back to the most basic problem of all, we understand that the source of most fear or rage — and the illnesses that arise from these in many guises — is our separation from God. In our search for the soul, or the true self, we end up mending that apparent separation and feeling whole once more.

Healing requires an in-depth look at what your life is about: what is your purpose and meaning, and how you can more fully express who you are in this lifetime? In traditional therapy, the client often looks to the therapist to provide the answers to life problems. In *healing*, the therapist empowers clients to take responsibility for their own healing and provides the tools for self-discovery and personal transformation. In the process, the healer does use energy techniques to assist the client, but this is done as a partner with Spirit and with the client, and can only be done because the client has chosen to ask for this kind of help.

When something stirred in me and sent me to India, I was waking up to something new — to a personal transformation that all of us need to experience in our process of getting well, and that therapists need to help their clients experience in order to truly heal them.

The Indian family I spent so much time with told me that I was being taught by a master so that I could return and teach others, and I believe that — to one degree or another — awakening to and passing through personal transformation brings any of us from the stage of student to the stage of teacher. As you read this book, you may be in the process of waking or passing through this stage; or you may already consider yourself healed and ready to guide others with your unique gifts and goals.

Either way, this book hopes to share with you why people need transformation, and how transformational therapy can help them to achieve progressive change. We'll talk about the various stages of life and what can happen that blocks people from transformation ... *and* how to address those blocks. You'll read specific stories from my clinical experience showing how effectively therapy can address them.

With this holistic approach — discussing background, solutions, and specific stories — I hope that I can bring to life for you the system of therapy we have used and taught for decades that has helped thousands in their personal processes of transformation. I also hope that you can look to these techniques for yourself, or perhaps become inspired to learn and share them with others in our collective process of helping to awaken the entire world.

Chapter 1
Values Questionnaire

I. Check what your values are. Prioritize the top five (give each a number).

✔ 1-5

☐ ☐ A. Health
☐ ☐ B. Honesty
☐ ☐ C. Courage
☐ ☐ D. Beauty
☐ ☐ E. Goodness
☐ ☐ F. Playfulness
☐ ☐ G. Independence
☐ ☐ H. Money & Abundance
☐ ☐ I. Intimacy in Relationships (sharing, cuddling, closeness)
☐ ☐ J. Sexual Connection
☐ ☐ K. Parenting children
☐ ☐ L. Nature
☐ ☐ M. Love
☐ ☐ N. Solitude
☐ ☐ O. Culture: Art, music, drama etc
☐ ☐ P. Other: _____
☐ ☐ Q. Other: _____

II. What activities make you happy or bring you pleasure, satisfaction, joy? After each one, name the values from above which the activity addresses.

A. _____

B. _____

C. _____

D. _____

III. What memories fill you with joy? List them and then see which value from above they address and write it down in the second column.

A. _____

B. _____

C. _____

D. _____

IV. Which traits, talents or qualities do you most like about yourself? What are your natural gifts? What characteristic makes you most glad to be you?

A. _____

B. _____

C. _____

D. _____

V. What work or career could you imagine that would incorporate your values and talents most completely?

A. _____

B. _____

C. _____

D. _____

VI. Check any unhealthy "rewards" that you have used to dissociate, numb or avoid feelings or to unconsciously punish yourself.

❑ Television
❑ Smoking
❑ Drugs (marijuana, cocaine, heroine, speed, etc.)
❑ Alcohol
❑ Pornography or sexual addiction
❑ Compulsive eating/dieting/exercising
❑ Compulsive spending/shopping
❑ Gambling
❑ Excessive telephone use
❑ Compulsive internet/computer usage
❑ Rescuing or care-taking others
❑ Other _____
❑ Other _____

Your Project: List three new behaviors to choose from to do each day to reward yourself in a healthy way.

1. _____

2. _____

3. _____

Chapter 2
Returning to the World, Discovering Hypnotherapy

I had been a psychotherapist before my trip to India, and when I returned, some of my former clients heard that I was back and tried tracking me down for appointments. But after so much time in India, where I was surrounded by poverty, the concept of having someone pay me $100 to listen to them for an hour was part of an enormous culture shock.

I had to adjust though, so I sat and listened as I had been trained to do. Now, however, I could see so much more about them than I had before. In India, my third eye had opened. The problem was ... I didn't feel I could tell them all that I saw. And during most of the sessions, I found myself longing to spend time in meditation, merging with God, rather than being present with my client. The longing for belonging was tangible.

One thing I noticed was that people were bringing up more spiritual issues than they had in my practice before my pilgrimage to India. They were dealing with their relationships with God, with religion, and with searching for the meaning in their lives.

As I spent time outside my appointments actually *in* those meditations I desired so much, I also listened to what I call the Christ energy, and in doing so, I felt guided to start teaching some yoga and meditation classes. If people were moving in the direction of spirituality, so much the better — by sticking with what I had grown so fond of, my transition back into American culture would be easier and I could begin to teach so much of what I had learned in India. This began a process, for me, of bringing together Western psychology with Eastern knowledge.

Even so, Los Angeles was no easy place to adjust to. LA had a frantic energy, and there was an atmosphere of manipulation and dishonesty. And as I settled in, I found myself missing my daughter, who had stayed with her father during my trip to India. I decided to go and visit her in Washington State.

I'll never forget leaving Los Angeles in the airplane and seeing the smog that covered the atmosphere. It was so brown and dense and dirty. Then I saw Seattle as we approached our landing, and it was green and clear and magnificent. I cried in the airplane as I saw the beauty and magnificence of the mountains.

As we drove through the beautiful Cascade Mountains, I was reminded of the beauty of the Himalayas in India. There, in the humbling presence of the Cascades, I felt like I was home, even though I had never been there before. It was clear to me right away that I would move to Washington

State to be with my daughter and to live in a place with this kind of majestic presence.

Soon after, I made the move to Washington and, needing work, got a job at a community mental health center. I took this job because I felt it would be a secure, long-term position. The job provided me with the link back into the therapy field that I needed. But more than that, it helped me to reconnect with my profession in ways that would later be essential to discovering my true life's work.

The job at the mental health center helped me to build a good reputation in my new community with clients as well as other professionals. I was working with families and children, and after my experiences in India, this helped me to get back in touch with the problems being addressed in everyday family situations in America. Also, because of the spiritual path I had been following, I felt behind in the latest knowledge on therapy. This job gave me the chance to catch up with the latest therapy journals and books that had come out during my "leave of absence." And it was comforting to be in a secure job like that.

Or that's what I thought it was.

It is during this time that I met David Hartman. He was on the board of directors of the mental health center and he was also a friend of my ex-husband. He was a nice man, very intelligent, and interested in my travels to India. In the small mountain town where I was living, there were few people who knew much about meditation, spiritual paths, or higher consciousness. David and I began to connect through his interest in meditation and development of a spiritual path.

Lost in the bliss of enjoying a spiritual companion and an honest job in therapy, I was completely caught off guard when the news came through that President Reagan had cut mental health budgets across the country as part of his new economic package called "Reaganomics." This sent a shockwave through the mental health center, because it meant that some people would be laid off. It turned out that, since I had been the last one hired, I was one of the first to be laid off.

At first I was upset. I was partly reacting with many of my co-workers who felt that they needed me there to work with the families and children. They wanted to protest and called a meeting of the board of directors. But since it was a "federal government" decision, there didn't seem to be much that anyone could do. Not even David.

Experience always opens new doors, though. During my time at the center, I had become an advocate for abused children in the community and had developed a sexual abuse network. Through that network, one of the local churches heard that I had been laid off and offered me an office for beginning my therapy practice and continuing my work with abused children and their families. I had referrals immediately and soon was earning more than I had at the mental health center.

Discovering Hypnosis

It wasn't long before I found myself talking with a sexual abuse client, and during her session, she slipped into hypnosis. At the time, I didn't know what was happening, but she began to regress and speak in the voice of a little child. She started describing past abuses and her feelings spilled through as if they were happening right there in my office.

I was amazed, and I was changed forever. I immediately vowed that, whatever this was, I was going to learn more about it.

When our time was up, I wasn't sure what to do. My client was still very deep in this regression. I asked for inner guidance and then remembered a hypnosis stage show I had once seen. So I said, "One, two, three wake up!" It took her a few moments to come back and realize where she was. We talked for a while and she told me that her previous therapist had used hypnosis with her and that she must have just "slipped" into a trance state. I told her that I found it fascinating and that I would get training in it so that I could be more helpful to her.

I immediately found the best hypnotherapy teacher in Seattle and drove three hours each way every weekend for six months to receive the training. That training opened a new world of therapy to me and exposed the misconceptions that so much of the public has about hypnosis.

Hypnosis, for instance, gets a bad rap in many people's minds because of the stage show variety. Those who have never looked into hypnosis at least have the image — from TV or Las Vegas or some other setting — of someone being put into hypnosis on stage before a crowd and then strutting around the stage, clucking like a chicken at the hypnotist's command. This kind of hypnosis and the hypnosis used by therapists have almost nothing in common except use of the mind's different states of consciousness.

In order for stage show hypnosis to work, a number of elements have to come together. First, the person being hypnotized is someone who wants to put on a show already. Otherwise, he would never get up on stage. This may mean that he's had a few drinks ahead of time, lowering inhibitions. It may just mean that he really wants a chance to perform for people. Second, he needs to be able to go into a hypnotic state. That's not hard since *all people* enter hypnotic states *many times* every day of their lives. In fact, it's been estimated that we spend as much as 80% of our waking hours in hypnotized states! And finally, the person needs to *want* to follow each instruction. If he wanted to perform in the first place, he would probably be open to most performance instructions. *But he always remains in control and can refuse any instruction given to him.*

The reason for this is simple: the stage hypnotist isn't *commanding* anyone. He's *suggesting.* And in a hypnotic state, people are more open to suggestion. This is precisely why hypnotherapy can do such deep work — it is done in partnership with the client's subconscious mind rather than with the conscious mind, and it is the *sub*conscious mind that drives us. It tells us what to do, and the conscious mind more or less figures out how to do it. This is why it's so hard to break any habits just by deciding consciously to do so — the conscious mind isn't the one calling the shots!

Still, people tend to think of themselves in terms of what they're consciously aware of. They believe their thoughts are what they consciously come up with. And because of this, they might even think that tapping into the subconscious mind is wrong (i.e., the work of the devil), dangerous, or unscientific. These beliefs are based on misunderstandings of how hypnosis taps into the mind.

An important thing for people to know, especially if they are considering whether to undergo hypnotherapy, is that the hypnotic state is perfectly natural. We actually go in and out of it all the time. Think of how often you're driving in the car when you suddenly realize that you haven't consciously been aware of the last several miles of your journey. Or think about how often you find yourself "zoning out" in front of the TV, or "slipping into" a good book. All of these are instances of entering the hypnotic state, where your conscious mind no longer has a distinct awareness of your surroundings. Your body settles into auto-pilot, so to speak, and your subconscious mind has come to the forefront. In this kind of state, you are highly suggestible, and this is why companies spend countless millions on advertising to you while you're watching TV. They know that the message will get in deep and will help to drive your later actions, even though you're consciously unaware of it.

And how is it that we slip into this alternate state so easily? It's because this state is induced by eye fixation. When we concentrate our eyes on just one thing, we can shift into a trance, or a hypnotized state. So driving, watching TV, reading a book, staring at the computer screen, and so on can readily take us into a trance. This is why it's estimated that we are hypnotized during so many of our waking hours.

Once you understand that about hypnosis, it's suddenly very clear that hypnosis has nothing to do with the work of the devil. It certainly isn't dangerous, or we'd all be in great peril every day. People worry that they might not come out of a trance, and yet it's done all the time. In fact, there is *not one documented case* of someone failing to come back from such a trance. And if you were watching TV and someone asked you to cluck like a chicken, would you do so without wanting to? Finally, how can hypnosis be unscientific when it primarily requires relaxation (so that your conscious mind doesn't have to pay attention to the body) and eye fixation to bring someone into a hypnotized state?

Any danger in day-to-day life or in a therapist's office has nothing to do with the fact that you're hypnotized. If there is a danger, it has to do with how others relate with us while we are so suggestible. People say things while we're consciously zoned out to them and, if we're not careful, we can take what they say and make it part of our belief system. An example that I have heard from many of my clients happens most often when they have been successful in losing weight. They would eventually go home to family environments during the holidays. Most often, jealous mothers or sisters would give them negative suggestions such as, "Wow, you've lost so much weight! You look sick. You're too thin. Be careful or you'll end up getting sick!" Or, "You probably won't be able to keep it off during the holidays!" These are negative suggestions, that often have the effect of encouraging the person — subconsciously of course — to put the weight right back on.

Families and friends, who are around us all the time, can have an enormous influence in this way, which is why it's so important to always be supportive of one another. If you've grown up listening to people say negative things about you, especially while in a hypnotized or dissociated state, there's a good chance you can start to believe what they've said and your whole life can begin to revolve around those beliefs.

And yes, the same kind of danger is present if your hypnotherapist isn't qualified to do therapy in the first place ... just as there would be danger in visiting *any* counseling therapist who wasn't qualified. If the therapist doesn't understand the mind, body, and emotions, she shouldn't be working with people. And since hypnotherapy is just beginning to be regulated in most states, it's important that clients verify a therapist's credentials before going to see her. It's important to make sure that she's got at least a master's degree in counseling, psychology, or social work, and that she's had more than a weekend's course in hypnosis or hypnotherapy. And of course if you are the therapist yourself, you should make sure you have these qualifications.

And remember, no matter what, *a person can always reject any suggestion given, even in hypnosis.* Again, we are suggestible in hypnosis, but we're still aware of what's being said and done. It's not hard for a client to know if her therapist is promoting positive, life-affirming beliefs or something that's not in the client's best interest.

A qualified therapist can use the suggestible state of hypnosis greatly to a client's advantage. She can not only help to re-form thoughts around positive messages, but she can also help to eliminate those negative beliefs that have hindered a client for many years ... perhaps for all the client's life! This is the power of reaching into the part of the mind that really drives a person. This is the power of hypnosis.

Making Use of Hypnosis ... and Beyond

After every weekend's hypnotherapy training in Seattle, I then returned to my clients and began practicing what I had learned with a number of them. The results were exciting and renewed my interest in therapy. What had been the same for so many years was suddenly brand new work. Hypnosis fascinated me because it allowed me to look into my clients' motivations. It felt much more accurate than talking with people's conscious minds only. I was filled with excitement and energy as each session became a learning experience. But as I used hypnosis, I also found myself going beyond that, drawing on the spiritual knowledge I had gathered while in India.

An example comes from one of my early clients — a woman of low self-esteem. She had read books, taken self-esteem classes, and attended therapy for years. Nothing seemed to help, and eventually I felt as if I were offering her very little. Not knowing what else to try, I asked her if she would like to experience hypnosis.

As it turned out, she was eager to try it. She was an excellent subject and immediately entered a deep trance state. I instructed her to go back to the source of this feeling of disliking herself. She regressed to her childhood and found herself being sexually abused by her stepfather. While he was abusing her, he was telling her that this was all her fault and that if she hadn't been such a nasty girl, this would have never happened to her.

This instant replay of her childhood abuse was unbelievably powerful. She would speak in her little girl's voice and then she would speak in her stepfather's voice. It was all so spontaneous and real that there was no way this could have been made up. She would cry just like a little child, beg him to stop, and then go limp as if she had dissociated from the pain of it all. I asked her where she was when the crying stopped and she said she was floating up on the ceiling. I was amazed that I had witnessed exactly how dissociation works. Later, I would learn that this is usually a time when a part of the person splits off, and both the soul and the emotions become disconnected from the person's immediate bodily experience.

As I watched on, her feelings of self-hatred made perfect sense. She felt guilty and dirty about the sexual abuse as if it were her fault. Being a small child, she believed her abuser when he said it was her fault. I didn't want to end the session there, and this is where my spiritual learning began to pay off. Internally, I asked for guidance about how to help heal the situation. I sat for a few minutes before perceiving the message that I needed to create a nurturing, internal parent to protect the little girl and take her out of that situation.

To do so, I gave her a soft pillow and told her to pretend that this was her as a little child. I directed her to find the loving nurturing parent within her who could hold and comfort and protect this little girl. A very soft, tender smile came over her face as she rocked the baby (the pillow) and spoke softly to her "inner child." I had her change the negative messages that her stepfather had given the little girl, telling the girl instead that she was blameless, innocent, and loveable.

At the end of her session, I was directed from within to have her put her hand over her heart and feel the unconditional love. I did that and a strong, spiritual energy surrounded her. I could actually perceive her aura, which was turning from deep purple to bright white light. I knew that I was in the presence of God's healing energy and I began to say something to that effect on the tape that I was making for her. I knew that what was coming through me was her healing angel's message for her, and I wanted her to have a recording of it.

When she consciously came back to the room, she was glowing. We both knew that some powerful healing had taken place during the session. It was difficult to speak for a while, so we just sat there for a few minutes in silence, basking in the spiritual energy. And I began to realize that this was the difference between therapy — even *hypno*therapy — and healing. Therapy is about the therapist and client working through issues on the conscious level. Hypnotherapy is about getting down to root causes, buried within the subconscious mind. It appears to be far more powerful than therapy alone. *Healing*, however, involves the therapist and client connecting on the conscious, subconscious, and even the superconscious levels, where our spiritual helpers guide us.

As I learned over time, bringing spiritual intuition, connection, and care into hypnotherapy makes a great deal of difference in terms of true, core healing. In most hypnotherapy training, spirituality is not brought into the equation because it's not considered scientific. And I agree that training for hypnosis itself should be scientific. But the therapy that follows should go beyond that to truly heal a client. By doing so, one is able to integrate the powers of Western psychology with Eastern spiritual practices. *This integration is what Heart-Centered Hypnotherapy is all about.*

In the years that followed, I would in fact find myself weaving in plenty of Western psychology, from the humanistic and Gestalt psychology that I learned from Fritz Perls to the Transactional Analysis from Eric Berne and the spiritual psychology of Carl Jung. In time, Heart-Centered Hypnotherapy would take form, every session refining the process so that the therapy could be applied to many different situations. I had no idea at that time that the opportunity would arise to teach this process to thousands of therapists all across the country, just as my spiritual teacher Maharaji had foreseen. And I had no idea that, as I taught the model to psychologists, psychiatrists, and counselors in Asia, Africa, and the Middle East, it would begin to take root across the globe.

It all started with those early experiences, with clients much like that woman who used a pillow to heal her inner child. And sometimes, I found that one such healing would open up other issues that a client still needed to clear. For instance, two weeks after her healing, that same woman returned and told me that, over the past week, she'd had a strange feeling and kept seeing an image of what looked like "bars" in front of her face. She said the image was most present when she was driving her car. I explained to her that often, when people are driving, they are staring at the road and slip into a trance state known as highway hypnosis. I told her that I would help her to experience hypnosis again and find out what was happening.

I put her into a trance and it didn't take long before the bars were in front of her again. I asked her where she was and what was happening. She began slowly revealing details of her surroundings. She was describing a small room with a blanket on the floor for a bed, and bars. All of a sudden she screamed. "Oh my God," she said, "I'm a man and I'm in prison." Thoughts started racing through my mind about what this could be. Then she said, "It's another lifetime." I was amazed that she was so easily able to access the feelings of this man in prison. Suddenly, she screamed again. "No! Oh no! I've raped a child." I sat there in shock trying to fit all of these pieces together.

But I didn't have to fit it all together, because her own awareness was clearly coming through. She began talking about karma and realizing that this was the reason she returned as a small child to be abused in this lifetime. At first she saw this lifetime as a punishment for what she had done in that previous lifetime, as "an eye for an eye" style justice. But I asked for guidance, and what came through was that her soul needed to experience sexual abuse so that she would never again do that to a child. She was able to reframe this experience so that she could see this life as a soul lesson rather than as a punishment. It was an important lesson that her soul needed to learn for its growth towards higher consciousness.

As I sat there with her, I remembered the original problem she had come to therapy to address. It was low self-esteem and never feeling good about herself. Now these feelings of low self-esteem were even more understandable. We had gotten past the personality level, which had been about the sexual abuse by her stepfather and his words to her. In this session, we were down to past life issues and an even deeper level of her karmic or soul issues. And all of this occurred in only two sessions!

The more this sank in, the more I saw what a narrow focus traditional therapy had. In our country, therapy had become focused on "problems" that needed to be solved. The solutions were mainly one-dimensional, especially since managed health care had begun requiring that we do short-term, solution-focused therapy. This short-term therapy was done on the conscious level and mainly involved putting a bandage on enormous wounds. Mental health treatment in our country had deteriorated into giving drugs to cover up emotions and providing temporary solutions.

With the right kind of hypnotherapy, I began to realize that in-depth, soul-level healing could take place in only ten sessions instead of ten years. Clients began telling me that they got more out of one session of hypnotherapy than they did in many years spent with psychiatrists. Of course this doesn't mean that people were healed in single sessions, but that — by getting down to core issues within a few sessions — we could more quickly start addressing problems where they began, rather than merely covering those problems up by treating only the symptoms.

Personal Transformation: Assembling the Puzzle Pieces of Your Life

As I watched the healing that my clients experienced with hypnotherapy, I decided to use hypnotherapy for my own weight issues. I discovered the work of Donald Keppner, Ph.D., who was using hypnotherapy with eating disorders at the University of Georgia. I went to study with him and to receive treatment from him at the same time. He taught me Hypno-Behavioral Therapy, which combined hypnosis with powerful behavior modification techniques. It worked well for me and I was able to use this to maintain healthy eating patterns afterwards.

During my work with Dr. Keppner, I described a pattern to him: whenever I began to lose weight, there was a part of me that rebelled and was almost afraid to lose the weight. This part seemed scared and wanted to hold on to the weight. He led me into a hypnotic regression, taking me back to the source of this feeling, and I was surprised by what we found.

In the regression, I began to experience a life in Germany when I was taken to the concentration camp at Auschwitz. I was terrified and had very strong emotional reactions. I was crying and trying to find my mother. I was in some kind of a cattle car on a moving train. People around me were crying, confused, and scared.

The scene then shifted and I experienced the night before we were going into the gas chamber, only we didn't know it at the time. I was cold, starving, and tired. I was in Auschwitz and I could hear all the little children crying. They were all very hungry, and I would take my gruel and give it to them to try and stop their tears. The smells of urine, feces, and intense body odors were excruciating. There was no such thing as a fresh breath of air. I reached down and felt my ribs sticking out of my body. There seemed to be no muscle on my body at all. I was starving to death. We were all starving.

Later that night, we got the word that we would be going into the "showers" in the morning. Some of us knew what that meant, others did not. There were many children that I, as a young girl in that life, felt responsible for feeding and comforting. For some reason they had been put in my care and I felt that I had to feed them and protect them from further pain. Since they were separated from their own mothers, I had become their surrogate mother. We were all in so much pain, fear, and angst that we could barely get through the night. None of us could sleep, and we spent the night huddled together to feel a little comfort.

The next morning, we were led into the showers. I could smell the gas. I slowly lay down and began going through a tunnel towards a very bright light. Suddenly I felt wonderful. I felt an incredible sense of peace come over me and I realized that I was leaving my body. I began laughing as it seemed to be another cosmic joke. The biggest thing we all feared was being put to death. Yet death was the most wonderful experience that I had since being taken from my family by the Nazis.

During the hypnotic regression, I discovered that my soul had made an "agreement" to come back to earth as soon as possible and to help heal human pain and suffering. It was a soul agreement that I hadn't been consciously aware of during my life until then. And yet, as my consciousness increased, I began to realize that this agreement was really a powerful driving force in my life. It is what I later came to see as my karmic agreement.

Learning about this past life put many puzzle pieces of my life together. First of all, I realized the connection with my urge to eat since, in that lifetime, *losing weight meant death*. Now it all made sense that, every time I began to lose weight, this past life experience was unconsciously triggered and I would start to panic. With Dr. Keppner's help, I changed this pattern in my unconscious, and told my unconscious mind that it was okay to get to my healthy body weight. He also told me, in the trance state, that I was no longer in that lifetime and that I was now safe. The unconscious mind has no concept of time and, as a result, things that happened in the past can be triggered and seem as if they are happening now.

This also helped me understand why I always had a deep connection with prisons and prison work. As I mentioned before, when I first went to college I was immediately attracted to a major in criminology. Many of the courses were about prison reform and "institutions." I was fascinated with all of these courses, and both my internship and my first job out of college were — not surprisingly — in a prison. As a young intern, I was passionate about trying to reform those who were in prison as well as the prison system itself.

Even the movies I always like best are prison movies, like *The Birdman of Alcatraz*, which I have probably watched twenty times. I'm also fascinated with Nazi movies and especially anything about the concentration camps. I went to Washington, DC, to experience the Holocaust Museum, and the place fascinated and stunned me. It all felt frighteningly familiar. I am also drawn to movies about sexual abuse and rape, which I now know also goes back to experiences in the war camps. Rape there was a common experience, and sex was the only bargaining tool a young girl had. Today, most of my therapeutic work has focused on healing sexual abuse and trauma in myself and others.

After that lifetime, I immediately returned to earth to keep my karmic commitment and avenge the inhumanity that was happening in Germany at the time. I was reborn in 1943 to a Jewish family in the U.S. My father had to leave for Germany to fight the Nazis when I was only six months old. My mother worked in a war factory making weapons to use in the war against the Nazis. All through my life, I have taken up the causes of persecuted peoples and never understood why. During my college days, I was active in the civil rights movement of the 1960s. Later, I fought for women's rights, children's rights, and a cleaner environment. Now I see how these activities were part of my soul's agreement to help heal the pain of humanity.

These kinds of "clues" can lead you to your past lives and ultimately to your karmic purpose here on earth. What kind of movies do you tend to watch? What themes are important to you? What causes are you drawn to? Do you know any people you feel that you've "known before"? Take a look at the patterns in your life. The conscious mind may not have the capacity to put this all together clearly, but you can at least start to get a sense of things.

The ideal, though, is of course to get more than just a *sense* of one's soul purpose, and hypnotherapy is an important step in looking to the past and clarifying the future. But again, the problem with Dr. Keppner's program — as all other hypnotherapy programs I came across — was that they failed to bring in the spiritual element. This meant that they couldn't properly address experiences like past-life regressions, which is integral to understanding the overall story of a person's soul. By adding that spiritual element and creating Heart-Centered Hypnotherapy to produce a true personal transformation, we *have* been able to give people more clarity and have helped them to connect with their destinies, so to speak. Depression lifts, apathy vanishes and clears, and one-pointedness can start to guide a person's journey. That is the transformation.

The approach, however, has just one obstacle in its way: here in the West, where traditional Christianity is so prevalent, many people believe in one life on earth followed by life after death in either heaven or hell. This in turn is supposed to negate the possibility of past lives and reincarnation. The Personal Transformation that we encourage in our therapy doesn't *depend* on people believing in these, because past life experiences in hypnosis are often convincing enough in themselves to help heal people, regardless of their beliefs.

But the disbelief *can* keep people from wanting to try hypnotherapy or denying whatever truths they may find in that process. I am not a crusader in the sense of wanting to force others to see things as I do, but I'm also aware of the power that Personal Transformation gives to people. Luckily, you don't need anyone to change their belief systems to have them accept the possibility of past lives. Instead, all you need is to have people *better understand* their belief systems.

The surprising thing for most people to learn is that, if you really study Judaism and Christianity, the metaphysical or mystical traditions within both religions support the notion of reincarnation, even if it isn't commonly accepted by their leaders and members.

The Jewish belief system includes a series of ancient, mystical teachings known as the Kabbalah, and reincarnation is a part of these teachings. So why don't many Jewish people believe in reincarnation? Because by tradition, only rabbis who are at least forty years old are meant to embark on a study of Kabbalah, and, even then, only a few are interested to walk that path. The teachings themselves are extensive and detailed, but because of their depth and because they deal with so much that is unseen, Kabbalah was never something for the masses. It was a secret, spiritual teaching that has only recently come into the public light thanks to the Hasidic movement within Judaism.

According to the *Universal Jewish Encyclopedia*, reincarnation is a universal Hasidic belief.[5] A passage in the Hasidic play, *The Dybbuk*, reads:

> If a man dies prematurely, what becomes of the life he has not lived? What becomes of his joys and sorrows, and all the thoughts he had no time to think, and all the things he hadn't time to do? No human life goes to waste. If one of us dies before his time, his soul returns to earth to complete its span, to do the things left undone and experience the happiness and griefs he would have known.[6]

This statement later continues by saying:

> .... vagrant souls which, finding neither rest nor harbor, pass into the bodies of the living, in the form of a *Dybbuk*, until they have attained purity. . . The souls of the dead do return to earth, but not as disembodied spirits. Some must pass through many forms (bodies) before they achieve purification.[7]

So really, for Jews, the idea of reincarnation doesn't need to challenge their faith at all. It is already a part of it. They just haven't been taught about it in this way, and as they come to understand this, then I believe they'll be more open to past life experiences if they come up in their healing process.

The Christian situation is even more interesting because reincarnation is staring right out at them from both the Old and New Testaments, and I think that biblical talk of heaven may have led to confused interpretations.

The fact that we call a certain place in the spiritual world "heaven" doesn't imply in any way that a soul cannot return from the spiritual world to do more work on Earth. In other words, it doesn't have to be one or the other. And according to metaphysical interpretations of the Bible, it seems that souls *do* return for more work.

For example, the Hebrew prophet Elijah lived in the 9th century B.C. Four centuries later, Malachi recorded this prophecy in the closing lines of the Old Testament: "Behold I will send you Elijah the prophet before the coming of the great and dreadful day of the Lord."

In the first book of the New Testament, Matthew refers to this prophecy on three occasions and the remaining gospels speak of it seven times.

> When Jesus came into the coast of Caesarea Philippi, he asked of his disciples, saying, "Who do men say that I, the Son of man, am?" And they said, "Some say that thou art John the Baptist, some say Elijah, and others, Jeremiah, or one of the prophets."[8]
>
> And as they came down from the mountain, Jesus charged them saying, "Tell the vision to no man, until the Son of man be risen again from the dead."
>
> And his disciples asked him, saying, "Why then say the scribes that Elijah must first come?"
>
> And Jesus answered them, "Elijah truly shall come first and restore all things. But I say unto you that Elijah has come already, and they knew him not, but have done unto him whatever they have listed. Likewise shall also the Son of man suffer of them." Then the disciples understood that he spoke unto them of John the Baptist.[9]
>
> Jesus began to say unto the multitudes concerning John, "… This is he, of whom it is written, 'Behold, I send my messenger before your face, which shall prepare the way before you.' Verily I say unto you, Among them that are born of women, there hath not risen a greater man than John the Baptist. … And if you will receive it, this is Elijah, which was to come. He that hath ears to hear, let him hear."[10]

It is obvious from the questions asked of Jesus that the Jews of this period were expecting the rebirth not only of Elijah, but of other prophets. Jesus not only failed to "correct" them on this notion, but he actually seemed to confirm that Elijah had reincarnated as John the Baptist!

Again, Matthew isn't the only prophet who talks about this. Both Luke and Mark talk about Herod being confused because he kept hearing things about Jesus being John the Baptist (whom Herod had beheaded) or Elijah or one of the other prophets. And when an angel prophesied to Zacharias about his future son, John (the Baptist), the angel told him that he would go forth "in the spirit and power of Elijah".[11]

These and other biblical references must give pause to the honest theologian who denies that reincarnation is an integral part of the Christian faith — especially considering that these are not obscure passages, but that they're right in the heart of the Christian story.

For Christians, then, the idea of reincarnation and past lives would seem to be a legitimate possibility. For the process of Personal Transformation, however, they don't even have to *believe*, though it can help if they are open to the idea. I think that when hypnotic regressions to former lives start making sense of their current lives, Christians and Jews (and other Western faiths with these types of passages, such as Muslims) will simply find that it makes sense to believe.

Still, it's okay for those who just cannot accept the concept of reincarnation. If they experience in hypnotherapy what feels to them like a past life, we simply ask them to see it as a metaphor for their life, or to use it as they would dream material. After all, the material is still emerging from their own unconscious minds. I have learned to trust each person's unconscious mind to be the ultimate authority in what each person needs to explore and process. Another explanation for this material is what Carl Jung called the *collective unconscious*. As Fritz Perls stated so many times, whatever *emerges* is the *emergency*: in other words, what needs to be addressed without delay.

Whether you're here to heal others and/or yourself, once you're past the hurdle of reincarnation (if it is even a hurdle — many people already believe), it helps to understand the whole birth and death process, which includes time spent prior to earth life preparing for everything the soul needs to experience while incarnate. Every stage of a person's life — beginning before conception, continuing in utero, and finishing with old age and death of the physical body — is part of the overall development of someone's soul. That developmental process, played over and over through past lives, affects every person living today, creating scenarios that need to be worked out, giving strengths and weaknesses, and giving purpose to people's lives. Understanding those stages and their effects, then seeing how Heart-Centered therapy can help, is of course the point of sharing this book with you, and we'll start with looking at just what happens between earth lives, in preparation for physical birth.

Chapter 2
Right Livelihood Questionnaire

Which of the statements are true in your life? Prioritize the top five (giving each a number).

T   1-5

❑ ❑   A. I am meant to work in ways that draw on my natural talents and abilities.

❑ ❑   B. Work is the key to my self-expression, and fulfillment in life.

❑ ❑   C. I work because I have to without thought as to whether it is correct for me.

❑ ❑   D. My work is doing my best at what I am good at and what I enjoy most.

❑ ❑   E. My work is consciously chosen, not what family and culture expected of me.

❑ ❑   F. I do my work with awareness and care, not mindlessly with indifference.

❑ ❑   G. My work is more than a job, even more than a career: it is my spiritual path.

❑ ❑   H. My work embodies self-expression, mindfulness, and conscious choice.

❑ ❑   I. My work adds to my high self-esteem, worthiness, and feeling trustworthy.

❑ ❑   J. My work is intrinsically fulfilling emotionally, mentally and spiritually.

❑ ❑   K. Money, security, and approval have ceased to be my only rewards.

❑ ❑   L. I accept my talents, and do not seek approval and direction from others.

❑ ❑   M. I become deeply involved in my work, releasing me from mind chatter.

❑ ❑   N. My work contributes to my sense that I count, and I treat myself like I do.

❑ ❑   O. Through my work I serve humanity and contribute to the light on the planet.

❑ ❑   P. My work is in alignment with my beliefs. I am in integrity at work.

What work activities make you happy or bring you pleasure, satisfaction and joy? After each one, name the values from the Chapter 1 Questionnaire which the activity addresses.

A. _____

_____

B. _____

_____

C. _____

_____

D. _____

_____

Your relationship with your life's work – which one fits best?

❏ A job is something you do everyday mostly to earn money. You often wonder what you are doing there and may feel bored, restless and increasingly unhappy.

❏ A career is daily work that is moving you toward a goal and feels more meaningful than "just" a job. It also makes use of your skills and education. The money you earn seems to be an important part of it. You seem to need raises in order to continue to feel successful.

❏ Life's work is spiritually, emotionally and mentally fulfilling. Each day you look forward to what you are doing. You feel challenged, excited and stimulated by what you are doing. It is wonderful if you can earn money doing your life's work, but you would continue to do it even if you didn't have the need to earn money.

Your Project: Send yourself a telegram

Write yourself a telegram, from someone who represents an authority to you, authorizing you to engage in a job or a venture that allows you to do your life's work. Make it as detailed as possible, with specifics regarding the mission, the work itself, the financial aspects, and timelines. Be bold. Incorporate all that you most want in your work life and career.

Chapter 3
The Interlife

Through the years, I continued using hypnosis in my healing practice and came across an incredible variety of experiences, as I continue to today. Many of my clients' regression sessions take them back to childhood, and sometimes even into the womb! Others take them into former lives where they discover the real origin of some hurt or fear or other issue — for example, when I regressed back to my life that ended in a German concentration camp. The healing that accompanies many of these experiences alone helps to validate these regressions. In many cases, though, other people who were present at the time, or a study of history, can validate regressions that a client never had insights on before.

But hypnosis can give us more than just information on someone's childhood or past lives. In some cases, it can tell us about the "interlife" experience as well. This is what I call life on the other side — where we live after death and before our next incarnation. There is a great deal that happens between lives, and we have a whole lot more details to that world than most people recognize. During the interlife, the primary purpose is to learn from the life just completed and prepare for the life to come. But there are many instances, too, when the interlife directly affects people here on earth.

A good example of all this comes up in the story of one of my clients. Molly remained in an unhealthy relationship for years with a man who never met her emotional needs. But any time she tried leaving him, some crisis came up making it necessary to stay with him. She might have an accident or get sick with asthma, making her so needy that she couldn't leave.

In fact, the asthma seemed to be triggered any time someone left her. At work, whenever a fellow worker retired, Molly got so sick that she was unable to breathe. She would end up at the doctor's office requiring a breathing machine and a multitude of drugs.

In my work with her, she regressed back to the time of her birth. During this session, Molly found herself struggling through the birth canal when her mother was given an anesthetic. When the anesthetic hit, Molly felt numb and emotionally abandoned. She felt as if her mother had just disappeared and Molly had to get through the difficult birth process all alone. Because of the anesthetic and the long struggle through the birth canal, she was unable to breathe well and she thought she was going to die. This abandonment was exactly what she felt when other people left her, even as an adult ... and her response of being unable to breathe (asthma) was just the same as well.

Another regression brought us to her next feeling of suffocation. When Molly was eight years old, her alcoholic father was laying on top of her, trying to force himself sexually on her. She was trapped beneath him and couldn't breathe, and she felt furious that her father would do this to her. A series of other events in her childhood reinforced her feelings of victimization and helplessness.

When Molly was fourteen, the most traumatic event of all happened to her and her brother. They came home one day from school to find that their father had drowned himself in the bathtub as an act of suicide while in a drunken stupor. Molly was horrified and in a state of shock to discover him face down underwater. She shouted at him to wake up as she shook his cold and rigid body to no avail. Interestingly, he died because he was unable to breathe.

During another Heart-Centered Hypnotherapy session, we worked to help her deal with all of these experiences. In this regression, Molly had the distinct sense that her father's energy was attached to her in a desperate attempt to remain connected to her even after his death. She felt that he was choking her. She cried and yelled for him to leave her alone. As she released her anger and grief, she was finally able to release *him*. She then began to feel her breathing open up, as if her father had finally released the stranglehold he had on her. She has not had another asthma attack since that session.

When Molly first came into the Personal Transformation work, she believed that her husband was unable to meet her needs. But as she released the energy of her abusive father, she realized that she had been projecting her fear and mistrust of men onto her husband. Through her release work, Molly has been able to open up to her husband and let him know her needs. This makes it possible for him to respond to her in a whole new way.

The story of this one client is enough to show us how flexible hypnotic regression can be, and it tells us just a little bit about the interlife. It's not clear to me whether Molly's father had truly latched onto her after his physical death; that may have just been her experience, though in either case, the release was important for her. But this kind of attachment *can* take place when people leave their bodies — they can want to cling to this world for many reasons, or can even just be confused about what they are supposed to do. In the case of alcoholics and drug addicts, for instance, it is possible that the disembodied soul has a substance craving that he cannot satisfy from the other world, so he literally attaches himself to someone still living and encourages him or her to partake, just so he can get his fix. Many drug users and alcoholics are influenced by addicts from their life who have passed away and have become attached to the living addict.

The attachment, in that case, is one of addiction to a substance, but there are many other reasons for entities to remain attracted to this world and therefore to become attached to those still living. Powerful emotions, either positive or negative, can tie entities here. For instance, anger, shame, jealousy, guilt, remorse ... or even love can make those who have died wish to remain here and continue feeding that emotion, or perhaps even to try resolving it. These are the *dybbuk*, the "vagrant souls which, finding neither rest nor harbor, pass into the bodies of the living." The problem is, overcoming negative emotions and traumas is only possible during life *in this world*. When entities attach, they may *continue* a negative emotional relationship — as in the case of Molly and her father — but they cannot *complete* it.

Another common and interesting example of a spirit attachment comes in the case of organ transplants. We recently helped a woman named Jeri who had a kidney transplant, and since the transplant, she began noticing some very strange things about herself. All of her life, she had enjoyed boating and water sports; suddenly she was terrified of the water and couldn't go anywhere near her boat. She also began to have environmental allergies and asthmatic symptoms of difficult breathing. She began having trouble sleeping at night and would wake up with night terrors; she started experiencing terrible headaches; and she felt that "someone very big was taking up her entire chest cavity."

It is quite common for people who get organ transplants to take on qualities of the person whose organ they have received.[12] Because donors have usually died suddenly and don't know that they've left their body, it's common for them to assume they have taken over the body of the person who receives their organ. We hypnotized Jeri and asked to "speak" to the organ donor, who was called Mickey. He told us he was in a serious boating accident during a storm, was hit over the head by the corner of the boat, and drowned suddenly. He could remember his head hurting and not being able to breathe. He had been terrified. When asked about his size, he said he was about 6 feet tall.

We directed him to leave Jeri's body and thanked him for his kidney. We told him that his death had brought life to another person. We explained that he would be much more peaceful in the light rather than hanging on to this poor woman's body. Once Mickey left her, Jeri felt total relief and her life returned to normal. Today, the headaches and allergies are gone. She is able to breathe freely again and feels like she is the only one in her body now. Plus, her fear of the water is gone and she can enjoy using her boat and going to the ocean again. She is sleeping peacefully and is grateful for the removal of this attachment. Her kidney is functioning better than ever.

With a sudden death, there are often traumas and/or strong emotions involved that can lead to attachments, or in some cases, the entity doesn't realize that it has died. Entities might also remain because of mistaken beliefs about the afterlife (or interlife). For instance, if they do not believe that there is life after physical death, or they believe that they're going to spend eternity in hell, they may not want to head towards the light in case that leads to hell or oblivion.

Finally, attachments can be intentional or accidental. If Molly's father was truly attached to her, then that was probably an intentional action on his part due to the strong emotions between the two of them. In other instances, though, simple proximity (i.e., being near someone at the time they die) may be enough to trigger an attachment if the dying person has strong ties to the world for reasons mentioned above. And these attachments are *not* uncommon, no matter how oblivious most of us are to them. Some experts on the subject suggest that 70–100% of all people will be unwitting host to an attachment at some point in their lives.[13]

These attachments may have positive, neutral, or negative intentions behind them, but they are all parasitic in nature and do cause a physical and/or mental energy drain on the living host. Obviously this is no small matter, and later in this book, we'll talk about how one can pass through the dying process without becoming stuck to the world in this way. When more practitioners begin implementing this work with those who are getting ready to depart this world, we will dramatically reduce the magnitude of this spirit attachment issue.

Helping departed people past their attachment to this life also gets them more quickly to the real purpose of the interlife, which is what we'll talk about in the rest of this chapter. Understanding this purpose and how the interlife works is critical to the work we do. It is, after all, a time when past life experiences are brought together and when the life to come — with all its inherent lessons — is planned. And all of this plays out in the challenges and potentials everyone faces in life.

You may not "believe" in past lives, or spirit attachment, or interlife experiences such as those described here. However, they arise in hypnotic regressions, whether they are literally true or are metaphor, dreamscapes, or contents from the collective unconscious, and we work with them.

Near Death Experiences

We have evidence about how the interlife works through many sources. We have the messages of both historical and modern day seers; we have the writings of certain spiritual giants; we have the clinical evidence of those under hypnosis whose testimonies are often confirmed by outside sources; and many of us even have personal spiritual experiences.

Among the latter, we have to give some credit to Western medicine in the sense that many more people are brought back from the other side who, earlier in history, would have passed from this world. So many people who are brought back like this tell a similar story of what happened on the other side, and this is of course known as the Near Death Experience (NDE) — something that 12 million Americans said they had gone through according to a 2000 Gallup poll. The consistency of stories (although not alike in every respect, because the experience seems to rely in part on one's religious or spiritual expectations) gives us ample suggestion about the first stages of the interlife.

Descriptions of NDEs reveal that the "consciousness" separates from the body, remains fully aware of its physical surroundings, and perceives everything in precise detail, usually from some vantage point in the room where the body is. As this separated consciousness, many report being greeted by deceased friends and relatives. They often encounter a tunnel, a brilliant Light that beckons, and a spiritual figure which — for Christians — is often Jesus. At this point, a decision must be made about whether to go to the Light or return to Earth to continue with this lifetime. When the latter decision is made, the consciousness of the person rejoins the physical body. Sometimes this happens apparently under the efforts of a medical staff; often, however, it happens to the shock of the medical staff who have already given the person up for dead.

Not everyone who survives an NDE reports seeing the Light. Some report more of a hellish scene, which is said to be the activity of the Lower Astral Plane and is referred to in the Bible as the place of "the gnashing of teeth." This is the place of demons, dark-energy beings, mischievous spirits, and earthbound disincarnates. Many of these spirits are actively seeking some unsuspecting or naïve being to attach to for their own purpose.

In either case, however, the undeniable experience of so many millions of people is that the individual consciousness survives physical death, fully aware as a discrete entity — a spirit.

The Interlife Process

Again, from many sources including extensive clinical learning, we know a great deal about what happens between one lifetime and the next. At the time of physical death, the etheric or subtle body lifts out of the physical shell. Contained within the subtle body are the energetic patterns of the emotional and physical residues of that life experience. Still encased in the subtle body, the conscious being that *is* the actual person moves toward the Light. Light is always present at death, though sometimes it seems close and sometimes far away. It depends on how preoccupied we are with attachments to "what used to be" and "what might have been" and "what I can't live without."

When you pass from this world, you continue to carry with you the beliefs, habits, fears, and desires that were yours in life. That can be good news or bad news, depending on your mental and spiritual health at the time of death. If you are angry and judgmental in life, you will find yourself experiencing those qualities immediately after death. If you are a sex addict in life, you will continue to be obsessed with sex after death. If you avoid change and cling to the status quo in life, you will do the same after death, and perhaps attempt to attach to someone from your life, or attempt to act as if you have not died and are still living.

Now, the traditional sequence of experiences after death, in the interlife, only comes about if you allow yourself to proceed through them. Those who prefer constancy and the status quo to instability and change must still face the inevitable changes, but they will attempt to avoid each transition. This avoidance can come in the form of indecision, ambivalence, and procrastination. It can come in the form of impulsively jumping headfirst. It can come in the form of reflex — habitual responses that allow one to act on automatic pilot, and thus to avoid any conscious experience of the transitional space. It can come in the form of entering the transition and never leaving it, "hiding out" in drama. It can take the form of retreat into traumatic shock.

In short, those who have a fear of the unknown, no matter how nice the experience could be, will avoid the traditional sequence of stages in the interlife. On the other hand, those who have lived consciously, mindfully, peacefully, and with integrity will likely go through the interlife in a similar way.

The traditional experience after passing from this world begins with moving toward the Light, where guiding spirits come to assist. These spirits may look like angels without wings dressed in white robes. They may look like shining lights. They may be spiritual figures from your particular belief system. Or spirits of deceased relatives or loved ones may arrive. Whoever arrives, they are there to guide you to the Light. Although this is a very gentle and non-threatening event, it might make sense to wonder whether the spirits approaching are the right ones for you. But this is a protected process, and unless some obviously negative entity were to approach, those who come to help will be right for you.

After you meet with these special guides, they lead you toward a Gateway, which is probably the reason for the common symbol of the "Pearly Gates." You aren't judged here, however. There is no one keeping you from passing through the Gate. In fact, you *have* to pass through the Gate if you wish to come fully into the Light. Until you pass through that Gateway, you still have a connection with the physical world and you have the opportunity to return to your body, so long as it is still physically available. Once you pass through the Gateway, the Silver Cord connecting your spirit with your physical body is severed and, at that point, you have made the decision to experience the interlife — to gain from the Earth life just lived and to prepare for the next Earth life to come.

Once fully in the Light, you're actually on the astral plane. Depending on the quality of your life and the choices you made on Earth, you can arrive on various levels of the astral world. What traditional religion refers to as hell, purgatory, or the "gnashing of teeth" is simply the lower levels of the astral plane. These experiences are described as "fiery" simply because, esoterically speaking, you must go through a process of "burning off" the outer shells of the astral matter surrounding your body. As you do so, you are able to reach the higher levels of the astral plane. Those who lead their lives with more love and wisdom, however, will find themselves arriving on the higher planes of the astral world without having to go through this temporary purging of the outer shells or lower levels of this world. This explains why there is value to traditional teachings, which encourage people to live better lives "lest they experience hell or purgatory." But the threat of eternal damnation is misleading and causes an inappropriate fear of the afterlife.

The middle to higher regions of the astral world are what religions tend to call Heaven. The heaven world allows for a period of relative rest, and we call this the "Resting Stage." After the Resting Stage comes the Review Stage, during which time you assess (with the help of counselors) what was accomplished in the previous life, what was not resolved, and what needs to be examined in the Planning Stage for the next lifetime. There are Great Halls of Learning where you can prepare for the next life. Finally comes the Planning Stage, then conception, and on to the beginning of another physical life.

Being aware of this process is important because, in many cases, those who get stuck after leaving their physical bodies are those who don't understand what they're supposed to do. In our chapter on death, we'll talk more about how people can prepare for the initial stages of the interlife. This process can often be facilitated by a Heart-Centered therapist, who knows that this preparation is part of finishing up the business of this life — an important part of the transformational process of someone's soul. The Review and Planning Stages, however, are preparations for a life to come (rather than the completion of a life), so we'll take a look at those now as the first stages of any life on Earth.

The Planning & Review Stages

Again, in the Review Stage of the interlife, you get a chance to go back over the life just lived. Different spiritual sages have described this process in different ways. Some suggest that you basically go through your life as if it were a movie, although you would experience it again much more quickly than it took to live. Others suggest that events would actually unfold in reverse order. Some have said that, rather than seeing things through your own eyes a second time, you would experience each event from *other* people's perspectives, in order to better know how your actions affected others.

Perhaps this stage takes place in one of these ways, or perhaps it takes place in different ways for different people. The *purpose* of this stage, though, is always the same: to understand the impact that your last physical life had; to know what you accomplished and what you failed to accomplish (in a non-judgmental sense); and to better see what goals you ought to set for the next life to come. This brings you into the Planning Stage.

The Planning Stage gives you a chance to actually sketch out the probabilities and possibilities of your future life. It pre-destines nothing, but essentially provides a board on which to play the next game. All of those with whom you may open spiritual contracts (loosely describing the relationship you will have together if both of your life choices bring you together at some point) are present in this stage.

Counselors are also present to help analyze how best to address unfinished business and unresolved emotional conflicts from former lifetimes. Possibilities for interacting with others and for addressing past life issues are all affected by choices regarding race, gender, health, parents, affluence or poverty, geographical location, and so on. With so many variables to consider, it makes sense to have counselors available to assist.

In fact, even events and opportunities are arranged that will give everyone involved the opportunity to resolve conflicts and balance any karmic debts existing from former lives. This is the foundation for the concept of karma, the law of cause and effect. In the Christian tradition it is represented by the phrase, "As you sow, so shall you reap."

Another important aspect of the Planning Stage is the design of the Lifeline, extending from conception to maximum age attainable. This includes *all the possible choice points* for checking out or choosing death. This can include death due to illness, accident, disaster, murder, old age, or anything else, and of course the circumstances surrounding someone's death not only affect their next interlife, but they provide learning opportunities for those left behind as well.

The value of understanding this Planning Stage is that, when you know that you've participated in your own life plan, you can look at things differently. You don't have to blame others for your experience; you can know that there are lessons in everything; and you can know that you have *always* provided alternate routes to choose from. In this way, you are never a victim, but a planner and creator. At any time, you can change everything because various paths are already laid out for you. But to do so, you'll usually need to complete contracts and pay off karmic debt in one situation in order to move into the next choice. This puts responsibility and healing into your own hands.

Development of the Ego and Personality

After the Planning Stage, the time has come for the consciousness of your spirit to say a "final goodbye" to the spirit world before conception, and to come into physical form and find its place on Earth. At the time of transition from spirit to flesh, many people feel angry, sad, or ambivalent. The ambivalence is about whether one made the right decision to come here, wants to be in this earthly life, wants to go back, or hesitates to go forward. Alternatively, some people feel ecstasy and exhilaration at this momentous time. William Emerson has coined the terms *divine homesickness* for a longing to return to the spirit world, and *divine exile* for a feeling of rejection at having been expelled from Heaven.

Ready or not, your spirit comes into physical form and finds its place on Earth. During this lifetime, the subconscious mind records everything that happens while the conscious, judging mind constantly assesses the environment for any real or imagined threats to survival. Besides this dual action of the mind, we also have an "emotional self" that we call the personality, and this interacts with everyone else's personalities.

As the personality develops, the *real* you — the inherent soul within — begins to associate itself with the personality and the mind. Since the function of the mind is survival, and since you begin considering that you are actually the personality, your mind begins to focus on survival of that personality. As a result, the mind tries to make the personality as strong as possible.

In the early stages of life, this leads to bragging; when we are too old to brag (if we're to be socially accepted), we start putting other people down in order to boost ourselves and keep the personality valid. For those who get beyond this stage of putting others down, there is still another technique for keeping the personality alive, and that is through accomplishments. This is especially true if we can get our names affixed somewhere that is relatively concrete — whether in newspaper articles, in patents, in copyrights of books or CDs, in world records, or anything else that can keep us alive even after our bodies are gone. This effort to keep the personality alive at all costs is called the ego, and this error of the mind leads to seemingly endless human suffering.

In short, the ego seeks to survive by (1) competing; (2) validating its own point of view and invalidating other people's points of view; (3) making itself right and others wrong; (4) justifying its own behavior; (5) judging the behavior of others; (6) self-aggrandizing.

You can see how this list fits most of us to some degree, though some have certainly overcome these tendencies more than others. For instance, consider how certain writers, singers, artists, inventors, and engineers develop products for wealth (which can purchase a legacy) or fame while others have developed the same kinds of products with more or less altruistic motives. The more advanced a soul, the less it is concerned with whether it gets the credit for a particular action, but instead how much that action helps the cause of human and world development. President Harry S. Truman said, "It is amazing what you can accomplish if you do not care who gets the credit." For the most part, few people do things *only* because of ego; and few people do things *only* because of the soul. Most people's motives are mixed because we are all working towards enlightenment, no matter how slowly or quickly.

The ego drives our personality through its judgments, assumptions, self-delusions, conclusions and decisions: all clouded by this need to keep the personality alive. We blame others in order to make ourselves look good; we avoid taking personal responsibility; and in some cases, we even make ourselves "more important" than we really are by assuming the guilt for someone else's suffering! The mind doesn't care *how* it has to go about making the personality important and alive; it just pursues the job of survival in any way it can. Thus, the ego is the basis for all human suffering as it carries errors from one lifetime to the next. And through the stages of life that we'll explore in the next chapters, this is what each of us must strive to overcome.

Chapter 3
Relationship Karmic Purpose Questionnaire

Which of the statements are true in your relationships with men and women, reflecting your basic life patterns? Prioritize the top five (giving each a number).

M   F   1-5
❑ ❑ ❑   A. Trust/commitment issues
❑ ❑ ❑   B. Control issues
❑ ❑ ❑   C. Expressing anger
❑ ❑ ❑   D. Fear issues
❑ ❑ ❑   E. Dependency issues
❑ ❑ ❑   F. Fears of rejection/abandonment
❑ ❑ ❑   G. Fears of engulfment
❑ ❑ ❑   H. Victim, rescuer, persecutor patterns
❑ ❑ ❑   I. Difficulty taking your power in healthy ways
❑ ❑ ❑   J. Asserting control in the area of money
❑ ❑ ❑   K. Asserting control in the area of closeness/distance
❑ ❑ ❑   L. Expressing your feelings directly
❑ ❑ ❑   M. Being who you truly are, not playing a role
❑ ❑ ❑   N. Seeing people from your past in those in your life today
❑ ❑ ❑   O. Using your full creativity to express yourself

What relationship activities make you happy or bring you pleasure, satisfaction and joy? After each one, name the values from the Chapter 1 Questionnaire (page 23) which the activity addresses.

A. _____   _____

_____   _____

B. _____   _____

_____   _____

C. _____   _____

_____   _____

D. _____   _____

_____   _____

What are the karmic or past life purposes for your relationships? What do you need to learn? What karmic wound are you healing? Name the person that may fit each category.

❏ To fulfill unrequited love from another lifetime

_____

❏ To bring particular children back into the world

_____

❏ To complete a relationship that was interrupted

_____

❏ To make a spiritual journey together

_____

❏ To learn non-attachment through the relationship

_____

❏ To learn unconditional love

_____

❏ To work through any of the above power issues

_____

Your Project: Send three letters

Write a letter (you may choose to actually send it, or choose not to) to the three people in your life who you have struggled with the most, explaining what lessons you have learned from your relationship with them. Take the opportunity to express your gratitude, as hard as that may be.

Chapter 4
The Womb Experience

After the Planning Stage for a lifetime, a soul only needs to wait until its chosen parents on Earth succeed in becoming pregnant, and then its introduction to this world begins. That soul brings with it all of the wisdom as well as the errors and challenges of former lifetimes, and these will have an effect on how the coming life progresses. This is important to understand in the old question of nature vs. nurture.

Of course nurture plays its part as well, and it starts doing so the moment a soul begins attaching to the dividing cells that eventually become a fetus. Not only do we have plenty of scientific information to back that up, but clinical experience tells us this too. For instance, hypnotic regression not only takes people to experiences in former lives or in their early childhood years, but it can also take them right back into the womb, where both the internal and external environments have a profound effect on their development.

I have countless examples of this happening in my own practice. One that illustrates the point well is when I worked with a woman named Lynn. Throughout her time in the womb, her mother was being abused and she experienced constant fear for her own life as well as for the life of her baby. The mother also felt shame that someone would find out about the abuse and consider her an unfit mother. So she hid the abuse and the fact that she was pregnant for as long as she could. She wore tight fitting girdles and loose clothes. When Lynn was born, it was quite a surprise to the many people who didn't even know her mother was pregnant.

When Lynn was first born, she didn't cry much and didn't connect well with people. Her mother and grandmother labeled her as "shy." When babies and young children are said to be shy, it can mean that they're carrying around the shame and fear that they experienced for nine months in utero. Baby Lynn soon developed extensive fears that were displayed most fervently when she was in the presence of men or when she and her mother were separated for even a short time.

When I met Lynn, she was an attractive, intelligent woman with painfully low self-esteem. Her husband, Howard, was a pilot who abused her, was cold and distant, and had many affairs which he flaunted in her face. When they came in for marriage counseling, however, Howard angrily told me that it was her problem and that he wasn't really interested in anything but a divorce.

I watched month after month while Lynn came in, continuing to be victimized and seemingly drowning in her shame and pain. She was unable to tell even her best friend what was happening to her and didn't even know the meaning of support. When her parents came for a visit, she pretended that everything was alright until her young three-year-old mentioned "daddy's lady friend." Even then, Lynn tried to get her parents to think the child was making up stories.

After three months of attempting traditional marriage counseling with this couple, I decided that only hypnotherapy could reach the deep patterns of shame and victimization that were preventing any real therapeutic progress. I began to see Lynn individually and introduced the concept of hypnotherapy to her. I let her know that her patterns of being victimized by her husband were stored in her subconscious mind and, if she was to find any happiness in her life, they would have to be changed.

I explained that the unconscious mind stores these patterns like a computer program and then replays this program over and over again. Freud called this "repetition compulsion"; only, at that time, he wasn't aware yet of our modern and scientific forms of therapy such as Gestalt, Transactional-Analysis, and behavior modification. Since combining some of the Humanistic theories with the hypnosis that Freud began working with and that Milton Erickson popularized, we now have some dynamic psychological tools that are much more effective than analysis alone.

I told Lynn that talking therapy, counseling, and analysis had brought her some conscious awareness of her problems; but as she knew, that hadn't changed the pervasive victim patterns in her life. And although she clearly saw and understood how unhealthy her relationship was with Howard, she seemed too paralyzed to make any changes. She agreed with my points and admitted that she had continued feeling frustrated; angry; and filled with hurt, shame, and grief.

We began hypnotherapy by exploring the shame that Lynn felt when telling her parents of her marital abuse and the consequent psychological abuse her children suffered as witnesses. Using Heart-Centered Hypnotherapy, I assisted Lynn in following that feeling of shame back into her own childhood. The age-regression revealed many scenes where she had watched her mother being abused by her stepfather over and over again. She regressed back to ages thirteen, eight, and even four to replay these scenes of violence, physical and emotional abuse, and degradation. This was the constant reality of her formative years and, as a result, part of her believed that this was how women were supposed to be treated by men.

The anger and pain she expressed from all of this was so deep, however, that I sensed there was still something more involved.

So I continued to regress Lynn, looking for the core issue behind this problem, and she began experiencing what I knew was a return to the womb. At first it was dark for her, and then the feelings began to slowly emerge. She began to describe her own shame and fear as her mother was abused throughout the pregnancy. "What was the shame about?" I asked.

And suddenly Lynn knew. She understood for the first time *why* her mother felt so much shame that she tried to hide the pregnancy. She understood for the first time that the pregnancy itself was a major reason behind the abuse. Her stepfather believed that Lynn was the result of her mother's affair with another man, and he was furious about this assumption.

So what was Lynn going through today? She was carrying her mother's shame about the pregnancy. She had done so for her whole life and in every cell of her being. That shame was transferred while she was yet unborn. Until this powerful hypnotherapy session, Lynn had been unaware that these feelings went back so far or that they were engrained so deeply — her whole nine months of fetal development took place in the midst of the *internal* belief that she was unwanted and shameful.

Wanting her to now understand her existential issue, I asked during her regression what conclusion she had drawn about herself by learning all of this. She replied that she wasn't safe in this world, and that the only hope for getting by was to be very good and not get in anyone's way. Her life's decision was that, in order to be safe, she would have to be invisible.

Of course this explained why she was so shy as a child and why she did nothing to stop her husband from having blatant affairs or abusing her. She couldn't risk making a fuss. But using the Heart-Centered Hypnotherapy model, I was able to extinguish Lynn's original feelings of shame so that she could reclaim her dignity and take back the power that she had deserved all her life. This powerful healing process felt like a sacrament to me. The spiritual energy was profound.

This episode was just one of countless experiences I could use to demonstrate the point — in other words, regression into the womb is not at all uncommon, and according to research, it can be highly accurate. In 2000, John Ham and Jon Klimo reported on research showing a high correlation between the womb experience recalled by individuals under hypnosis and the birth mother's account of the pregnancy. In the study, the researchers verified that the relevant information had never been shared with the subjects, ensuring that their only source for the information was their first-hand experience. In this study, subjects recalled — and birth mothers verified — a wide range of emotional states, including the emotions of happiness, joy, aloneness, sadness, frustration, resentment, disgrace, shame, disappointment, fear, and love.[14] Many in traditional psychology treat consciousness as if it begins at age 2 or 3 years with the first autobiographical memories. However, current research distinguishes somatosensory (emotional and body) memories from autobiographical memories. The right brain (feelings, senses, intuition) develops faster during the first three years, embedding a trail of somatosensory memories; at around the age of three, growth of the left brain (language, rationality) becomes dominant, allowing the creation of autobiographical narrative memories.[15] Traumatic memories are also experienced and stored as somatosensory, and they have been termed *situationally accessible memories* because they cannot be accessed intentionally, but instead are triggered by reactivating stimuli.[16] We will discuss the factors that both enhance and impede the development of early memories later in this chapter. Hypnosis uniquely provides access to past memories of such emotional and somatic events,[17] and is therefore an invaluable tool in the transformational healing process.

Fetal Development and Environmental Stimuli

The fact of how profound the pre-natal period really is may surprise people who don't understand how developed and aware fetuses and newborns are. For instance, as early as 13 weeks gestational age, fetuses show individual behavior and personality traits that continue after birth. In 1992, Alessandra Piontelli observed four sets of twins by ultrasound periodically over the course of the pregnancies. Each set of twins seemed to manifest a unique relationship together: one set was loving, another contentious, and another was passive. The fourth pair consisted of a brother who was active, attentive, and affectionate, and his sister who would passively follow his lead. The boy in this pair kicked and wrestled with the placenta, actively pushing for space and looking disgruntled. However, at times he would reach out to his sister through the membrane separating them, caressing her face or rubbing her feet with his. His sister would reciprocate when he initiated contact.

Piontelli then conducted follow-up observations of each set of twins through age four and found that behavior after birth for each child, and in the relationship between each set of twins, continued remarkably unchanged.[18] It is also well documented that fetuses dream, as exhibited by rapid eye movement (REM), as early as 23 weeks gestational age.[19] The dreaming activity in both fetus and premature baby is vigorous, involving coherent movements of the face and extremities as well as changes in heart rate and respiration. The dreams are, as with adults, expressions of inner mental or emotional conditions and are markedly pleasant or unpleasant.[20] This alone tells us that fetuses have the ability for mental and emotional responses. But someone might *still* wonder if that includes responses to external stimuli.

First of all, the fetus responds reflexively to touch by around 8 weeks of gestational age, and by 14 weeks most of its body (excluding its back and top of the head) is responsive to touch. The fetus responds to light with changes in body movements and heart rate from 26 weeks. So we know that the fetus is physically aware of these stimuli. More specifically, Kanwaljeet Anand and Paul Hickey specified the anatomical pathways and mechanisms for pain perception from the seventh week after conception onward. They pointed to the early origins of the neurochemical systems associated with pain, especially substance P, which appears in the brain and spinal column at 12 to 16 weeks. And perhaps most importantly, they noted the consistent and predictable effect of prenatal pain on the cardiorespiratory system; on hormonal and metabolic changes; and on motor responses, facial expressions, crying, and other complex behaviors ... *including long-term memory.*[21]

In fact, a fetus is actually capable of discriminative learning, which requires some form of sentient awareness. And memory for prenatal experiences is present immediately after birth. For example, newborns prefer a lullaby their mothers had sung to them in the womb to an unfamiliar one sung by their mothers[22], and prefer to hear stories that were read to them in the womb, rather than unfamiliar stories.[23] One study found that newborns of mothers who had consistently watched a particular television soap opera during pregnancy responded, when hearing the theme song after birth, by stopping crying, becoming alert, and changing their heart rate and movements. The newborns did not respond to other unfamiliar television tunes.[24]

But we can go even earlier in fetal life. The unborn human develops the capacity to respond to the environment at least by the age of four weeks. The central nervous system's limbic system, which is critically involved with the storage and retrieval of memory,[25] is partially mature at four weeks of gestation,[26] and further development requires use. In other words, development of the central nervous system is completed long after the fetus begins processing information and responding to it. And according to recent research, with the capacity to respond comes the ability to store experiences in memory for future use.

What's more, we don't even need to get to the point of a developing limbic system for a fetus to start taking on the effects of its environment. Every cell in the body has a memory of its own, and each stores a record of all the positive and negative impacts on the growing fetus. In Thomas R. Verny's words, "Before our children have even rudimentary brains, they are gathering within the cells of their bodies their first memories."[27]

These cellular memories and the wiring of the brain itself do not just store information about the physical and emotional environments (diet, pollutants, stress levels, etc.). They store everything about the *thought* environment as well. Thoughts are stored in the cells of individuals and are transmitted by the breath. So what happens is that a woman's thoughts are recorded in the fetus *and are often responded to later in life.*

These thought imprints are very real, and have extraordinary consequences. For instance, research and years of experience indicate that suicidal thoughts often come from the pre- and perinatal experiences. When a baby is conceived and that conception is unwanted, the mother herself may begin thinking about having an abortion. Even though the mother has never told the child about these thoughts or feelings, the process of conscious, connected breathing can bring this knowledge to the conscious awareness of the breather (the child of that mother) in therapy later on. Unaddressed, such thoughts of abortion — transmitted by the mother to the child — can become a death urge which may plague the child throughout life in the form of depression, feeling apologetic about living, or even suicidal thoughts.

To illustrate the point: Andrew Feldmar studied a number of adolescent patients with a history of more than five suicide attempts each, always at the same time of year.[28] He eventually determined that the suicide dates of four patients corresponded to the month in which their mothers had tried to abort them. The adolescents had no *conscious* knowledge of the abortion attempts that they were *unconsciously* acting out. Feldmar discovered that they had even used a method of suicide similar to the method of the abortion — chemicals, for example, or instruments. After discovering that their suicide attempts were seasonal intrusions of prenatal memory, the patients were free of the suicidal compulsion. They never attempted suicide again, even when their 'anniversaries' returned.

Violence in children can be explained by these internal memories as well. Of course many talk shows discuss this topic and present various theories to explain it, blaming peers or the families, etc. But these theories don't hold much water since so many parents notice that their children have been angry from a very young age. It is this rage that attracts them to peers who are also angry and violent. The peers may then support their rage, but they are not the cause of it.

A great deal of research has been done on this topic. William Emerson surveyed a number of experts, among whom were R. D. Laing, Frank Lake, Barbara Valassis, Barbara Findeisen, Stan Grof, Michael Irving, and others, to determine the prenatal, etiological basis for violence and aggression.[29] These researchers reported on the kinds of regressive experiences that their aggressive and violent patients had uncovered and that were central in the success of their treatment. Several common threads of consensus emerged:

(1) pre- and perinatal experiences were paramount in aggression and violence;
(2) childhood experiences seemed to reflect and reinforce prenatal traumatization;
(3) aggression and violence were related to the severest levels of pre- and perinatal trauma;
(4) themes of loss, abandonment, rejection, and aggression were consistently related to aggression and violence; and
(5) certain pre- and perinatal traumas were consistently related to aggression and violence.

More specifically, here are some of the details they came up with:

Conception. When aggressive and violent clients are regressed, they frequently encounter the experience of traumatic conception. The most frequent traumas involve forced or manipulated sex; rape or date rape; substance or physical abuse; dismal familial, social, or cultural conditions; and personal or cultural shame, such as being conceived out of wedlock.

Implantation. Regressed aggressive and violent clients often experience implantation, the biological process whereby the conceptus attaches itself to the uterine wall. They report experiencing the terror of being near physical death and/or the feeling of being unwanted with no place to belong. The uterus does not feel receptive to them, and it is here that they first 'decide' that the world is a hostile and unsafe place.

Discovery of Unwanted Pregnancy. When aggressive clients regress to the prenatal period, they frequently go to the time when the pregnancy was discovered and find that they were unwanted. The discovery of being unwanted typically leads to the realization that lifelong episodes of depression, self-destructiveness, or aggression are a direct expression of prenatal rejection. Common responses to being unwanted are to collapse into helplessness and hopelessness, to rage at others and the world's injustice, and/or to refuse to engage in life. These responses are due to "discovery shock." A subsequent book by the author will address the complex subject of the psyche-soma split we call "shock."

Prenatal Aggression. Many adults with problems in aggression learn that they were exposed to various forms of aggression during the pre- and perinatal period. Some common forms of aggression are warfare, gang fights, domestic violence, physical or sexual abuse of parents or siblings, annihilative energies, intrauterine toxicities, and/or abortion attempts. Prenates who experience one or more of these aggressive conditions are at risk for manifesting aggression and violence later in life.

Adoption. Adoption trauma refers to a broad range of painful experiences that are common to adoption. One is abortion trauma: there may have been direct attempts on life, abortion plans with no attempts, or abortion ideations but no plans ... all traumatizing to the fetus. Others are conception shock/trauma (child unwanted at time of conception), discovery shock/trauma (child unwanted at the time of discovery), or psychological toxicity (child exposed to mother's annihilative or ambivalent feelings, or to socio-cultural shame). Being unwanted not only has lifelong consequences of behavioral problems, but actually increases the short-term risk for infant death. Infants born of unwanted pregnancies are more than twice as likely to die within a month of birth than wanted infants.[30]

Parental Influences on the Baby In Utero

Understanding how distinctly the fetus is influenced by its environment, we can easily see what kind of impact Mom and Dad (when present in the mother's life) have. During this lifetime, while the subconscious mind records everything that happens, the conscious, judging mind constantly assesses the environment for any real or imagined threats to survival. Besides this dual action of the mind, we also have an "emotional self" that we call the personality, and this interacts with everyone else's personalities.

As the personality develops, the *real* you — the inherent soul within — begins to associate itself with the personality and the mind. The real you also begins to identify with the world into which you have descended, and that is largely a reflection of your mother (attitudes, beliefs and emotions carried in her egg) and father (attitudes, beliefs and emotions carried in his sperm). At the time of fusion of the sperm with the egg to form a fertilized cell, the prenate (you) may experience an eagerness to move forward with the journey into human life, or dread, or ambivalence, depending largely on the attitudes of the mother and father. As we've discussed, the parents' feelings about becoming pregnant at the time of conception has a profound impact on what the soul, begins to identify as self. The "unwelcome child," for instance, may react with shame and overpowering anxiety regarding his very right to exist.

While an initial shot of either positive or negative influences come at the moment of conception, one of the first major events for the newly developing life comes about one week (six to nine days) after conception when that life descends through the fallopian tube to the uterus — a journey of about four inches. The experience of leaving the snug fallopian tube to enter the vast cavity of the uterus can feel like tumbling or falling, and the new life must stop its fall by grabbing hold of something solid. The individual begins questing for a suitable site to implant, one that offers fertility, nurturing, and welcome.

But again, depending on the father's and mother's attitudes, the individual may instead experience the uterine wall as barren, toxic, or engulfing, like quicksand that sucks one into satisfying the mother's needs; or as full of rigid conditions and demanding expectations; or as unwelcoming, carrying the message of "I don't really want you" or "You are a burden." Any of these compromised sites for implantation could result in a feeling of not belonging, of confusion and ambivalence about "being here" in this life, and could activate defenses of avoidance, control, or preoccupation.

Themes of the implantation experience are creation, survival, and the life-death struggle. It is also during this phase of development that some individuals encounter the spirits or energies of previously conceived lives that have passed through this womb; particularly siblings that have been miscarried or aborted. Many people also experience the loss of a twin who does not survive implantation.

After 5 to 7 days of being completely absorbed by the mother in the uterine wall (in implantation) — about two weeks after conception — the conceptus begins to grow back out of the uterine wall, separating from the mother's flesh. The separation can bring relief and a sense of freedom and accomplishment, but it can also initiate a profound sense of alienation, rejection, and loneliness. In a hostile or ambivalent uterine environment, the conceptus may experience a sense of impending death, carrying a "death imprint" that contaminates the life-oriented impulse to move forward in life.

During the time from conception until the mother knows she is pregnant, the new life may experience a number of things. If there is fear of not being accepted, the prenate may experience existential despair ("No one knows or cares that I exist") or shame and anxiety ("I must hide and be still so they don't know I'm here"). The defenses of withdrawal, hiding, and dissociation can then become imprinted as lifelong patterns.

Once the mother knows with certainty that she is pregnant, the embryo experiences unconditional welcoming or varying degrees of rejection. Rejection may take the form of ambivalence, anxiety, shame, or even abortion thoughts or attempts. Or the rejection may take the form of realizing that "my parents, rather than wanting *me*, actually want me to be a surrogate for their own unfulfilled dreams, or as a replacement for a lost child." The embryo feels terror or despair at the threat to its existence, concludes that "I'm in danger of annihilation," and defends itself by hiding its very existence, adaptively becoming "no bother," or feeling rage at the disappointment of rejection.

Other specific examples of a mother's emotions or physical well-being affecting the life within her are provided by numerous studies. For instance, Nicholas Allen and associates[31] showed that:

- Major depression in a child is predicted by maternal emotional problems and/or rejection during pregnancy.
- Anxiety in a child is predicted by a maternal history of miscarriage and stillbirth.
- Disruptive behavior disorder in a child is predicted by poor maternal emotional health during the pregnancy, as well as by birth complications.
- Substance abuse by a child is predicted by maternal use of substances during the pregnancy and/or the birth.

Meanwhile, Geraldine Downey & James C. Coyne[32] showed that depressed maternal emotional health during pregnancy also increases the child's odds for future conduct disorder and attention deficit disorder. Obstetrical complications appear to be significantly related to psychopathology later in life as well. These pathologies can include schizophrenia[33], personality disorders[34], antisocial behavior[35], and bipolar disorder.[36]

It's already well-established that a mother's nutrition and exposure to toxins during pregnancy has lasting effects on the development of her baby. But now we can see how much more we really have going on. *Everything* about a mother's pregnancy experience affects the baby to a degree. And of course this means that the father (and other people, to the extent that they're involved with the mother) can have an enormous effect as well. If a woman is in a physically, emotionally, and mentally supportive environment, then the baby's development is greatly supported too. But if a woman is abused, fearful, depressed, stressed, and so on, these conditions can manifest in all the problems in the child that we've talked about.

We should take special note of stress, here, because while abuse and depression are — sadly — widespread problems, stress is present in *everyone's* life, and therefore affected *all of us* to some degree when we were yet unborn. One study[37] showed that, when a mother is under stress, her hormones change — particularly the stress hormones — and that in turn alters brain circuits of the offspring in a permanent way.

There is even growing evidence that stress affects the fetus differently depending on when during the pregnancy it occurs. Research now seems to indicate that moderate stress in mothers during pregnancy during the period from 24 to 32 weeks gestation could actually enhance the development of organs,[38] whereas stress for the pregnant mother between 12 and 22 weeks gestation may be related to a variety of negative outcomes for the baby, including greater likelihood of developing ADHD.[39] Research has also shown that the flow of maternal hormones in the fetal brain during this critical second trimester of pregnancy (weeks 12 to 22) result in the formation of natural variations of sexual identity and orientation,[40] and that another period of high vulnerability for determining sexual identity and orientation is the three months immediately *prior* to conception.

As you can see, a child's brain can be permanently imprinted while in the womb, and depending on the imprint, we can see various results. A basic terror could be imprinted at this early stage, for instance, and may appear decades later as panic attacks. A pattern of depression may begin in the third or fourth month of gestation when the mother's depression sends stress hormonal changes to the fetus. Trauma from the fetus' environment can lead the child to develop learning disorders, dyslexia, ADHA, chronic depression, stuttering, and many other conditions.

Examples of these Effects in Real Life

A good example of response to in utero influences comes from a woman who once attended our training. Like many people, she had spent nine months in what we call a "toxic womb" and, because of this, had symptoms of environmental allergies as an adult. And typical of those with this background, she wanted to control the environment around her so that she wouldn't suffer.

While at our training, this woman complained violently about the environment. She reacted to the perfume of the woman sitting next to her and she didn't like the incense we burned one morning during a meditation. She was overwhelmed when we used sage to cleanse the room as we had been taught to do by our Native American shaman teachers.

At one point, we asked her if she would be willing to work on this reaction and she said she would. So we had her join us in a hypnotherapy session and she first went back to age three when there was a fire in the family home and her parents refused to leave the building because they didn't want to lose their possessions. They forced her to stay inside until the firemen arrived, even though she felt overwhelmed by the smoke.

We then regressed her further and she went right back into the womb experience, where she *again* felt overwhelmed by smoke — this time by her mother's smoking. She was extremely angry at being trapped in this toxic womb for nine months without any way to escape the fumes.

Through our work with her, she was able to complete a lot of release work and get out her anger at her mother for these situations. We "cleaned out" the womb for her and let her experience a non-toxic womb for the first time, and she felt a powerful healing within. The next day in class, she was beaming and had no problem with our use of incense or sage, or with anyone's perfume. This goes to show how real and how lasting the womb experience is.

Factors Influencing Memory Retention

With so much evidence about parental effects on a growing fetus (especially from the mother), it almost makes you wonder why anyone would want to get pregnant. But the story is not really as frightening as it sounds. It is *instructive*, because it encourages us to treat an entire pregnancy as a sacred period; and when problems do arise, it points us to a possible root of these problems, helping healers to assist their clients.

But just as with adults, the impact of a fetus' environment on the fetus depends on various factors. For instance, if you were talking with someone you barely knew and they called you stupid, but you were widely respected for your thoughts by everyone else you knew ... well, the impact of that one insult wouldn't be very deep. But if everyone you knew, or if someone you held in especially high esteem called you a fool, it might not be long before you began to wonder. So it is with the fetus. There are, in fact, factors that both enhance *and impede* the development of early memories. Here is a summary of both:

Influences that *Enhance* Encoding of Early Memories

Intensity. The more intensely experienced an event is, the more likely it is to be recorded as a long-term rather than short-term memory. Long-term memory is recorded in cells with entirely new proteins and new connections among nerve cells, whereas short-term memory is created when proteins in nerve cells are modified only temporarily. A dramatic example of the effect of intensity on creation of long-term memories is the phenomenon known as "flashbulb memories." Most people retain an enhanced memory of where they were and what they were doing when President Kennedy was assassinated, or when the space shuttle Challenger exploded, or when the attacks occurred on 9-11. The dramatic intensity of the experience enhanced the memory storage as long-term.[41]

Repetition. Neural circuits in the brain are connections between cells, pathways created to record an experience. Increased traffic over that pathway — i.e., more frequent use of the connection — makes the connection stronger, faster, and more permanent. A connection used infrequently atrophies and is eventually abandoned: "use it or lose it." For example, children who are rarely spoken to, read to, or played with in their early years will likely develop poor language and social skills. On the other hand, any experience that is repeated frequently will become deeply embedded in long-term memory.

Fear. When an experience generates fear, it is more likely to be recorded in long-term memory.[42] Memory of the fear is deeply embedded and easily generalized to other stressful situations, even if they are unrelated to the initial, fearsome incident. According to Verny and Weintraub[43]:

> Memories of abuse are different from normal memories, and research bears that out. Locked away in the recesses of our brains so we are shielded from their intensity, these memories are more difficult to retrieve than other memories, but also more difficult to alter and erase. Because these unconscious, implicit memories are so powerful, they influence behavior throughout life.

Verbal processing. A child's memories of anything are more enduring when they have been talked about reflectively with caregivers at the time of occurrence.[44]

Influences that *Impede* Encoding of Early Memories

Hormones (oxytocin and cortisol). Studies show that, in high concentrations, the maternal hormone oxytocin extinguishes memory.[45] The mother's body (and therefore the baby as well) is flooded with oxytocin prior to birth, and this continues as long as she breastfeeds. Oxytocin facilitates uterine muscle contraction for birth and lactation, and also serves as an "anesthetic for the mind"[46], protecting us from remembering the traumas of birth. The mother also secretes the stress hormone cortisol at birth, which acts to extinguish recall of traumatic memories.

Age of onset of the trauma. The younger the child, the more likely he is to dissociate from traumatic events and repress memory.[47]

Imposition of secrecy. Being told not to tell effectively inhibits the child from speaking through immediate fear, and contributes to memory loss (repression) because it makes verbal processing less likely to happen.[48] This is why so many men and women don't have conscious memories of abuse, but they do have "body memories." For example, a woman will tense up when a man begins to touch her sexually if she has been abused. She doesn't consciously know why this happens, but her muscles and skin remember that this is not safe.

Degree of perpetration violence, including the number of perpetrators. The more "unspeakable" the experience, the more violent and the greater the number of perpetrators, the more likely the child is to dissociate from it, obscuring any memory.[49]

Degree of intimacy between the perpetrator and the victim. The greater the sense of personal betrayal involved — i.e., the more intimate and trusted the perpetrator — the more likely a child is to dissociate from the abuse.

The Healing Process

Considering all that can affect a fetus, the good news is that the fetus prepares for environmental stress early in its development: beta endorphins, a prime resource for responding to stress, are already in production by seven weeks of gestational age, and are present in the fetal pituitary before 15 weeks.[50]

At the same time, however, children's response to trauma is much more intense than an adult's response to the same trauma. One study[51] showed that babies undergoing surgery have five times the stress response of adults undergoing similar surgery, with heart rate, blood pressure, and hormone levels skyrocketing. The same is true for emotional trauma as for surgery.

Fetuses and children, like adults, can deal with a certain amount of pain, which is why intensity and repetition are two of the factors necessary for something to become overwhelming. When this happens, the memories can be lodged into the long-term memory, or repression may occur and memories are buried into the subconscious. When lodged in the conscious memory, a person has the option of dealing with the pain. This leaves the person with the choice of whether to respond in positive or negative ways, but there is a choice. But when memories are repressed, they need to be accessed before the person has any choice about the matter and before any real healing can begin.

In the course of Heart-Centered therapies, we use several techniques to go about that healing. Hypnotherapy is of course central to much of what we do, but we also use other techniques such as birth simulation and re-parenting. These allow us to help our clients experience buried traumas and memories and to correct them — all with the "Heart-Centered" theme of healing the soul. We'll talk in more detail about these techniques later in the book, as the techniques are used to heal problems that come up in any stage of growth and development. So first, it's important that we continue looking at the stages that follow conception and womb-time, next of which is that astounding miracle called birth.

Chapter 4
Womb Experience Questionnaire

The world at the time of your conception

Research the world that your mother and father lived in at the time of your conception, in the family, locally, nationally, worldwide. Was it wartime or peacetime, prosperous or a depression? What was going on in your parents' lives? Was there fear, anger, was there a death in the family, were you occupying a womb that had recently been occupied by another? What were your parents' feelings about becoming pregnant with you, happy, anxious, resentful? Were you welcome or unwelcome?

A. In the transition of leaving spirit world to enter earthly life, I likely felt:
- ❑ 1. *Divine homesickness* (rejection and shame at leaving, and longing to return)
- ❑ 2. *Divine exile* (rejection and rage at being expelled from or forced to leave Heaven)
- ❑ 3. *Regretful choice* ("I made a choice to come here, but it was a really bad choice")
- ❑ 4. *Foreboding* (a pervasive sense uncertainty, but expecting it to turn out badly)
- ❑ 5. *Depression and anxiety* (dread, impotence, and ambivalence to engage life)

B. I had shame and overpowering anxiety regarding my very right to exist:
- ❑ 1. Parental rejection (contemplated or actual adoption or abortion)
- ❑ 2. Parental belief that I was a burden (financially or emotionally)
- ❑ 3. The womb felt barren, toxic, or engulfing rather than nurturing and welcoming
- ❑ 4. Separation (from spirit world) a profound sense of alienation and loneliness

C. When my parents discovered that they were pregnant with me, I experienced:
- ❑ 1. An existential despair ("No one knows or cares that I exist")
- ❑ 2. Shame and anxiety ("I must hide and be still so they don't know I am here")
- ❑ 3. Rejection (rather than wanting *me*, they want a replacement for a lost child)
- ❑ 4. Terror ("I'm in danger of annihilation," so I become no bother)
- ❑ 5. Rage at parental ambivalence or apathy about my being here

D. The womb environment (mother) was suffocating, toxic, disconnected, or nurturing:
- ❑ 1. I am impatient to get out
- ❑ 2. I am starved for nurture
- ❑ 3. I am lonely and feel regret for coming here
- ❑ 4. I feel content

Your Project: Write about the world at the time of your conception

_____

_____

_____

_____

_____

_____

_____

_____

_____

_____

_____

_____

_____

_____

_____

_____

_____

_____

Chapter 5
The Birth Experience

There's no question that the time spent in the womb has a substantial influence on someone's life — either positive, negative, or usually a combination of these, because most women have both positive and negative experiences while pregnant. The effects are cumulative, so that no one experience can be the single womb-influence on the child's life.

When it comes to birth, however, things are very different. Birth happens in a comparatively short period of time — generally not more than 36 hours, and usually much less. So any given aspect of that birth really can have a substantial, long-term effect on the baby's life. And once again, through hypnosis, we're able to learn a lot about just how the birth experience plays out over the years.

For instance, a woman named Sally came into my office and was white with fear. She began to explain how, every time she was about to travel on an airplane, she began to feel terrified. Her anxiety would rise and she couldn't think of anything else. As the day of departure drew nearer, she felt more and more terrified. She would usually get sick just before going ... so she could "legitimately" cancel her trip.

Sally was tired of this pattern, as it greatly limited her life. She and her family couldn't go on trips and her husband was growing disturbed by her limitations. She knew that these fears were "irrational" and that they were controlling her life. But I had previously relieved a friend of Sally's from a fear of heights, and now Sally hoped for similar results.

When I put Sally into hypnosis, I found that she was readily able to slip into a relaxed state. I asked her to go back to the most recent time when she had experienced her fear and describe things to me. At this point, I was trying to narrow down what her fear of going on airplanes really was. For some people, it's claustrophobia, or the fear of suffocation in small places. For others, it may be the fear of death. For still others, it may be separation anxiety.

As Sally went through the virtual experience of buying her plane ticket during hypnosis, she began feeling panicked. She knew she was going to die on that plane, and she didn't want to go. We moved things forward so that she was driving to the airport and the panic increased — on a scale of one to ten with ten the highest, I asked how high her anxiety levels were. She was at a seven.

So we moved her right onto the airplane, and now her anxiety levels hit the roof. Physically, her breathing rate increased and the blood drained from her face. "Now, I'm going to tap you on the forehead and count you down from ten to one," I told her. "With each number, feel yourself getting younger and younger, going to the source of this problem. When you get there, raise your finger."

When she raised her finger, she began describing herself as being in the womb. She said she could feel herself coming out the birth canal and seeing fear on the faces of the people in white standing around her. In fact, they were afraid that the baby (which was her) was going to die.

There was a silence for many moments, and then a beautiful smile and almost a "glow" came over Sally while she sat in her hypnotic trance.. I waited for a while to let her enjoy the experience, then asked her what had happened. She told me that she had "died" and gone to heaven with the angels. She was definitely in a state of bliss. Suddenly, the smile slipped from her face and she looked disappointed. "What happened?" I asked.

"They brought me back," she said. "I didn't want to come back, but I had to." Again, she saw faces of fear, with doctors and nurses who thought she was gone. When they realized that they had her back, a great relief spread over them. But by then it was too late. Sally had already taken on an extraordinary fear of death because of her first experience upon entering the world.

Because we used hypnosis to discover the root problem, however, I was able to use a hypnotherapy process called "Extinguishing the Fear" to eliminate her problems with flying. When Sally returned from the hypnotic state, she was so excited to have visited her own birth experience and to have been able to release this fear that had haunted her for years. Some months later, she and her husband fulfilled a lifelong dream of going to Europe. For the first time in her life, she felt free to travel.

This is an example of how birth issues can affect people their whole lives without them knowing it. And the *reason* this is so goes right back to our last chapter — fetuses and babies are *not* unconscious beings that suddenly gain the ability to think, feel, and remember at age two or three. They are aware, to various degrees, from the moment of conception so that, by the time they are born, the birth experience is both powerful and lasting, even if it is all held in the subconscious mind.

For instance, when babies are exposed to musical passages or even tastes and smells while in the womb, they demonstrate familiarity with these immediately after birth. (And of course they are familiar with their parents' voices right away too.)

As another example, one study had parents speak daily to their babies in their native languages over a period of time while the babies were in utero. After birth, the babies were introduced to one person speaking the native language and to another speaking in a foreign tongue. Each time, the babies were readily drawn to the person who spoke their own language.

In fact, that relatively short period of time called birth creates a template for someone's life because it holds the message, "Welcome to the real world. This is how things work here." Imagine the baby who is pulled out by forceps or brought out by Caesarian delivery, for instance, whose primary first message is, "Other people will take care of the hard work for you." And of course these are just two of the many twists and turns of modern delivery.

So, if the birth experience has such a powerful impact on someone's life, it's important that we understand this experience as best we can for a more thorough approach to healing.

The Birth Experience

For years now — to the point that we now tend to call this a "traditional" birth — hospital births have basically involved a woman getting anesthetic or an epidural, then lying on her back and waiting until she's told to push. The baby is often helped out with forceps to speed the process and make Mom's experience a bit less uncomfortable. This is a relatively passive arrangement for both Mom and baby, and the focus is less on the mother's empowerment than on the medical professionals' convenience. The baby is considered a passive, unconscious bystander.

Contrary to this standard practice, research shows that labor progresses better when the mother is more active, physically and mentally. Passivity (including epidurals) commonly keeps the uterus from contracting properly, and the frequent remedy is to artificially induce labor with hormones. Lying flat on the back is probably the worst position for labor. Pressure of the uterus on the large aorta and vena cava arteries may interrupt the blood supply (and therefore oxygen) to the womb.[52] And pain-killing drugs or anesthetics — which lead to a number of risks as well as long-term life problems — are often administered prematurely, ignoring the natural, non-intrusive chemicals in the placenta, the natural morphine-like beta-endorphins.

Not only that, but "tradition" has the baby whisked away from the mother right away so that doctors and nurses can perform a number of tests and place drops of silver nitrate in the baby's eyes. But research shows the grievous error in this approach as well. Except in the case of medical emergencies, there is great value in handing the baby directly to the mother for skin-to-skin and eye-to-eye contact, umbilical cord still intact.

All of this shows how unnatural the process of birth has become for many women and babies. Nature seems to have had very good reasons for designing birth as it did, and our interference has many ramifications. To understand this better, we'll take a look at birth from a baby's perspective, and then we'll talk about some of the issues and traumas that can come up from a negative birth experience.

The Baby's Experience

From the baby's point of view, birth consists of four discrete stages.[53] Of course any of these stages can be modified by the mother's experience (for instance, stress hormones or anesthetics can be passed to the baby through the blood stream) or interferences such as forceps. But for natural birth, these are the four stages:

Fetal State. The first stage is really just the last moments of the blissful fetal state — a state of unbounded, mystical union. In general, the fetus has felt only sensations of floating and limitlessness, security, warmth, and satisfaction. It has known total autonomy, experiencing its environment, the placenta, uterine walls, and umbilical cord, as extensions of itself. All of its needs have been automatically met.

Onset of Labor. The fetal state comes to a sudden end with the second stage, the onset of biological labor. The bliss is disturbed by chemical signals and then by muscular contractions. Since the cervix is not yet open, there is no way out, and this creates a feeling of engulfment and claustrophobia, physical torment and existential crisis. The first experience of something "not me" foreshadows the separation to come. For the first time, the fetus' consciousness asks the question, "Do I want to do this?"

Passage into the Birth Canal. The third stage of birth begins with the cervix opening and the uterine contractions propelling the fetus down into the birth canal. The experience is a tremendous struggle for survival: the birth/death struggle. The baby wonders, "Will I be annihilated by the suffocating and crushing pressure, or will my purpose and resolve to live prevail? Can I use the immense primal energy surrounding me to move forward, or will exhaustion and fear stop me?"

Delivery. The final stage of birth is delivery from the struggle, relief and relaxation, and emergence into the light. The terror of separation from the womb, from everything known, is tempered by the ecstasy of deliverance into this new, limitless independence. The joyful experience of victory is only compromised if the baby then feels rejected or otherwise not fully welcomed into the new environment. This can come of the mother's direct rejection or, sadly, of the modern decision to immediately remove the baby from Mother's loving embrace.

Birth Issues

As we discussed in earlier chapters, certain major decisions about someone's life actually happen prior to birth. We call these "Life Decisions." If we could maintain clarity about these life decisions, we could base our daily choices on our intuitive knowledge, wisdom, and love. This clarity, however, is affected by the pre- and perinatal period, the birth experience, and all the events leading into adulthood. Anytime an event plugs "fear" into the equation, clarity is compromised and we begin acting from that fear. During the birth experience, six primary fears can be triggered.

Fear of Abandonment

This can result from prolonged labor or delayed birth, premature birth and placement in neonatal intensive care. The most consistent source of abandonment is twofold: first the disconnection with Mom upon the use of anesthetics; and second, the common practice of immediately separating the baby from mother after birth for hospital procedures. Also, parental fears about lack of money or resources often lead to contemplation of abortion or adoption. With this ensuing fear of abandonment come the coping strategies of becoming highly adaptive and people-pleasing, as well as leaving others before they can leave you.

Fear of Engulfment or Suffocation

This can result from breech birth or a prolonged labor or delayed birth. The longer a fetus is in the birth canal, the more suffocation issues that person will have. A prolapsed umbilical cord, the cord wrapped around the baby's neck, or having the cord cut too soon can certainly result in fear of not enough oxygen. A multiple birth, which follows the experience of becoming more and more crowded as two or more fetuses have grown, can feel very suffocating to the babies.

One young client came to us with anxiety/panic attacks in which he couldn't breathe. When he called, he was speaking about his job and a female boss whom he felt he could never please. He kept saying, "I've got to get out, I've just got to get out!" In our hypnotherapy with him, he subsequently went back to his birth experience where his mother was in labor with him for four days! Apparently, she loved being pregnant because it was the first time she ever felt connected with anyone. So she didn't want to give birth and go back to the emptiness she had felt all her life. The midwife finally told her that, for the baby's health, she had to let go. And so this baby boy was born. As a result, these suffocation issues, panic attacks, and claustrophobia had followed him throughout his life. Bringing resolution to those old wounds allowed him to stop using the anti-anxiety medications he had needed to cope with life's everyday stresses.

Parental stress, especially over the gender of the baby or about the baby's or mother's health and safety, can also cause the parents to become overprotective, which can result in engulfment. The major coping strategies include becoming counter-dependent and relying on passivity.

Fear of Needs Not Being Met

This can result from analgesics, anesthetics, or forceps at birth; breech birth; prolonged labor; and delayed or induced birth; or other incidences at birth. Caesarean birth can especially cause this fear since the baby does not learn the very first lesson in life, which is how to push through obstacles to get needs met. Because the baby is "taken" from the womb, she grows up expecting to be rescued and therefore is often demanding that others meet her needs. A prolapsed umbilical cord or having the cord cut too soon reduces the baby's supply of oxygen, which also causes a fear of basic needs not being met.

Of course I've pointed out that infants are quite conscious when born, and any form of perceived parental rejection can create the fear of needs not being met. This includes the prenatal instances when parents are thinking of abortion or adoption, but also involves birth events such as when an infant is placed in neonatal intensive care, because the immediate need for connection with the mother isn't met. Another common practice with infants is to substitute bottle feeding instead of breast feeding shortly after birth. The baby has to suck harder on the breast to get the milk, which satisfies the infant's sucking needs (not to mention further connection with the mother). With bottle feeding, the infant often feels unsatisfied and may start sucking fingers to get this sucking need met.

Coping strategies for the infant whose needs have not been met include denying that one has any needs, withholding emotions, stubbornness, possessiveness, fear of change, and becoming overly dependent.

Fear of Intimacy

Fear of intimacy can occur whenever there is sudden and premature disconnection between the mother and baby, such as in the use of analgesics or anesthetics at birth. The birth process is meant to be a cooperation between mother (through contractions) and the baby (through pushing). When numbness takes over due to drugs, the contractions slow down and the baby is paralyzed and cannot push. Other birth issues that can lead to this fear include a long and painful breech birth, premature birth, Caesarean sections, placement of the fetus in neonatal intensive care, and any form of major parental rejection.

Coping strategies for this pervasive fear include dissociation from feelings; numbing behavior, such as addictions to drugs or alcohol to avoid stress; and relationship addictions, such as marrying a partner who cannot bond or connect.

Fear of Annihilation

This fear is most pronounced when parents are considering abortion prior to the birth process, but it can also result from heavy anesthetics at birth, a difficult breech birth, and prolonged labor. The lack of oxygen due to a prolapsed umbilical cord or having the cord cut too soon can certainly feel like death to the fragile infant. If the baby is placed in neonatal intensive care without the physical connection of the parents, the baby can gravitate to the experience of this fear.

Coping strategies later in life may include unwillingness to commit to a relationship and possibly an active death urge.

Fear of Being Unworthy (Low Self-Esteem)

This fear is most intensely felt by infants who are not valued because they are the wrong gender for their mother or father. This fear is also prevalent when the baby is considered a mistake (such as those conceived out of wedlock) or is unwanted for any reason (including change of life babies that were unplanned). Nearly any parental rejection, including contemplation of abortion or adoption, can result in this life-long issue.

Coping strategies for someone with this underlying fear can include compulsive perfectionism and the continuous attempt to win approval through adaptation and people- pleasing.

Living life based on any of these fears is an "ego expression." These expressions can look as different as grandiosity and shame, but both are self-centered, narcissistic, and ultimately fear-based. Living beyond these fears — with feelings of autonomy and worthiness, and with the clarity that was present at least early on in the womb — is a "spiritual expression" that is always confident *and* humble.

Of course the various traumas that trigger these fears are many, and they are common. We cannot and do not simply write someone off as stuck with their fears because of a birth trauma. Instead, we try to understand the various traumas and how they can affect people so that we're better able to analyze symptoms. This helps us to go back and address the root problems through transformational hypnotherapy. So let's take a look at the various traumas and what they do. Then we'll take a look at the healing process.

Birth Traumas

Birth traumas can take many forms. Some have been around forever, simply because things like multiple births or breech presentations have always occurred. Others are more recent because of medical intervention in birth. Each one can affect a person's life in a unique way. Following are detailed explanations of these elements.

Prolonged Labor

Difficulties can come with prolonged labor (over 24 hours) where, due to abnormal presentation, a large fetus, multiple fetuses, or emotional resistance, contractions are too weak to push the baby out. The fetus runs the risk of suffocating, and often imprints on feeling claustrophobic. The mother's resistance can create imprints for this child of procrastination and a tendency of being non-committal. Order and ritual may become a strong need for the child to function later on. The prolonged-labor baby often avoids setting goals and instead looks to processes.[54]

Induced Labor

Obstetricians may stimulate contractions with pitocin, a labor-inducing synthetic form of the hormone oxytocin. The fetus experiences the imposed contractions as non-natural in movement and timing, externally imposed, and painfully overwhelming. The induced baby often imprints on inappropriate response to external demands and on the sense of being rushed or pressured. Later in life, she may be oversensitive to the pains she is "causing" others. The overriding individual issue is feeling "overwhelmed" and powerless. This person uses language such as, "No matter how hard I try, I just can't get ahead," or "Stop pressuring me!"

Delayed Birth

The birth process is sometimes interrupted in the final moments, for example when the doctor is late to the delivery or the mother is en route to the hospital. It is an externally controlled birth with control taken from mother and fetus. Those in attendance often tell the mother to hold her legs together to prevent the baby from being born at that time. The baby can imprint on expecting to be held back by others while, paradoxically, depending on them for any progress. Growing up, such a child may have fears of abandonment and guilt about developing independence and self-sufficiency. This person uses language such as, "It's not my fault," or "I don't understand why I can't move ahead in my life."

Premature Delivery

Premature deliveries (babies born before 37 weeks) can create difficulties and may be caused by a young mother giving birth, heavy smoking, poor nutrition, infections, emotional traumas, and multiple births. This baby is usually isolated in incubation or placed in neonatal intensive care, often leading to disrupted bonding, an imprint on abandonment and mistrust, and a feeling of being pushed into independence before she is ready.

The preemie experiences less restriction in the womb and less stimulation in labor than mature babies because of her smaller size. As a result, this child experiences frustration and confusion in the face of any restriction or limitation later in life. She feels pushed into things, resists change, and avoids responsibility.

The premature birth relationship issues are fear of abandonment, fear of intimacy, and fear of commitment. These babies often have a sense that their needs will not be met due to the fact that they were separated from maternal bonding at the time when they needed it most.

Post-Mature Delivery

With late onset of labor, post-mature infants usually have developed to a larger size, causing complications going through a tight birth canal. As a result, the child may later tend to feel claustrophobic; overreacting when feeling confined or trapped, and may also avoid responsibility. If there are strong contractions to help the baby out, the longer preparation for birth can lead the "overtime" baby to be flexible in the face of change, independent, and strong. Often, however, contractions are insufficient to move the birth along, and this person may later use language such as, "I feel trapped," or, "There's no way out of this."

Prolapsed Umbilical Cord

A prolapsed umbilical cord occurs when the oxygen supply in the cord is cut off or restricted through pressure from the fetus' body. It can occur in a breech delivery, or simply when the cord gets tangled with the fetus. In this case, asphyxiation is a serious threat to life and may cause mental retardation, epilepsy, or cerebral palsy. It often results in the obstetrician's choice of either a forceps delivery or a Caesarean section.

For the baby, there are sensations of bondage, and she often imprints on suffocation fears, panic, and anxiety. The trauma is much more grievous if the fetus actually loses consciousness, indicating a near-death experience. This interruption in experiencing the whole sequence of birth events causes a tendency to disorganized thinking and confusion, and to dissociation and repression.

Breech Presentation

The positioning of the fetus during delivery is one common form of birth difficulty. In 96% of pelvic deliveries, the top of the skull comes out first (vertex presentation). The others may present with their brow, their face, their shoulder, or their buttocks or feet first. (The latter two represent a true breech position.)

Breech presentations occur in about 4% of all deliveries, and may be delivered vaginally or through Caesarean section. The major risk for the breech baby is suffering a lack of oxygen either due to a prolapsed cord or a delayed delivery. The contractions in breech births are strong and violent and can presage later tendencies to aggressiveness, impulse-control issues, emotional disconnection, and overreaction.

The breech baby born vaginally often imprints on life being very challenging, expecting to be pulled through every tight spot she encounters. She tends to set high expectations on other people without communicating this, leading to frequent disappointment in others. The breech baby born through Caesarean section often imprints on being rescued from challenges in life.

Because a breech birth is often very painful to both mother and baby, breech birth relationship issues involve: rescuing others (others' needs first at the expense of one's own needs); feeling responsible for others' pain; and being highly adaptive (a "people pleaser"). The overriding individual issue is "struggling" through life. This person uses language such as, "Life is a struggle," or "I just can't seem to get it right."

Sometimes the shoulder-presentation or the breech fetus can be turned before or in early labor, resulting in a common vertex delivery. The baby who was turned and born in opposition to her natural presentation seems to not be content in interactions with others. Either she manipulates them into giving what she wants, and feels dissatisfied, or resents that they don't honor her needs and comply with them.

Anesthetics

As I've mentioned, medical aids to delivery can often cause long-term harm, even though good is intended. For instance, anesthesia restricts a woman's ability to push her baby out, leaving the baby feeling abandoned in a time of great need. In fact, any approach that puts the mother in a position of passivity leads to poor, non-sequenced contractions. Such contractions push the amniotic fluid forward *into* the baby's mouth and lungs, rather than propelling the baby with a massaging motion that drives the fluid *out* of her lungs. This can also lead to the use of labor-inducing hormones, as discussed above.

What's more, anesthetization particularly affects bonding, because residual amounts of anesthesia are common in babies, even hours and days after birth. This residual anesthesia makes babies (and mothers) numb and therefore less available to the bonding process. Any traumatic experience causes a defensive dulling of mind and body in both mother and baby. In this case, the dulling is a conscious choice. Under such dulling, the quantity and quality of bonding are lessened, and the infant is less able to cope with stress. As a result, the baby can imprint on escapist behaviors to avoid stress.

The anesthetic birth relationship issues are codependency and powerlessness (expecting emotional abandonment in times of need) and difficulty in bonding. The overriding individual issue is dissociation, including addictions. This person uses language such as, "I just can't seem to get started," or "Nobody is ever there for me."

Forceps

Forceps are usually needed to pull the baby out when the mother is rendered ineffective through anesthetics or when fetal distress is observed, often in prolonged labor or delayed birth. Forceps babies tend to re-create dependency in relationships later in life, either by abdicating to external forces or by craving to always be in control. Thus, these children tend to become judgmental and to idealize themselves (grandiosity) or authorities (dependency).

The forceps baby often imprints on the world as intrusive. Many people who were delivered with forceps feel stuck in their head and overly-intellectual. The forceps delivery relationship issues are: rebelling against authority and feeling "violated." The overriding individual issue is lack of personal power. This person uses language such as, "You're always hurting me," or "It's just too hard for me."

Caesarean Section Delivery

Experiencing contractions in birth is profoundly important to the development of boundaries. The contraction is the first occasion for the fetus to experience physical limits, and on the release of the contraction to experience freedom. This first awareness of limits to personal control, or boundaries, is a major building block for developing a definition of self in relation to others.

This first experience of mutual effort — whether cooperative, competitive, or passive — impacts the development of skills in forming relationships for a lifetime. Adapting to the contractions with persistence prepares the fetus for autonomy in the world, and loss of this experience through Caesarian delivery often leads to later passivity in the baby's life. A Caesarian-born may, when conflict arises in relationships, leave or immediately opt for a divorce instead of wanting to work things out, often just taking the path of least resistance.

What's more, the umbilical cord is usually cut more quickly in Caesarean births than in vaginal births for fear of hemorrhaging in the mother. This causes suffocation, panic, mistrust, and separation anxiety for the newborn. The Caesarean-born expects the help of others anytime, especially in the face of obstacles or challenges, and tends to blame failures on those who aren't helping enough. Caesareans have missed a vital step in the birth process, and therefore have difficulty following the sequential steps in any process in life and have a low tolerance for frustration. They may be enthusiastic, yet erratic in implementation.

People born by Caesarean delivery tend to have unclear cognitive boundaries, may be unable to define ideas precisely, and have confusion about body- and self-image. Grandiosity is a condition that allows no limits or boundaries, and can come of not experiencing contractions in birth.

The Caesarean relationship issues are: entitlement or expecting to be rescued by others; taking the easy way out; having difficulty overcoming obstacles; invading others' boundaries while reacting strongly to having their own boundaries violated; resenting authority figures; and failing on follow-through. The overriding individual issue is "Why won't somebody help me?"

Caesarean birth affects the mother as well as the fetus. After a Caesarean delivery, it's common for the mother to feel fear, frustration, disappointment, failure, loss of control, and loneliness. These emotional reactions are bound to impact the newborn's emotional experience of confidence, intimacy, and bonding.[55]

Finally, Caesarian birth also affects the individual's spiritual experience since, when we die, we face the same process of "moving through the tunnel" toward the light. People who have not had that experience at birth may not know what to do at death, and may become what we call a "lost soul" whose spirit wanders uncertainly, waiting for outside help.

Cutting of the Umbilical Cord

Just as contractions help the baby to develop a first definition of self *in relation to others*, the cutting of the umbilical cord provides a primal beginning to differentiation, the experience of self *separated from others*. At this event, one begins learning to differentiate "my experience" from that of others, "my needs" from those of others. This is a vitally important developmental process, rehearsed in the rapprochement phase between eighteen and thirty-six months of age and integrated in the passage from adolescence into adulthood.

The baby's reaction to the cord cutting will foreshadow its eventual success at differentiation. The umbilical cord and placenta has been literally an extension of the fetus' body, a life support system providing extraordinary autonomy and security. The abrupt, precipitous loss of this major organ of the body becomes the prototype for all losses to come in life — indeed the fear of death itself.

If the cord is cut before the baby is ready to breathe on her own, she feels suffocation and panic, and may imprint on distrusting that her needs will be met in life. This loss is also the primal basis for castration anxiety and penis envy; the boy's penis has become a substitute for the cord, which was in fact cut off, and the girl seeks a substitute for it. Both boys and girls experience something missing and attempt to find other security substitutes, such as the ubiquitous "security blanket" or the mother.

The resistance to let go, which Freud attributed to anal fixation from toilet training, may in fact really derive from the loss of the umbilical cord and the security and autonomy it represented. Feelings of holding back, stubbornness, possessiveness, stinginess and hoarding, and also the fear of change, are reactions to and re-enactments of that primal loss. Of course, as we have already seen, that basic "resistance to life" may well have been initiated before birth, even before conception. Such a predilection adds trauma to the loss of the umbilical cord, becoming "the straw that broke the camel's back" following prolonged or intense traumas such as abortion being considered or toxicity in the womb or earlier (in pre-life experiences). Loss of the cord may be a challenging but non-traumatic developmental step, however, for the newborn that has a basic sense of security.

We find that many people "hold themselves back" from fully participating in their life. Passion, exhilaration, excitement, joy, and meaningful fulfillment seem to be lacking for them. We call this condition "resistance to life," and the image is that of a cat being forced into a carrier: all four legs stretched out, claws drawn, saying "No!" There is a lack of hope for them, a flat feeling or a sense of being stuck in a process of mourning that knows no end. Carl Jung refers to this condition as similar to the diminution of the personality known in primitive psychology as "loss of soul".[56] He states that we label the similar experience in our civilized culture as an *abaissement du niveau mental*, and describes it as "a slackening of the tensity of consciousness, which might be compared to a low barometric reading, presaging bad weather. The tonus has given way, and this is felt subjectively as listlessness, moroseness, and depression."

Incidentally, we find that addictions can be symbolic attempts to reclaim the connection of the umbilical cord. Smoking, overeating, bingeing and purging, and alcohol or drug use provide the individual with the self-stimulation, nurturing, and sense of control reminiscent of the functioning umbilical cord before it was cut. Impotence or compulsive sexuality is also common as a result of poor response to the cutting of the cord since it is often cut too quickly. Recovery from these addictions involves giving up dependency itself and accepting the autonomy that birth, separation, and differentiation offer.

Multiple Births — Twins

In the case of multiple births, the infants must deal with crowding in the womb, and often with delayed labor. As long as the pregnancy goes to term, there is only a minor increase in risk with twins, and this risk is generally to the second born.

As the twin fetuses grow and develop together, they enjoy an ultimately intimate closeness and connection. As their space becomes more limited, however, they may also feel cramped, trapped, and suffocated. With the birth process, the twins must deal with who is to come out first.

Other issues will include things like which twin wins that first, adoring look from the mother, and which gets the first taste of Mother's milk. This is the beginning of either competition or putting the other's needs first. The second twin born usually has trauma: the regret of holding back in deference to the other, and/or the frightening first time of being alone, of being abandoned.

The relationship issues for twins are codependency and separation. The overriding individual issue is the question, "Who am I?"

Loss of a Twin or "The Vanishing Twin Syndrome"

Embryological research indicates that loss of a twin may be much more common than previously thought. Current research indicates that at least one in eight births begin with twins (and may be even more), and thus for every live-born twin pair, ten to twelve twin pregnancies result in single births.[57] The death of one of these embryos very often occurs so early after conception that it's unknown to the mother. People who experience the loss of a twin manifest several common dynamics:

- First, there is an ineffable but profound sense of loss, despair, and rage. These feelings are usually held in, but are sometimes acted out against others.
- Second, there is a chronic but unarticulated fear that loss will happen again, a pervasive insecurity. The threat of loss is defended against by distancing from others, or by engaging in codependent relationships.
- Third, the ability to bond with others is deficient or neurotic because there is a lack of trust in relationships, or the belief that relationships will not last.
- Fourth, there is often an over-compliance in life, based on the unconscious feeling that "If I don't do what is expected or wanted, I will die." Over-compliance feeds hostility and aggression toward others, since one cannot take care of oneself when constantly complying with others.
- Finally, prenatal experiences of near death and/or loss are sometimes turned against oneself or others, resulting in masochistic behaviors such as suicidal thinking and attempts. The surviving twin often displays depression from a very young age, which baffles psychologists, parents, and teachers.

Neonatal Intensive Care

As we've talked about in earlier sections, our modern-day deliveries customarily take a baby away from the mother, disrupting the bonding process that's so important immediately after birth. For the sick or premature baby who is placed in the neonatal intensive care unit, the isolation is vastly compounded by invasive naval and windpipe tubes and electronic monitors. Placement in intensive care is frequently experienced by the newborn as a terrifying, lonely, over-stimulating, and painful abandonment. This baby imprints not only on abandonment by human contact but also on bonding with the sights and sounds of mechanical life support. Their warmth literally comes from a machine and later on in life, they may bond with their computers, cell phones, iPods, and the latest technological devices.

Menopausal Births

Babies born to a menopausal mother tend to be harshly judgmental, directing this judgment both at themselves and at others as inadequate. Factors at work here may include the hormonal environment in the menopausal womb, the presence of elderly and perhaps more authoritarian parents, and the higher incidence of birth complications. What's more, the issue that the baby may be a surprise and even a burden to an older family can have the effect of the infant feeling rejected and not belonging in this family.

In Vitro Fertilization

Because there is a high incidence of prematurity, low birth weight, and twins in this population of newborns, the factors for those conditions apply to many "test tube babies." Also, mothers of IVF children are generally older than mothers who give birth without medical intervention. Mothers with children conceived by IVF express a higher emotional involvement with their children, and a higher quality of parent-child relationship than mothers with naturally conceived children.[58] While there is little research on the longer-term effects for the child (the first IVF birth was achieved in 1978), this child is probably destined to ask, "Who am I and how did I get here?"

Parental Stress, Shame, and Rejection

We spoke of the affects of parental stress, shame, and rejection in our last chapter on the womb experience. For reasons covered there, stress during delivery (i.e., hormones transmitted through the blood stream) can also affect a baby during delivery.

Babies facing these different parental issues react in a number of ways. Relationship issues are: never feeling loved for oneself; becoming highly competitive and highly adaptive; having difficulty bonding; feeling jealousy and envy; trying to be someone else; and experiencing love as suffocating. The individual issues are: an overwhelming lack of self-esteem; a constant feeling of inadequacy; lifelong grief and an unexplained depression; and a disturbing identity disorder, for instance never having one's own identity.

The Unwanted Child

Some pregnancies are unwelcome. This may be due to interpersonal conflict between the parents, the circumstances of the conception (such as rape, or a "mistake"), unfavorable conditions in the world (such as war or poverty), or beliefs about the prenate (such as potential birth defects or being the "wrong" sex). Whatever the reason, the new life in the womb experiencing this rejection faces a difficult choice. She must either blame herself for the rejection, believing "there is something profoundly wrong with me and I do not deserve to live" or becoming defiant and taking the stance that "I will defy you and do whatever it takes to survive."

Once born, this infant may become seriously disturbed, periodically exhibiting a freezing defense in which she remains immobile and glassy-eyed. This passive defensive dissociation in prenates and newborns may even, at the extreme, account for death. Infants born of unwanted pregnancies are more than twice as likely to die within a month of birth than wanted infants.[59] This is sometimes labeled SIDS (Sudden Infant Death Syndrome), which the medical profession is unable to explain. We believe that there is an unconscious explanation why infants suddenly die for no apparent reason. Believing that they are unwanted may be one of them. An early psychoanalyst, Sándor Ferenczi, wrote a paper in 1929 entitled *The Unwelcome Child and His Death Drive* which relates the struggle between a tendency to self-destruction and the inhibition on it by the wish to live.[60]

Here the relationship issues are: fear of rejection; fear of abandonment; codependency; adaptive people-pleasing; and fear of commitment. Individual issues tend to be: existential angst; never feeling that one is good enough; anxiety disorders; and pervasive shame.

Abortion Trauma

Knowing herself to be an "unwelcome child" is devastating to an infant and may lead to the re-creation of rejecting relationships later in life. Abortion is the ultimate form of parental rejection, and considering or attempting an abortion stamps a child with this deeply embedded belief of being "unwanted."

The abortion survivor relationship issues are: fear of abandonment; codependency; adaptive people-pleasing; and fear of commitment. The overriding individual issues are: an active death urge, including suicidal thoughts or attempts; existential angst; never being good enough; impotence; anxiety disorders; terror of annihilation; pervasive shame; and the feeling that life is always a "double bind."

Adoption Trauma

Parental rejection can also take the form of contemplated or actual adoption. We discussed some forms of this in the previous chapter. For instance, adoption trauma generally includes discovery trauma (the child is unwanted at the time of discovering the pregnancy); conception trauma (the child is unwanted at the time of conception); or psychological toxicity (the child is exposed to the mother's annihilative or ambivalent feelings, or to socio-cultural shame); and of course the abandonment of adoption itself. This unborn child is aware of being an "unwelcome child" and reacts with shame and an overpowering anxiety over her right to exist.

Adoption relationship issues are: abandonment anxiety; rebellion against authority; the willingness to sell one's soul for love ("looking for love in all the wrong places"); and the fear of commitment. Individual issues are: shame, depression, difficulty bonding, a highly adaptive nature, and an active death urge.

Oxygen Deficiency

During birth, there are a number of situations in which a baby can suffer from anoxia (the lack of sufficient oxygen). This can happen when:

- The mother is given anesthetics, especially if she is unconscious. The anesthetic acts directly on the fetus' survival functions, particularly interfering with the access to oxygen.
- The umbilical cord is wrapped around the baby's neck or otherwise prolapsed.
- The umbilical cord is cut prematurely, stranding oxygen needed by the baby in the mother's placenta.

The struggle for oxygen when too little is available produces Fetal Distress Syndrome, with symptoms of rapid heart rate, high blood pressure, and frantic breathing. The child's instinct represses feeling, mental concentration, and awareness, using an exaggerated impulse control in order to quell the "frenzy," conserve oxygen, and ultimately save the baby's life. This instinctual repressive response may become an imprint, and surface later as the response to any stressful situation.

Birth trauma from anoxia can result in childhood illnesses, allergies, asthma, epilepsy, ADHD, Cerebral Palsy, and Sudden Infant Death Syndrome (SIDS). This trauma can lead to problems in adolescence and adulthood as well, including depression, suicide attempts, Chronic Fatigue Syndrome, panic attacks, phobias, paranoia, and psychosis. In one study[61], respiratory distress lasting one hour or more in infancy was correlated with a high risk of teenage suicide. In another study[62], fifteen of the sixteen most violent, male criminals in Denmark had traumatic, oxygen-deprived births.

According to one study on diminished oxygen levels during birth, nearly every newborn has an oxygen loss similar to that of a sprinter after a run.[63] The human fetus is squeezed through the birth canal for several hours, during which time the infant is intermittently deprived of oxygen by compression of the placenta and the umbilical cord during contractions. Of course, in deliveries where the umbilical cord is pinched, the oxygen supply is more severely restricted.

Additionally, every baby faces a potential respiration trauma when the source of oxygen converts from umbilical cord to lungs upon the first breath. Because the circulation of blood reverses direction with the first breath, the stakes are high at this crucial moment. Depending on the treatment the newborn receives, this moment can lead to imprints of exhilaration and triumph, or dependence, violence, disconnection, and separation.

Whereas a lack of oxygen at birth can cause trauma, excess oxygen at birth has been shown to increase IQ and muscle coordination, and hasten overall development.[64]

Lack of Warmth

The fetus has lived in a well-regulated, cozy 100° oven until it emerges into the world. The normal delivery room is kept at a temperature of 68° for the comfort of the hospital staff, and that is the shocking welcome offered to the newborn. If she is then removed from the mother for weighing, Apgar testing, heel sticks, eye drops, or placement in the neonatal intensive care unit, the troubling lack of physical warmth is compounded by a lack of emotional bonding.

Lack of Touch

The infant's need for touch was documented by Spitz[65] in his work in orphanages. Children die during their first year of life if they do not receive sufficient touching. Ideally, the newborn is placed immediately — before the cord is cut — on the mother's breast, and is cuddled by her or the father until she falls asleep. Children fail to thrive if they do not receive sufficient bonding, and the first minutes and hours are the most important for imprinting on unconditional love, intimate connection, reassurance that needs will be met, and whole-hearted bonding.

Research indicates that an infant is more responsive to touch in its first five days than to any other form of stimulation. We know that gentle touch for an infant reduces stress responses and increases anabolic (constructive) processes, and that there's less output of stress hormone when the infant has been gently stroked and touched prior to the onset of stress.[66] Research with premature infants shows that there is a greater output of somatotrophin growth hormone, which stimulates the immune system and promotes growth, when tactile stimulation is provided to them soon after birth.[67]

Circumcision

Although circumcision technically comes after "the birth experience," it is closely enough connected with it to consider its long-term effects alongside the other traumas dealt with in this chapter.

Except in the case of Judaism, where circumcision is a religious ritual, the practice of circumcising newborns was apparently introduced into the United States as a means of controlling or preventing masturbation. This is because the foreskin is the most sensitive (pleasure-giving) part of the penis, and it may have been hoped that, without it, there would be less incentive to engage in masturbation, which was considered socially unacceptable. The medical community then began to try justifying this procedure by saying that it was done for health reasons.

Today, after a number of studies, doctors are admitting that there is no medical reason to remove live, healthy tissue. (Some in the medical community will still say that circumcision can reduce the likelihood of urinary tract infections, but studies on this are generally in question.) Nature provides all parts of the body for a reason, and the foreskin is there to help provide and maintain lubrication during intercourse.

As with the traumas resulting from human intervention during birth, the mutilation of nature in circumcisions has a substantial impact on a child. For example, some theories based on extensive therapeutic knowledge from working with mutilation victims show that circumcision may be the reason for so much sexual sadomasochism in our culture. The connection of pain with sex may begin with this painful process of cutting the foreskin off of the male sexual organ at such an early, vulnerable age. Many men may have sexually bonded with pain through this experience.

One of the great errors that may have allowed this practice is the belief that babies don't experience pain. But we've already shown just how aware and conscious babies are ... even when they are still inside the womb. In fact, babies experience pain more intensely than adults, and films of babies going through the trauma of circumcision show them screaming at first and then going into severe dissociation or shock afterwards. You can observe a horrifying, vacant stare in their eyes and realize that this may be one reason why so many men experience being disconnected from themselves. From the extensive soul retrieval work that we have done, it seems that the pain of circumcision may trigger fragments of the soul to leave the body, and thus cause the emptiness that many men experience.

Therapists who have worked on this issue with their male clients report that the men may not consciously be aware of these feelings. But during age regressions and birthwork, these feelings come up. Often, men who have had difficulty with pre-mature ejaculation and impotence have found that it may be due to sexual anxiety — the source of which has been traced back to circumcision. Therapists also report that, during regression, men often feel betrayed by their mothers, whom they depended on to protect them. This may also be one source of deep-seated rage and mistrust that men have about women — a rage that needs to be released.

I've reflected on the extensive body shame that so many men have about their penises. They often blame it on the size, but could it be that the shame comes from the inner realization that part of the penis has been cut off? Could this penis shame actually be about having a "mutilated" or "deformed" penis?

Many of us are horrified when we hear about the female circumcision being done in Africa. We attribute this practice to their ignorance of following harmful rituals that have been blindly followed for many years. I don't see any difference between what is being done in Africa to young females and what we do to our sons every day in every hospital across America.

What can we do about it? Therapists can help male clients to express and work through the potential post-traumatic stress disorder (PTSD) which may be the result of early trauma, shock, and dissociation due to circumcision. Nurses and doctors can begin to tell parents the truth about circumcision — about why it's become tradition and why we have no reason to inflict this on children from this point on.

The Lifelong Effects of Birth Trauma

It's easy enough for us to see all of the above traumas and understand *why* they would be traumas. Going from the predictable state of nurture inside the womb into situations where you can't move, can't breathe, are grabbed by the head (having your work done for you), brought into a relatively frigid environment, separated from that which has sustained you for nine months, and so on … it's not hard to imagine how traumatic the situation may be for a newborn.

On the other hand, how powerful and lasting these traumas are may or may not be intuitive. There is a great deal of research into these matters, even though the traditional field of psychology has tended to ignore it until recently. I'll give you just a taste of what's available.

To begin, let's take a look at a thirty-year study.[68] This research looked at those who had suffered from birth and childhood traumas. Among the group with both types of trauma, there were about three times as many health problems as the overall group average. The effects of early trauma diminished over the years if the child formed a close, nurturing bond with at least one caregiver. Even then, early trauma is still stored in the body in the form of high stress hormone levels and low serotonin levels, and it has lasting effects.

Birth trauma is positively correlated with stress[69]; anxiety[70]; conduct and antisocial personality disorder[71]; learning disabilities[72]; behavior problems in children[73]; psychosis[74]; suicide attempts[75]; youth suicide[76]; mental illness[77]; childhood neurosis[78]; schizophrenia[79]; schizotypy[80]; drug and alcohol abuse[81]; psychosomatic illness in children and adolescents[82]; infantile autism[83]; violence[84]; insidious trauma[85]; and dysfunctional relationships.[86]

Not only is birth trauma a causative factor in adult self-destructive behavior, but the *form* of trauma is related to the form of behavior.[87] In 1987 at the Karolinska Institute in Stockholm, Sweden, Bertil Jacobson and associates gathered birth record data for 412 forensic victims comprising suicides, alcoholics, and drug addicts born in Stockholm after 1940 and who died there between 1978 and 1984. They compared the subjects with 2,901 controls, and mutual comparison of categories showed that:

- Suicides utilizing asphyxiation, such as hanging, were closely associated with asphyxia at birth.
- Suicides by violent mechanical means were associated with mechanical birth trauma.
- Drug addiction was associated with numbing by the use of ether gas, opiate, and/or barbiturate administration to mothers during labor.

And unfortunately, birth trauma appears to be fairly common. In a 1987 study, Dr. William Emerson found that 55% of a sample of 200 children showed signs of moderate to severe birth trauma. Barnett[88] surveyed previous research into the negative birth experience (NBE) and noted that the incidence of NBE is constant at about 30%, and that nearly 20% of all psychotherapy patients suffer from symptoms due in part to prenatal trauma.

But while unresolved traumas affect the spiritual and psychological development of children, those who had no trauma, or whose traumas have been resolved, are clearly unique. They are more spiritually evolved, manifest higher levels of human potential, and are developmentally precocious. They exhibit higher self-esteem and get better intelligence test scores. They are more empathic, emotionally mature, cooperative, creative, affectionate, loving, focused, and self-aware than untreated and traumatized children.[89] So how can we help our clients to resolve their birth trauma issues?

Healing Birth Traumas

When it comes to healing birth trauma, it's critical to understand something about how long-term memory is stored. To become part of that memory, an experience must engage the hippocampus.[90] Since the hippocampus does not fully mature until the third or fourth year of life, only the *quality* of early experiences, but not their *context*, can be remembered later in life. These memories are organized as somatic sensations (body memories), behavioral reenactments, nightmares, and flashbacks.[91] Therefore, working to heal people who have stored terrifying information on a visceral level means helping them remember the fragmented memories and then attaching context and meaning so they can be processed like ordinary memories.

Learning like this, called state-bound learning, is *always* the learning that an infant goes through. In other words, it's not just the case with trauma. For example, the fetus may experience that its mother, whose stress levels are always high, *only* calms down when the fetus also experiences nicotine or sugar or alcohol in the blood supply. This lesson is learned at the deepest layer of the developing fetus' nervous system. The memory is not verbal or conceptual, but is viscerally imprinted. And it influences choices later in life when the fetus — now a maturing child or adult — uses substances to "calm down." This explains one reason why it may be so difficult to give up nicotine, sugar or alcohol.

So how do we help to heal people who cannot access these experiences through the normal memory process? How do we help them to put these experiences into proper context and help them to heal? The only means of accessing this deep-seated learning for possible change is to return to the state in which it was learned: re-living the original experience *as it was first experienced*. Barring a spontaneous, transpersonal experience, one can generally only do so through hypnosis.

Successful hypnosis can, in turn, partially reactivate the stress-released, hormonal information that originally encoded that event in a state-bound condition. Since the client's *mind* cannot recall what happened, this helps the *body* to remember actual physical sensations. In this way, the state-bound information is brought into the *mind's* consciousness, where the client's ordinary cognitive and verbal ego can process it. This allows the state-bound or dissociated memories of the traumatic event to be accessed, processed, and therapeutically released. Again, this is done by placing the now-conscious event into proper context for the client. We always have the "wise adult" make new, healthy decisions for the infant. And we always develop an internal nurturing parent to provide an internal corrective experience for the individual.

And does it work? Can hypnosis successfully take people back to their birth traumas and allow them to release that which has been such a negative effect in their lives? I think it's useful to quote from Claire Etheridge, Ph.D., because her comments are very cautious about hypnosis while emphatic about the results. Dr. Etheridge specializes in prenatal psychology, dissociative disorders, and clinical hypnosis. She writes:

> At present, it cannot be proved that prenatal consciousness exists or that a person's prenatal recollections are true. The validity of a person's early memories, while in hypnosis or otherwise, can always be questioned, even when verified by a third party. What is certain is that therapeutic

change occurs after a person re-lives his/her traumatic early experiences and heals the memories of them with the help of a qualified therapist.[92]

She's absolutely right. There's really no way to *prove* what a baby has gone through from his or her perspective during birth, even if you ask the mother about it. But third-party confirmation has repeatedly shown an *apparent* accuracy to these therapeutic age-regressions, and the therapy works. I think that nothing proves a theory or a technique quite so well as the fact that it consistently works.

So it is that we are able to bring about transformational healing to all those who have faced trauma during birth. But there is much more life ahead of that child. And for all the positive events and experiences to be enjoyed, there is also opportunity for more traumas that need to be healed. Let's go on, then, and take a look at the next phase in life.

Chapter 5
Birth Issues Questionnaire

I. Which of the following situations "trigger" a response within you?

   A. Do you have "suffocation issues"?
- ❑ Do you feel anxious in closed in spaces such as elevators, airplanes and small cars?
- ❑ Do you get carsick?
- ❑ Do you always have to sit by the window in cars and airplanes?
- ❑ Do you have an intense fear of flying?
- ❑ Do you have difficulty driving over bridges?
- ❑ Do you have asthma, chronic bronchitis or trouble breathing?
- ❑ Are you uncomfortable in rooms without windows?

   B. ❑ Do you have difficulty setting boundaries with other people?

   C. ❑ Do you have oral fixation (overeating, drinking, smoking, nail biting, thumb sucking)

   D. ❑ Do you often struggle through situations rather than ask for help?

   E. ❑ Do you make things more difficult than they need to be?

   F. ❑ Do you often feel responsible for or guilty about other's pain?

   G. ❑ Do you often "take the easy way out" or give up something you want without a struggle?

   H. ❑ Do you tend to bond with material objects (things, machines, computers, vehicles)

   I. ❑ Have you always had a sense that "something is wrong with me?"

   J. ❑ In relationships do you sometimes push people away and then want them back? (push-pull)

   K. Do you have "abandonment fears"?
- ❑ Do you get upset when someone in your life doesn't show up on time?
- ❑ Do you often leave relationships because you think the other person is going to leave you?
- ❑ Do you feel anxious or angry or fearful when spouse or children are late coming home?
- ❑ Do you always imagine that the other person is going to reject you?
- ❑ Do you get extremely jealous and accuse your spouse of cheating on you for no reason?
- ❑ Do you often check up on your spouse to make sure he/she's told you the truth?

II. Birth experiences (check if appropriate)
- ❑ My mother used anesthetic during my delivery.
- ❑ At my birth, at least one of my parents wanted a baby the opposite sex of mine.
- ❑ At the time of my birth, I don't think my mother (or father) wanted a baby at all.
- ❑ I had a long delivery and was stuck in the birth canal too long.
- ❑ I am a twin.
- ❑ I was premature and in an incubator.
- ❑ I am adopted.
- ❑ My parents considered aborting me.
- ❑ I was born Caesarian.
- ❑ I was delivered with forceps.

III. I have a sense of the connection between my issues identified in I. above, and the birth experiences identified in II. above. Those connections are:

A. _____

_____

_____

B. _____

_____

_____

C. _____

_____

_____

Your Project: Research your birth

Get all the information you can about your birth. Talk to parents, older siblings, other relatives. Get your birth records from the hospital. Were there previous occupants of your womb, and if so did any not reach live birth? Become familiar with that time in your life and in your parents' life. What was their experience financially? Were their close relationships supportive or burdensome? Was the culture they lived in at peace or war, stable or chaotic, prosperous or destitute?

Chapter 6
Developmental Stages and the Traumas of Life

By now, we've pretty well established that the direction of our lives is profoundly affected by the womb and birth experiences. Positive influences during these times will strengthen us and help us to more easily achieve the goals our souls planned for us before we arrived. Negative influences can weaken us and tend to hinder us from achieving these goals. The good news is that healing is available, through corrective experiences such as those provided in transformational therapy. There's nothing quite like first impressions, and that is certainly true when it comes to the power of these first life experiences.

But that doesn't render the rest of our lives inconsequential in determining our life story. Every stage of our lives impacts the years we still have to live, and a trauma in *any* of these stages will tend to affect us — often in subconscious ways — even while positive experiences can strengthen us. Take the example of a young woman named Judy.

Judy came into our program kicking and screaming. She was excessively negative and angry concerning nearly every experience. Her constant complaints and negativity pushed people away and tended to keep her isolated and alone in the group as well as in her life. She had a firm belief in victimization that permeated every aspect of her life. She had few relationships and was in such poverty that she had to move in with her father in order to have a place to live, even though she worked as a professional therapist.

Her ego was so fragmented that she openly told us she hated herself. Her overt self-destructive behavior confirmed this: she was overweight, smoked cigarettes heavily, and picked sores until they bled all over her body. She was literally the image of self-hatred and powerlessness.

As we began Heart-Centered Hypnotherapy with Judy, she regressed back to several situations where her father was extremely critical of her and was "always picking on her." When she was very young, her mother died and literally left her alone and unprotected with her critical, abusive father. We always ask during age regressions, "What conclusion about yourself did you draw at this time?" Her response was, "Everyone I love always leaves me," and, "Even God is not here for me." Another conclusion was, "I deserve to be picked on," which was the underlying belief that caused her to pick sores all over her body for most of her life.

At the end of each age regression, we had Judy approach that hurt and abandoned inner child to give her the love she needed. The inner child she found stuck in each situation essentially made up many "inner children" — aspects of her fragmented ego. We had her change her self-limiting beliefs into something new: "There is always plenty of love for me." It was difficult for her to accept at first. Sometimes she could barely even say the new words because they felt so foreign to her.

Judy's fragmented ego affected every aspect of her life. Her relationships were the most dysfunctional part of her life. She did not possess a basic trust in the Universe and especially in other people. She had deep fears about not having enough money, even though she had a master's degree in social work and a good job.

Judy deeply longed for a loving relationship with a man and wanted children. In her life, the few relationships she attracted were with men who were unavailable (married) and who reflected back to her the self-hatred that she projected. They were often abusive both physically and emotionally. She often remained in these relationships because she was lonely and feared that she didn't deserve any better.

During the first year of her work in the group, which met once every three months, Judy did some powerful hypnotherapy work, confronting deep-seated fears and reclaiming and integrating the lost ego parts. But it was during the second year — when we began using Heart-Centered Energetic Psychodrama — that Judy really began to integrate, to project and confront her deepest issues of abandonment. When another group member played Judy's mother who had died, Judy got in touch with the profoundly deep grief that the small child had previously been unable to express.

It was at this point that her anger at God came out. How could a child ever trust God when God had taken her mother from her, leaving her unprotected? It was from this point that the importance of the group connection came into play. Over the two years, Judy had bonded with the group members. They had consistently been there for her through her anger, her fears, and her many attempts to push them away. She began to realize that God had brought her to this group and to these people who loved her. A whole new sense of purpose came over her. She knew that she was on this earth for a reason and that her existence was not a mistake or a punishment, as she had previously felt.

The final integration in the transformation process is the spiritual one. During this work, Judy experienced that not only had her ego fragmented, but her soul had too. She lost connection with a big part of her soul when her mother died, and then her soul continued to fragment and split off during those abusive times with her father. Once she was able to go back and reclaim her soul, a spiritual transformation took place.

As a result, Judy's life changed. She stopped trying to kill herself by smoking and was very proud to give up that behavior. She stopped "picking on herself" and began healing the sores which had previously scarred her entire body. She began getting in better physical shape and was proud of being able to complete a triathlon held in her city.

Finally, Judy no longer embraced the victim consciousness. She now feels power in her life. She has turned around her financial situation, moved out of her father's house, and purchased a home of her own. She is open to attracting a loving, healthy man into her life so that she can create her own loving family.

This is the power of personal transformation. It involves integrating ego fragments as well as soul fragments. It involves going down to the hidden corners of the individual's psyche and facing the deepest shadow parts. It involves expressing the most powerful depth of pain, grief, fear, rage, loneliness, and abandonment. And when this work is done in a group, the individual can share that pain with others. When our pain is witnessed and validated by loving friends, it can then be fully released. This witnessing brings trust, intimacy and a deep bonding that most people have never experienced in their lives. As a result of this process, personal transformation takes place.

That kind of transformation is needed, of course, because of the kinds of traumas that happen either in the womb or during birth, or in later stages of life as we saw with Judy. So let's take a look at the various developmental stages that people go through after birth and how trauma can affect them.

Three Life Factors

Before we get into the stages themselves, I should point out three factors that apply throughout these stages. These are the three factors that, ideally, are strengthened in each stage, but that traumas can often undermine. The factors are independence, worthiness, and clarity.

Independence

A child is born independent and autonomous if she experienced feelings of support, nurturing, and welcome while still in the womb. Control and power become desirable to a child *only as a defense against the loss of autonomy* imposed on her by others — by caregivers who need to create emotional dependency or subservience. The child faced with this indignity needs to feel important and special, and becomes competitive and grandiose or — when expression is punished — submissive and passive.

Worthiness

A child is born feeling self-worthy as long as there are no traumas in the womb that bury such feelings. A sense of unworthiness can be created in the child through shame imposed by individuals, family, religions, and the cultural itself. "I am flawed" becomes the constant inner dialogue and prompts the split into a hidden "real" self (private self) and a stylized "imposter" self (public self). Healthy development always increases the convergence of these two selves into one re-united and worthy self.

Clarity

Finally, a child is normally born with an unfailing, innate sense of what is in its highest good: clarity. Only the imposition of dependency and unworthiness can interfere with that inner knowing and create confusion.

Understanding, then, that independence and worthiness — both contributing to clarity of one's purpose and highest good — are supported through positive development and hindered by negative development throughout life, we can take a look at the following life stages and see how each specifically impacts these three factors.

Developmental Stages

Erik Erikson postulated eight stages of psychosocial growth in the normal human, and suggested that when a child is frustrated in the completion of one, she becomes fixated on that stage, preventing her from mastering the stages that would normally follow. In other words, each developmental stage is a stepping-stone to the next, so that each depends on those that came before for the development of a healthy adult.

Traumas along the way can essentially halt or hinder a child's inner development. And of course unconscious parenting isn't the only cause of trauma. Violence, accidents, deaths, and natural disasters can cause trauma, and these can trap a child in the developmental stage in which he experienced the trauma. This can lead to shock, dissociation and repression; unhealthy relationships; a desperate sense of disconnection and isolation; or even substitute behaviors and neurotic symptoms … all to deal with the pain of trauma in a developmental stage of life.

The good news is that when a parent *does* support her child, the stages can build properly upon one another, helping the child to reach his potential. And of course traumas unresolved in childhood can be remedially accessed and healed, providing a healthy foundation on which the individual can not only survive and recover, but thrive.

Let's take a closer look at the specific stages and consider the affects of trauma in each one.

Psychosocial Developmental Stage 1: Bonding

The first developmental stage, from conception to 6 months after birth, focuses on bonding, basic trust vs. mistrust, and healthy codependence. The purpose of this stage involves learning how to express needs; accepting nurturing; bonding emotionally; learning to trust adults; and choosing to live.

Symptoms and substitute behaviors include: a failure to recognize physical needs or doing anything to get them met; addictive and compulsive behaviors, especially addictions to things ingested such as food, sugar, alcohol, pills, or tobacco; other eating disorders; the inability to ask directly for anything; a terror of abandonment; the need for external affirmation of one's worth; a deep, basic lack of trust of others and of having one's needs met; frozen feelings, numbness; worries about not enough money, food, time, etc.; the inability to bond physically/emotionally.

Psychosocial Developmental Stage 2: Exploration

The second developmental stage, from 6 to 18 months, focuses on *oppositional* bonding — i.e., "I need to trust you to discover me as separate from you" — and healthy counter-dependence. The purpose of this stage involves exploring and experiencing the environment; developing sensory awareness; expressing needs and trusting that others will respond; beginning to learn that there are options to problem-solving; and developing initiative.

Symptoms and substitute behaviors include: a failure to know what one wants; boredom; a fear of trying new things or experiences; the tendency to defer to others; a fear of abandonment and/or engulfment; a fear of making mistakes; an unawareness of one's body; frequent accidents or injuries; the tendency to be compliant and adaptive; obsessive/compulsive behavior; motivational problems; a reluctance to initiate things or assert oneself; a tendency towards being hyper-active or under-active.

Psychosocial Developmental Stage 3: Separation

The third developmental stage, from 18 months to three years, focuses on development of a separate identity, thinking and problem-solving, issues of autonomy vs. shame and doubt, and development of a healthy independence. The purpose of this stage involves establishing the ability to think for oneself; testing reality by pushing against boundaries and people; learning to solve problems with cause and effect thinking; expressing anger and other feelings; separating from parents and being welcomed back with love (rapprochement); and beginning to give up thoughts of being the center of the universe.

In this developmental stage, the child needs to be able to "leave" the mother and then "return" with full love and acceptance. If the mother herself feels abandoned when the child "leaves" and is thus angry when he tries to "return," the child will not develop proper independence and trust in relationships. Thus punished for attempting to become independent, the child will block his freedom, trust, and passion in relationships through immersion in shame.

Symptoms and substitute behaviors include: difficulty with boundaries or distinguishing one's own needs, wants, and feelings from those of other people; a lack of feeling separate or independent; codependent relationships; avoidance of conflict at any expense; the inability to say "no" directly, but using manipulative means instead; a tendency toward inappropriate rebellion; use of anger to mask other feelings; negative, oppositional, controlling, rigid, critical, or withholding relationship styles; intestinal and colon disease; a demanding personality; frequent feelings of being cheated; Borderline or Narcissistic Personality Disorders; Attachment Disorder.

Psychosocial Developmental Stage 4: Socialization

The fourth developmental stage, from three to seven years, focuses on socialization, identity and power, initiative vs. guilt, and belonging. The purpose of this stage involves asserting an identity separate from others while creating social inclusion; acquiring knowledge about the world, oneself, one's body, and one's gender role; learning that behaviors have consequences; learning to exert power to affect relationships; practicing socially appropriate behavior; separating fantasy from reality; and learning what one does and does not have power over.

In this developmental stage, getting approval is very important to the young child. If people don't get the approval they need in order to develop a healthy ego, they become starved for approval. They then give their power away by becoming willing to do anything just to get that outside approval. They may also deal with feelings of powerlessness by trying to overpower others in abusive ways.

Symptoms and substitute behaviors include: unawareness of the option for asking questions, relying instead on guesses and unchecked assumptions; incorrect or missing labels for feelings, with anger often labeled as sadness or fear experienced as anger; belief that incongruity between one's thoughts, feelings, and actions is normal; power struggles to control one's own and others' thoughts and feelings; a grandiose sense of one's own magical powers, e.g., "If I act a certain way, my father won't drink or my parents won't get divorced"; a magical hope of being rescued from challenges; manipulation of others to take responsibility for them; sexual identity problems; seductiveness as a means of getting needs met; metabolic and circulation disease; an obligation to take care of others' feelings (emotional rescuing) to avoid abandonment; the need to always be in a position of power, or fear and avoidance of power.

Psychosocial Developmental Stage 5: Latency
The fifth developmental stage, from seven to twelve years, focuses on industry vs. inferiority, concrete knowing and learning, healthy interdependence, and cooperation. The purpose of this stage involves learning skills and learning from mistakes; accepting one's adequacy; learning to listen and collect information; practicing thinking and doing; learning the appropriateness of having wants and needs; learning the structure of the family and the culture; learning the consequences of breaking rules; having one's own opinions and being able to disagree while still being accepted and loved; developing internal controls; learning about taking responsibility and knowing who is responsible for what; developing the capacity to cooperate; identifying with same sex role models and peers; competing and testing abilities against others.

Erikson linked the maturing ego with openness: a more mature ego becomes capable of a greater tolerance of ambiguity and diversity, while a less mature ego resorts to simplistic certainties and conformities in order to preserve a sense of security. He discussed four main features of immature identity related to this developmental stage:

- Problems of intimacy (unwillingness to risk abandonment which is seen as threatening one's already tenuous identity);
- A troubling sense of lack of progress toward goals due to time "flying by";

- A cognitive deficiency revealed by poor concentration;
- Formulation of negative identity (selected roles presented by parents or community as preferred or acceptable are rebelliously rejected — "my identity is defined by what I am not").

Symptoms and substitute behaviors include: a belief that one should know how to do things perfectly without instruction; lack of information on how to organize time for complicated tasks; procrastination; inability to negotiate, either giving in completely or insisting on having one's own way; perfectionism; inflexible values; the tendency to act without thinking; a discounting of one's own feelings; ulcers, headaches or high blood pressure; living in the past or future rather than in the present; the need for being part of a clique or gang, or being a loner; difficulty with rules and authority, rebelliousness; and the reluctance or inability to be productive and successful.

Psychosocial Developmental Stage 6: Adolescence
The sixth developmental stage, from twelve to eighteen years, focuses on identity vs. role confusion, sexuality, and healthy independence from the family. The purpose of this stage involves achieving independence and a clear separation from the group and the family; gradually emerging as a separate person with one's own goals and values; being responsible for one's own needs, feelings, and behaviors; integrating sexuality into one's identity.

Symptoms and substitute behaviors include: a desperate search for companionship to fulfill the emptiness one perceives in oneself; refusal to accept traditional standards of behavior; the flaunting of differences through extremes of dress or style, thumbing one's nose at society; either extreme dependence or isolation; a pretense of having no wants or needs; the forming of codependent, symbiotic relationships in which one loses a sense of separate identity; extreme rebellion; conflicts with authority figures such as police, bosses, teachers, the government, etc.; sexual games, sexual addictions, sexual dysfunction, confusion of sex with nurturing; use of psychological games to avoid real intimacy; self-absorption; the need to one-up others; a sense of vengeance; difficulty with completion; the experience of abandonment when beginning or ending jobs or relationships; a tendency to abandon others to avoid separation or completion; a confused sexual identity.

Psychosocial Developmental Stage 7: Young Adulthood
The seventh developmental stage, following adolescence, focuses on intimacy vs. isolation, creation of an ego strong enough to withstand the fear of loss inherent in true intimacy, and the creation of personal ethics strong enough to abide by commitments. The purpose of this stage is for the young adult to become attracted to starting a family, establishing a career, and making a home or 'nest' of his own. Successfully building a relationship with a mate completes the process of separation from the primary caregiver begun in the separation/individuation stage — rapprochement. The effort to create and maintain an identity becomes less the (negative) adolescent flight from the anxiety of alienation and more a (positive) quest to find a fulfilling role in the world.

Symptoms and substitute behaviors include: sexual dysfunction, dysfunctional intimate relationships, uncertainty about what direction to take in life, and poor ego strength.

Psychosocial Developmental Stage 8: Mature Adulthood
The eighth developmental stage, following young adulthood, focuses on generativity vs. stagnation, creation of meaning in one's life through relationships, contribution to the community, self-actualization, and spirituality. We must develop spiritually *and* emotionally in balance to experience true transformation.

If we develop spiritually but not emotionally, we become psychics blinded by personal projection, or ministers filled with rage rather than compassion, or meditators who take refuge in the safety of meditation at the expense of social obligations. If we develop emotionally but not spiritually, we become therapists who avoid our clients' spiritual experiences, or we become stuck in "meeting our needs" and isolated from the passion and peace of mind that come from selflessness in intimacy.

Erikson suggests that wisdom is the ego strength of the final developmental stage. He defined wisdom as "the detached and yet active concern with life itself in the face of death itself," and said that "it maintains and conveys the integrity of experience in spite of the disdain over human failing and the dread of ultimate nonbeing."[93] He believed that an individual fulfilled his life cycle by finding clarity in a final "existential identity." Existential identity is the ultimate expression of agency, of experiencing everything as choice, expressed as: "I choose my experience," or, "I am 100% accountable for my experience." It is a sense of sovereignty of the self. An individual who achieves this avoids the narcissistic beliefs of being the center of the universe, however, through a clear need for relatedness with nature, with others, and with his own conception of God.

The problem at this stage, of course, is in not achieving that sovereignty of the self before the end of one's life. Any dysfunctional or self-limiting behaviors in the person's daily life can be seen as substitutes for the missing meaning, satisfaction, and sense of fulfillment in life. What does a healthy achievement of this final stage of development mean? What does it look like?

Developing the Ego Enough to Surrender It

All of the developmental stages described by Erikson bring us into adulthood, but there is a tradition in many cultures of dividing life into two parts: in the first phase, from childhood to middle adulthood, we are becoming individuals, learning the ways of the world and asserting ourselves in the demands of family, work, and society. This is described by those first eight stages. In the second phase, however — which begins according to Carl Jung and Joseph Campbell with the "midlife crisis" — we begin turning inward, reconnecting with the center of our being. This would be essentially a ninth developmental stage — that of "the wise elder." This development focuses on creating meaning in one's life beyond what we can *do* and based instead on who we *are*. As Edward Edinger puts it:

> It is generally accepted among analytical psychologists that the task of the first half of life involves ego development with progressive separation between ego and Self; whereas the second half of life requires a surrender or at least a relativization of the ego as it experiences and relates to the Self.[94]

Both halves are important. If the ego is not developed and strengthened, it can not bow to the Self when that time comes. So we'll take a look at how it grows over the years and becomes strong, then faces this time of "surrendering" itself later on. In this discussion, we'll use the Jungian perspective, which suggests that the ego is the seat of the conscious personality, of subjective identity, the sense of "I". It is partial, impermanent, and changeable, but believes itself to be whole, permanent, and absolute. The ego is the *conscious* part of the total personality, the Self. The Self is the central archetype of wholeness, the unifying center of the total psyche, and includes both conscious and unconscious elements. It is that part of us capable of truly being a healthy sovereign, full of wisdom and experiencing everything as choice. The question arises, "How did our ego get so separate from our true essence, our Self?" That happens early in life in response to the reality of living on planet Earth with human (and that always means imperfect) caregivers.

Creation of Ego States: Integration, Possession, and Trauma

One of the basic processes in human development is *integration*, by which a child learns to put concepts together — such as dog and cat — thus building more complex units, in this case called animals. As the child grows in complexity, he begins to organize selected, similar behaviors and experiences as well. He looks for those with a defining common element and sets those into groups called *ego states*. "Every time I experience something like this, I am *mad at Mommy*." Or, "Every time I experience something like this, I am *eager to please*." This grouping of experiences is integration.

Think of a time in your adult life when you went from one way of being (ego state) to another very different way of being (another ego state) instantly. For example, John Watkins[95] describes such a switch when a father who easily crawls on the floor with his baby playing "peek-a-boo" in one ego state and, in a moment's notice, can respond to an emergency by giving sophisticated instructions to a nurse on how to manage a medical crisis. We can transition spontaneously in this way only because we groped our way through the process as very young children. You may recognize some people as not very good at this sort of shift; for example, someone who feels very awkward when he is with both his boss and his family at the same time, or with friends from church and friends from work at the same time. Such people probably have not integrated their various ways of relating (ego states), and probably the difficulty goes back to early childhood.

To understand how this lack of integration develops, we need to look at two other sources of ego states: 1) possession by or introjection of significant influences; and 2) reactions to trauma.[96]

Through possession or introjection, the child takes on clusters of behavior and attitude from significant others. If these are accepted and become identified as one's own, the resulting ego state is a clone of the other. If the trait or attitude is positive, such as honesty or compassion or generosity, then the child is well served. Unfortunately, too often it is the negative traits that tend to be powerful, intrusive, and captivating. For example, a child may internalize his mother's critical, judgmental perfectionism. Her constant dissatisfaction with him evolves into his own dissatisfaction with himself. Once internalized, the nagging parent becomes an interminable nag within, and the child becomes his own worst critic. Another way of saying it is that the child is "possessed" by his mother's critic. Years later, the man's internalized critical parent ego state can take over at a particular moment — irrationally, angrily — and lead him to abuse his own children, just as he was abused when he was a child. We call this "identifying with the persecutor," and it is nearly always in the history of any bully, rage-a-holic, or abuser.

Another variation of this possession occurs when the introjected ego state is not accepted and identified as one's own. Then the new ego state, the nagging parent within, is rejected and repressed. The child will suffer internal conflict because "part of me" is self-critical but "part of me" is not. This child may become depressed or experience authority issues because such internal divisiveness is exhausting, confusing, and maddening. The child becomes an embattled personality, highly demanding of himself and simultaneously resistant to compliance.

Another example is when a parent shames the child for wetting the bed or for crying. The child either identifies with the shamer, or identifies with the shame. In the former case, the child has introjected the "shamer," identifying with the abuser and mimicking that abusive behavior toward others. Or, in the second case, the child rejects and represses the abuser within, turning the judgments, blame, and abuse against himself by feeling unworthy and shameful. Children take on parental attributes like this because, to a child, the adult is always right

The other primary source of developing ego states is early trauma, when the child dissociates as a survival defense. If an experience is too awful to bear, he simply stops experiencing it by separating from part of himself. The disconnection may be from what he defines as the "weak" part of himself, or it may be from the "higher" part of himself, the soul. Obviously the estrangement between the ego personality and the Self, begun in the rapprochement stage, is not resolved in this case and the ego and Self remain isolated from one another. When this happens, the ego states in this individual's repertoire of roles are not choreographed flowingly by a healthy maestro; rather, they compete with each other for dominance and this competition appears in various ways in response to external conditions.

Development of Ego States: Differentiation & Dissociation

Now, while a child finds common factors used to group things (i.e., cats and dogs are both animals — integration), he also goes through a companion process in development called *differentiation*, by which he separates general concepts into more specific categories, such as discriminating between 'good doggies' and 'bad doggies.'

Likewise, while grouping experiences into ego states through integration, the child also creates boundaries between each of these states through differentiation. As he develops a repertoire of ego states, he begins experiencing each one as a separate, bounded state of "I". In other words, "these experiences lead me to ego state #1 which is distinct from ego state #2." For example, "When someone important criticizes me, I feel humiliated, insignificant, and self-loathing (ego state #1). When someone important praises me, I feel proud, valued, and self-loving (ego state #2)." Each ego state is essentially a different experience of who this person is, of his "I" in that moment.

This differentiation of ego states is accomplished through *dissociation*. Mild dissociation produces ego states with permeable boundaries that have agreements between them to take turns at being in charge (the "executive") according to the need of the moment. Remember the capability of the father who easily crawls on the floor with his baby and, in a moment's notice, can respond to an emergency.

Dissociation lies on a continuum from this example to the opposite extreme, as in the case of multiple personality disorder (MPD, now called Dissociative Identity Disorder, or D.I.D.) where boundaries are not permeable. And there are innumerable variations in between. In other words, rigid boundaries between each ego state create a situation where someone is one "I" or one person in this moment, and in another moment is another "I" or another person without any knowledge of the first "I". This is true D.I.D. With healthy, permeable boundaries, a person can make an intentional transition between each state. And again, there are various degrees of permeability, so that someone can be anywhere along the continuum of healthy and unhealthy transitions between states.

Do your ego states always cooperate? Do they always agree on what happened at the office party last year or on what your character strengths and weaknesses are? Which ones tend to be dominant, and in what types of situations (the shame one, the angry one, the one scared of rejection, the confident one, the playful one)? These questions can provide some insight into the permeability of these boundaries.

Complications of Ego States

Some of these competing identities or ego states may not be too compatible. A person may be determined to "be good" and stay away from sweets, for instance, but then another pops up and devours all the candy in the jar. Each is successively in control, and the greed or lack of discipline of the latter defeats the high intentions of the former.

Carl Jung saw most people as identified almost entirely with certain acceptable aspects of themselves (the *persona*), having denied and repressed the unacceptable aspects (the *shadow*). In fact, Jung refers to this identification with the persona as an instance of *possession*[97], as we discussed in the context of introjection. One identity (each of which he called a *complex*) hijacks the whole confederation of identities for a moment or two before another takes over. "Everyone knows that people have complexes," Jung wrote, but "what is not so well known ... is that complexes can have us."[98] So we find ourselves one day in a job we don't like in order to pay the mortgage on a home we resent. Who made the choice twenty years ago to live this way? Which complex hijacked you?

An example of this predicament is when two people fall in love with each other at first sight — feeling an almost eerie sense of familiarity — and then gradually realize that they actually hate each other. The familiarity may come from marrying one's unhealthy parent, re-creating a nuclear family just like the original family of origin. Or the familiarity may come from marrying someone who personifies one's own repressed shadow part. A person who is overtly outgoing and sociable, but underneath is actually self-conscious, marries that introverted part of themselves. This relationship re-creates the internal conflict that is waiting to be resolved.

Most people see the unwanted characteristics in the other, and "resolve" the conflict by divorcing, or leaving the job and that difficult boss, or moving to a new church congregation to get away from that irritating someone at the old church. A healthier strategy is to recognize the re-creation of this internal conflict as an opportunity to finally heal and resolve the issue rather than avoiding and running from it.

Personal Transformation

Being a multitude of "I"s is not in itself problematic, and can be highly adaptive. It allows for specialized focus on one area at a time, with the ability to temporarily defocus on others. The problem, however, lies in the fact that we *can* be hijacked by any given complex or ego state, or even "possessed" by the persona while trying to ignore or bury our shadow rather than dealing with it.

So it's hopeful that — after successfully establishing the first eight psychosocial stages of life — questions of "Who am I?" and "Who do I want to be?" start surfacing in one's consciousness ... and that answers begin to surface as well. Through moments of transcendence, we get glimpses of the vast possibilities beyond normal everyday consciousness. We experience ourselves through an egoless lens. This can be a peak experience induced by religious ritual, meditation, near-death experience, or many other means. We begin to discover, perhaps through psychotherapy or meditation, that there is a lot more to us than we ever suspected.

This can help lead us to recognize the limitations of our normal approach to life and, in doing so, a new door opens to us. When the ego — this never-ending procession of momentary "I"s who believe in their own supremacy — sees these limitations and this fragmentation, it can take new action. It can begin to accept all ego states and even the shadow as mere aspects of itself, and then acknowledge that there is a higher Self that is not any of these. The second phase of life can then begin, when the ego starts taking a back seat to the Self. We call this personal transformation, or transpersonal growth.

The first phase of life must be completed, however, or the second phase will not succeed. In other words, the ego of the seeker must be so strong and healthy that it dis-identifies from the various fragmented selves and surrenders itself to a higher purpose than its own self-promotion. Essentially, the person whose ego states are controlled by outside influences is not yet ready for profound transformation. If criticism from others calls out one "me" (perhaps the ego state fearful of rejection) and praise from others calls out another "me" (perhaps the ego state anxious to please others), then sovereignty is still elusive. One or more fragment of the self may be concerned for its own survival and fight against the transition or transformation in any way it can ... even by simply blinding us to new possibilities. If the ego is strong, well-tested, and secure in its abilities, though, then it is (we are) prepared to move beyond the realm of "I am what I do" and venture into a whole new level of self-exploration.

Of course, this new movement of the ego back toward the Self is a reversal of the original rapprochement process of the two-year-old. That is, the adult at the outset of this developmental stage develops an intense ambivalence toward her own potentiality as a *Self-oriented ego*. The conflict is based on a growing awareness of the ego's dependence on the

Self for meaning, purpose, and immortality, while still being pulled by its long-standing drive for autonomy and independence. The goals of the ego and Self *appear* at first to undermine one another: the desire for transcendence makes autonomy seem like *alienation* (loss of connection) and the desire for autonomy making transcendence seem like *annihilation* (loss of self). However, as we'll see below, the two can work together in a healthy collaboration.

The process of this new rapprochement has prototypes from earlier life experiences — in fact, prototypes in each of the life stages we've discussed until now: first, in the transition between the interlife and life itself; second, in the transition from womb to birth; and finally, in the gradual transition from infant to adult.

The first prototype for the mid-life transformation is the monumental step between the interlife and life. From the soul's perspective, this process can be conscious, with careful planning of the life ahead, or it can be unconscious, the thoughtless reflex of grabbing at the familiar. If at death one is addicted to pain or power or prurience, then it can be overpoweringly seductive to grab onto another life of the same. In other words, we carry our weaknesses, unresolved conflicts, erroneous beliefs, and unconscious reflexive reactions with us into the experience after physical death. That is the teaching of every major religion. And if we cannot overcome these in planning for a future life, then the transition into life is an unconscious one. An important question to ask ourselves is, which one of our ego states will be calling the shots at the moment of death?

Let me share an example with you. Candace was someone whose lifestyle was fast-paced and impatient. She constantly sought distractions to keep herself occupied in order to avoid experiencing a deep-seated sense of personal angst. In one session with us, she experienced an age regression to a past life with a similar life pattern. After going through death in that past life, Candace watched herself hurry through the celestial consultation available to her in the interlife, brushing aside any opportunity to reflect on lessons she could learn in her haste to "get on with it" and enter the next life — her life as Candace. The lesson in this session was profoundly unmistakable, and she realized ample reason to make fundamental changes in her tendency to rush life, avoiding periods of quiet by creating preoccupations.

Another prototype for the process of mid-life transformation is the process of birth. Leaving behind the security and predictability (and the extreme limitations) of the womb again requires a monumental leap of faith. The fetus willingly surrenders itself to the unknown force which will carry it to a new and infinitely expanded world. On the other hand, the fetus can fight this change and go through it in fear or pain or rage. The difference between these choices sets in motion influences of vast proportions during the lifetime to follow.

A final prototype for the process of transformation is the gradual growth of the infant and toddler from its identification with its mother or other caregiver into an autonomous individual. That process occurs over years through the psychosocial developmental stages. Throughout the process, the underlying momentum is meant to strengthen the ego without going overboard into narcissism.

In each of these prototypes, one is moving from what is safe and known into something that seems dangerous and unknown ... but if you make the choice consciously because you know it'll get you where you really want to go, then you take that leap of faith and find *true* freedom, because of course you have grown into a place of new power. Likewise, moving consciously through the mid-life transformation provides new strength and freedom.

However, if the ego isn't strengthened enough (where there isn't enough worthiness, personal power, or sense of identity) or gains too much strength (where there is overcompensation with arrogant ego inflation), then there are problems with mid-life transformation. So we need to take a look at how that ego is ideally strengthened and, if there are problems in that process, how we can guide someone through transformational hypnotherapy into an ideal state for real introspection and healthy collaboration between ego and Self.

"Strengthening the Ego" and the Therapeutic Process

A child is born experiencing himself as literally the center of the universe; that is, the ego is totally identified with the Self. In the beginning, healthy parenting eagerly meets every need, thus reinforcing the child's basic sense of worthiness and trust. Jung called this *ego inflation*. Soon enough, however, the world (and the parents) begin selectively meeting demands and rejecting others. A child whose ego inflation continues unchecked by boundaries and limits becomes "spoiled," and grows into an adult who exhibits ego inflation through grandiosity, demands for control, entitlement, selfishness and even narcissism.

Adults can also exhibit negative inflation — that is, unworthiness, guilt, ambiguity about their existence, and the need to suffer. This occurs when they experience abusive parental rejection, which is a rejection stemming from projection of the parent's shadow onto the child and the child identifying with it.

We can see an example of this from our clinical experience. Whenever George would cry or ask for help as a child, George's father saw him as weak and judged him to be pathetically incompetent. That was actually George's father's fear of his own condition, a belief that he developed in turn from *his* father's rejecting treatment of *him*. He overcompensated for his own rejection by acting out the emotional bully with his son, George. George identified with this introjection, seeing himself as weak and shameful, and judged himself at least as harshly as his father did.

A child's experience that he is *not* the center of the universe leads to an estrangement between the ego and Self. The ego is chastened and humbled. Initially, this is experienced as alienation, but a loving environment keeps the ego from being damaged in the process. That is, the ego dis-identifies from the Self while maintaining connection with caregivers and a sense of belonging in the community, which is desirable for healthy, continued development.

If, however, the child doesn't experience a loving environment, the ego's connection to Self is severed and serious damage results. In this case, the ego is disconnected from its origin, its inner resources. The person is no longer whole and integrated. Aspects of his essence, such as innocence, trust, courage, compassion, spontaneity, or artistic expression, are "lost." Healing that wound requires restoring connection with the natural inner resources of strength and acceptance (Self), without returning to the narcissism of identification with it (inflated ego). That balance is referred to as the individuated ego or the authentic self, and the process of realizing it is individuation or self-actualization.

In therapy, then, it's important to deliberately strengthen the ego in cases where someone's ego is not strong enough for the rigors of self-exploration. There are many techniques for ego-strengthening. One category includes techniques that assist clients to access a strong resource state within themselves, to relive successful experiences. These could include instances of particularly high self-esteem, of successes in mastering challenging tasks, or of the adulation of others.

Another category of techniques is the creation of an idealized self, not based on remembered success but rather on projected fantasy. This might take the form of an image of "how I could be if ...," or it might be the idealized person we hope to become at a specific time in the future (for example, the wise ninety-year-old).

Another category involves "borrowing" the strong persona of another — either someone in the client's life, or a public figure, or a mythic or fictional model with the desired attributes — until they are integrated into one's own self.

All of these, of course, are desirable therapies when needed, because mid-life transformation is an important part of one's growth, both for a person and for the person's soul. And as a therapist, I know that if someone is here on Earth and in relationship with me, he is here for growth of the true Self. And whether we are therapists with clients ready for that inner growth, or we are ready for that growth ourselves, it's important for us to look at the possible stages of spiritual growth and understand how that development can take place.

Chapter 6
Developmental Stages Questionnaire

A. In infancy (birth to 14 months), I most likely felt:
- ❏ 1. "Go back where you came from"
- ❏ 2. Fears of needs not being met
- ❏ 3. If I am powerful I will be abandoned
- ❏ 4. If I am weak I will be engulfed
- ❏ 5. Curiosity and exploring are dangerous
- ❏ 6. Safety in controlling and constricting

- ❏ 1. "Come into the world, you're welcome here"
- ❏ 2. Security that needs will be met
- ❏ 3. It is safe to be powerful
- ❏ 4. It is safe to be vulnerable
- ❏ 5. Confident to be curious, to experiment
- ❏ 6. Excitement is pleasurable

B. As a toddler (14 to 24 months), I most likely felt:
- ❏ 1. Authority is arbitrary or abusive
- ❏ 2. Fear of rejection (insignificance)
- ❏ 3. Survival depends on need for approval
- ❏ 4. Taking initiative leads to failure

- ❏ 1. Authority is trustworthy
- ❏ 2. Security that I am important, I matter
- ❏ 3. I am limited and dependent, and I thrive
- ❏ 4. Taking initiative leads to success

C. As the controller child (2-3) and the existential child (3-4), I likely felt:
- ❏ 1. Manipulate power to challenge parents
- ❏ 2. Fear of weakness
- ❏ 3. I must repress my anger
- ❏ 4. Self-reliance and mistrust of others
- ❏ 5. Self-doubt, feeling overpowered
- ❏ 6. Despairing impotence

- ❏ 1. Power is bestowed for being real
- ❏ 2. Security that needs will be met
- ❏ 3. I am encouraged to express my anger
- ❏ 4. Self-worth and other-trustworthiness
- ❏ 5. Confident to be included and well-treated
- ❏ 6. "I'm okay, you're okay"

D. As the pre-schooler (4-7 years), I most likely felt:
- ❏ 1. Fear of not belonging, not being accepted
- ❏ 2. Anxiety of feeling stuck and trapped
- ❏ 3. Non-acceptance leads to identity confusion

  - ❏ 1. I am important, I matter, and I belong
  - ❏ 2. The future looks rosy
  - ❏ 3. Identity is based on inclusion

E. In the latency period (7-12 years), I felt:
- ❏ 1. Perfectionism and procrastination
- ❏ 2. Discounting one's own feelings
- ❏ 3. Living in the past or future, not the present

  - ❏ 1. I discover and express my true self
  - ❏ 2. Self-esteem for my adequacy
  - ❏ 3. Being fully present in my life

F. As an adolescent (12-13 years), I felt:
- ❏ 1. Driven by the need for acceptance
- ❏ 2. Self-judgment (fear of vulnerability)
- ❏ 3. Games to avoid real intimacy
- ❏ 4. Needing to be one-up on others
- ❏ 5. Abandoning self to avoid separation
- ❏ 6. Desperate to fill the emptiness inside

  - ❏ 1. Secure in my rightful place, I belong
  - ❏ 2. Realistic self-assessment
  - ❏ 3. Willing to take risks of real intimacy
  - ❏ 4. Companionship based on cooperation
  - ❏ 5. Enjoyment in expressing my true self
  - ❏ 6. Confident and comfortable with who I am

G. As an adolescent (14-16 years), I felt:
- ❏ 1. Obsessed by the need to separate
- ❏ 2. Self-absorption (fear of intimacy)
- ❏ 3. Lose my identity in relationships

  - ❏ 1. Separate / individuate in my uniqueness
  - ❏ 2. Satisfaction in intimacy with others
  - ❏ 3. Relish my unique identity in relationships

H. As an adolescent (17-18 years), I felt:
- ❏ 1. Obsessed with fears of unworthiness
- ❏ 2. Lack of clarity regarding purpose in life
- ❏ 3. Projection and identity confusion

- ❏ 1. Secure in own sense of self-worth
- ❏ 2. Growing optimism about purpose in life
- ❏ 3. Expect to live up to internal standards

Can you see how the origins of these lifetime patterns can be traced to your early developmental experiences? Circle those that seem to apply in your life.

- A. **Abundance/lack issues**: 0-6 months
- B. **Intimacy/withdrawal Issues**: 0-6 months (survival, lack of bonding)
- C. **Commitment/commitment phobic**: 0-6 months
- D. **Worthiness/unworthiness**: 0-6 months (survival), and 18-36 months (security)
- E. **Sexual Shame/Passion**: 6-18 months (exploratory stage, nurture)
- F. **Victim/rescuer/persecutor patterns**: 18-36 months (security)
- G. **Authority issues**: 18-36 months (security)
- H. **Integrity/dishonor**: 18-36 months (security, separation)

Your Project: Write about your earliest memories.
To recall experiences before about age three, you will need to seek the facilitation of an age-regression hypnotherapist. However, you may be able to get some non-specific impressions of those earliest non-verbal experiences by quieting your mind and allowing your attention to drift back to that time in your life.

_____

_____

_____

_____

_____

_____

_____

Chapter 7
Stages of Spiritual Growth

At one point in my work, a woman named Loren came to me for help. Her childhood was very traumatic, as her older brother had sexually exploited her for many years. When she complained about this to her parents, they denied that it was even possible. This denial destroyed her ability to trust authority figures and ultimately to even trust herself and her own perceptions of reality. When parents deny the reality of children, they can cause "thought disorders" that confuse their children and keep them from correctly differentiating between reality and fantasy.

Loren did have difficulty feeling clear at times, especially when it came to interactions with others. She often perceived situations differently than those around her, and this led to problems with friends and colleagues. Her greatest disappointment was that she couldn't maintain an intimate relationship with a man and was ultimately alone. She was aware that she had a great fear of intimacy and that she maintained a wall of protection around herself, especially when it came to men. She often felt unworthy of love and was unable to accept love when it was truly there for her.

In her relationships with her women friends, Loren was very codependent. She would always look to them to solve her problems for her or to give her guidance in her life. Her pattern was to look outside of herself for answers since she didn't seem to trust that she had any inner resources. The more I grew to know Loren, the more I detected a deep emptiness within her. At first I assumed that this came from the sexual abuse and her parents' denial of her reality.

After some in-depth treatment, though, I saw Loren initially improving but then slipping back to her previous feelings of insecurity and inner turmoil. It was then that I knew the issues went deeper than the sexual abuse. Because of all the birth work I do, I started sensing that we needed to go back to the source of emptiness and unworthiness within Loren, which I knew might stem from her being unwanted as a fetus, baby, and/or child.

We began to pursue this suspicion by doing a Heart-Centered breath therapy session with her. This breath therapy is also referred to as "rebirthing" since people are often able to recreate their birth experiences through conscious, connected breathing. This is also a method for healing birth trauma and for releasing negative thoughts or self-limiting beliefs held in the "memory chip" of the subconscious mind.

At first it was difficult for Loren to "let go" enough to have an experience in the breathwork session. It became clear that holding on to control was important to her feelings of safety. In breathwork, learning to feel safe enough to let go is one of the main objects and is essential to its success.

During the session, Loren began to say she felt "stuck" and that she couldn't move. She felt paralyzed and trapped. Since this is a common experience in birth work, we felt that she might have been stuck in the birth canal and we encouraged her to push out. She said she could not, which was frustrating to her.

The breakthrough came later when we were teaching psychodrama. Loren was part of the group and she became emotional as she identified with another woman's session. At this time, she began getting in touch with deep feelings of abandonment and anxiety that she had experienced as a young child. As we began working with her, Loren finally (and easily) regressed to her experience as a two-year-old who was terrified every night about going to sleep. She was afraid of dying and did not want her parents to leave her side. She cried herself to sleep night after night and, during this regression, recalled a nightly dream of falling into a river with alligators. As the dream came to her, she felt her fingers becoming numb with the pain of attempting to "hold on" to a rope. In the session, her knuckles were actually turning white.

Loren described herself as being on a bridge with rope handrails when the bridge suddenly broke. She was hanging on by her fingers for her life. Then the handrail broke and she felt herself falling into the river. She described a "freeze frame" here as she disconnected from the experience of falling into the river to her death. This showed us why Loren was so afraid of letting go, which in that previous experience meant death.

Loren then described a fall that seemed to go on and on. At first she was falling through the air, then it felt as if she were a leaf falling into the water. When the falling ceased, she described herself as being in a cocoon and feeling stuck and trapped. It was the same way she had felt in her previous breathwork session, but now we understood how her birth experience was similar to this past death experience. Part of her was trapped in a former body because that death was so sudden; she didn't realize that she had died. And it was so traumatic that she had been unable to move beyond that life into her next journey. So she became stuck between lives.

While part of Loren stayed behind in a former life, stuck because of overwhelming confusion, part of her moved on and was born into her current life. As you may remember from our chapter on the womb experience, the conceptus drops from the snug fallopian tube into the vastness of the uterus soon after conception, and many people describe their regression to this experience as "the Fall." Loren experienced that Fall again, just like the leaf falling, when she was born into this life. Our healing now involved powerful energy work, assisting Loren to go back to the freeze-frame experience and release her body as it fell into the river. As the body fell, we could help direct her soul to the light.

We then began the process of Soul Retrieval, which energetically assists the person in bringing missing soul energy into the current body. Loren was able to see her soul floating above her and invited it to fully come into her body. This was a powerful process witnessed by the entire group.

What Loren went through explained why it had been so difficult for her to trust her inner resources; there had been few. When part of someone's soul energy is missing, she usually goes through life feeling empty and unworthy of love. What had been split was reunited; what had fostered ambiguity about living this life, what we call "resistance to life," had dissolved. With the recovered energy, though, Loren displayed a whole new glow in the days that followed.

The Spiritual Work of Healing

As we discussed in chapter 1, the *word* psychology really has to do with a study of the soul (*psyche* means soul in Greek), but the *field* of psychology has focused more on cognition, perception, and the personality than on the soul. While this doesn't take away from the value of what psychology offers us, it leaves an enormous hole in the process of healing. This is the hole that practices like ours seek to fill. In order to do so, we have to recognize and work with the entire body/mind/soul connection. Working with all three is essential to Transformational Healing.

An important way of doing so is understanding and working with the chakra system. The chakras are energy centers that transform universal life energy into physiologically usable chemical messages by activating the appropriate endocrine hormones. They progress from concrete, survival-oriented functions in the lower centers to subtle, spiritual functions in the higher centers.

The chakra system can teach us much about the whole human because each chakra is associated with a major gland in the body. Each chakra is either active or not active based on someone's mental/emotional development, and can be brought into activity by working through developmental issues, and the vitality of each chakra depends on the development of a person's soul. So by knowing the qualities of the chakras and what they indicate in a person, we can get a rough picture of the body/mind/soul connection.

There are entire books written on the topic of chakras, but you can get a sense of this system here. When we talk about the location of each, this is where they are located by mystics and students of energy healing; these are locations in a person's etheric body, which is considered a subtle aspect of the physical body. We also connect each chakra with the developmental stages of life described in our last chapter.

We also correlate these chakras and developmental stages with Abraham Maslow's Hierarchy of Needs[99] and with the Perennial Wisdom interpreted by Paul Foster Case in *The Tarot: A Key to the Wisdom of the Ages*.[100] These seven stages of spiritual unfoldment are represented by Tarot major trump cards 15 through 21, as summarized by Case.

Finally, if you study this topic further, you'll find that there is some variation between sources on the precise location and color of each, as well as the gland each is associated with. We're providing some basics as an introduction; differences on these points needn't keep us from using chakra knowledge in healing work, and greater study into the topic can certainly help to advance any of your own healing efforts for yourself or for others.

The First Chakra

Name:	Root Chakra (*muladhara*)
Location:	Base of the Spine
Color:	Red
Element:	Earth
Gland:	Adrenals
Maslow Needs:	Physiological (addressing hunger, thirst, bodily comforts, etc.) and safety/security (keeping out of danger)
Spiritual stage:	The first stage of spiritual unfoldment is the conscious recognition of bondage to illusion and the discernment between living "in the world but not of the world."
Developmental stage:	Conception to roughly 6 months

The first (Root) chakra represents our connection to the earth and to the tribe, community, or family we have chosen. The life force energy is stored in this chakra. Some teachings refer to this energy as chi, ki, or kundalini energy.

This chakra is located at the base of the spine and has to do with many issues of fear. The first chakra represents all of the prenatal and birth issues that follow us through life. The fear of abandonment is the core fear that begins at conception for every unwanted child. Another core issue here is the fear that your needs will not be met. So for example, I treated a woman whose mother did not want to breastfeed her because she was told that this was old fashioned and inconvenient. The mother was so busy trying to prove her own worthiness, that she often didn't even have time to hold the child during feedings. She would lay the baby down in the crib and prop her bottle up on a pillow.

When this woman came to an advanced training at our Institute, she was filled with fears but didn't even realize it. She would ship boxes of stuff ahead of time to make sure that her needs would be met. She would ship her own pillow and blankets. She even sent bottled water and certain foods that she might need. She would arrive hours ahead of everyone else to make sure she got the bed she wanted.

She did this even though we spent hours on the phone assuring her that we had bottled water, blankets, and pillows, and that we were very close to stores where she could buy food. Before she did the release work, she could not let go and trust that her basic needs would be met.

When your very first experience in life is that you can't trust your mother to hold you and feed you, these deep insecurities follow you and pervade all new experiences. These fears come up especially in new environments where you don't know what to expect and where you're not fully in control of your surroundings. Going to workshops or otherwise visiting new places often brings up these fears.

Another woman came to our training stating that she was always very angry at her family members and was actually abusive to them. She did not know how to control her rage and did not even understand what she was so angry about. When we did a session with her, it turned out that she was an adopted child. She regressed back to her birth where she experienced being furious at her birth mother for giving her away. She kept screaming, "How could you give away your own child?" She realized then that she had projected this anger onto her family members every time she imagined or experienced being rejected by them. For example, if her husband or children were late in coming home and forgot to call, she immediately experienced feeling abandoned. She had not realized that that was what she was feeling before she went through the session.

She also discussed her adoptive mother and said she had always been very angry at her, even though she was a very nice lady. After the session, she realized that it was her birth mother, not her adoptive mother, whom she was really angry with. She stated that she would go home and have a long talk with her adoptive mother and ask for her forgiveness. She also realized that it was actually the fear of abandonment that triggered her rage. In other words, anger was the secondary emotion, covering up the fear.

When the Heart-Centered work is used to break through these early fears, the client moves out of the ego issues into the spiritual place of connecting with the kundalini, or life force energy. Once connected with this energy, the individual actually experiences that all needs will be met and that, in fact, the only need that actually exists is the spiritual need to be One with God. The first chakra lesson is about fear of separation, and when you experience being One with God, that fear is healed.

In this way, we can see how developmental issues correspond with chakras and why it is so important to use ego issues as a vehicle to move toward spiritual enlightenment. As developmental issues are healed, so is the spiritually empowering activity of the chakras opened for use.

The Second Chakra

Name:	Sacral Chakra (*svadhisthana*)
Location:	Genitals
Color:	Orange
Element:	Water
Gland:	Gonads
Maslow Needs:	Belonging and love (affiliating with others and being accepted)
Spiritual stage:	The second stage of spiritual unfoldment is the revelation of the fallacy of one's personal separateness from all creation, and acceptance of one's interdependence.
Developmental stage:	Approximately 6 to 18 months

The second (Sacral) chakra can be blocked early in life, often from six to eighteen months of age, during which time an infant should be able to safely explore her environment. If she is in a dangerous environment, she may grow up with a need to control things in the future in order to feel safe.

This chakra is known as the chakra of sex and passion, and even after that early developmental stage, many people experience personal violations that affect the second chakra and keep them stuck in shame and control issues. A common example of a person stuck in second chakra issues would be someone who was shamed for early masturbation or who was sexually molested early in life.

For example, Carrie was sexually molested at an early age by her stepfather, which caused her to feel unsafe in her environment. The only way she could feel safe was to constantly attempt to control the things and people around her. This of course often alienated others and caused conflict. Her relationships usually ended up with difficulties in the areas of trust, money, and sexuality since she tried to control all these areas. She and her husband were even on the verge of divorce.

When she began to address her sexual abuse through therapy, she saw how strong her need was to feel safe. She began realizing how she had tried to control her husband and their sexual relationship because of her fear of being unsafe. As she worked through the issues in this chakra, it began to open up and so did her sexuality.

Before long, she was also able to trust those close to her and realize that they weren't going to abuse her. But more than that, she began to feel a whole new passion for life in general. Releasing the shame of her abuse increased her self-esteem, which allowed her to feel good about herself for the first time. The more she was able to love and accept herself, the easier it was to stop judging others and to develop loving, trusting relationships.

The Third Chakra

Name:	Solar Plexus Chakra (*manipura*)
Location:	Navel (Solar Plexus)
Color:	Yellow
Element:	Fire
Gland:	Pancreas, Adrenals
Maslow Needs:	Esteem (achieving, being competent, and gaining approval and recognition)
Spiritual stage:	The third stage of spiritual unfoldment is a calm following the storm, a period of quest and search amid the dim light of distant sources, and realizing the personal power that comes with integrity.
Developmental stage:	Approximately 18 months to 3 years of age

The third (Solar Plexus) chakra represents our place of personal power and emotion. The corresponding developmental stage is eighteen to thirty-six months, when security is established and when a child learns separation and individuation.

If children are shamed or punished for attempting to become independent or for expressing emotions (including saying "no"), then powerlessness develops. They are, after all, being conditioned to be passive rather than assertive, and this is often when they become victims. They can also become overly adaptive in an attempt to not be rejected. A child blocked in this way sells her soul for approval and may attract abusive, codependent relationships.

Our client, Carrie (who had the second chakra issues mentioned above), also had third chakra issues from the sexual abuse of her stepfather. People like Carrie, who experienced the abuse of power, frequently have third chakra blockage and confuse power with abuse. They often become codependent people-pleasers who experience fear about standing up for themselves and fail to tell their own truth in an effort to give others what they think they want to hear. Through years of these destructive patterns, the true self is lost and a false "victim self" is all that the individual is in touch with.

Another aspect of this pattern is the victim who attempts to feel powerful by rescuing others. This person subconsciously seeks out other victims and assumes responsibility for solving their problems. The victim, turned rescuer, often gives unwanted advice and may experience feeling overwhelmed by taking on too much. Rescuing others and being responsible for many problems actually creates a *false* sense of power.

The work in this chakra is extensive and involves learning to reclaim one's power through self-discovery, assertiveness, and self-expression. The emotional centers are located in this chakra, and as a person opens up to the healthy expression of emotions, the fears disappear and full self-expression can begin. This chakra is intricately related to the throat chakra in the process of opening to full expression of self.

Incidentally, although this chakra most directly affects the pancreas, it also strongly influences the adrenal glands, which are associated with stress. When we're overly stressed, the adrenals break down and cannot function. People often experience the most stress when they feel powerless in their lives. So reclaiming personal power in the third chakra can heal adrenal autoimmune functioning.

The Fourth Chakra

Name: Heart Chakra (*anahata*)
Location: Center of the Chest (Heart)
Color: Green   .
Element: Air
Gland: Thymus
Maslow Needs: Knowledge and understanding through exploration
Spiritual stage: The fourth stage of spiritual unfoldment is the incorporation of the knowledge gained thus far into the bodily organism: "Taking it to heart."
Developmental stage: Approximately 3 to 7 years of age

The fourth (Heart) chakra represents the guiding light for the entire energy system within us. It is the Heart chakra that shows the third chakra how to burn its raw energy in loving ways, that shows the second chakra how to manifest its sexual energy through the transmutation of love, and that shows the first chakra how to merge the physical with the Divine.

The Heart chakra (also known as the "Heart Center") is equidistant between the first and the seventh chakras, between earth and heaven. It is the center point of the primary emotional energy of the universe, which we call love. It is the gateway from the lower to the higher chakras, and balances those above with those below, all of equal importance.

The corresponding developmental stage is the socialization stage of three to seven years when the child is looking for belonging and acceptance by the peer group. If this doesn't occur, then the child begins to feel unworthy, left out, and resentful about being rejected. These feelings will often close the heart center and disconnect the child from love. She will then often confuse love with pity and performance, never having experienced true, unconditional love.

The Heart Center can also be blocked any other time love is restrained. For instance, when people hold resentment in their hearts, this certainly stops the flow of unconditional love. Often people ask if it is necessary for them to forgive their abusers in order to complete their healing. Our answer is always yes.

Forgiveness does not mean accepting that what a perpetrator did was right. Forgiving someone does not mean you have to like them or even be in their presence again. Forgiveness is a spiritual process where your soul recognizes the pain in someone else's soul that may have caused them to perpetrate something against you. Forgiveness is about recognizing that we all have shadow parts of ourselves that could have acted just like this person did against you. And forgiveness is about forgiving ourselves as well as others. It is the only way to finally release the hate and resentment in your heart that blocks your flow of unconditional love.

Another thing that blocks the Heart Center's flow of love is a feeling of unworthiness. When a person feels unworthy to be loved by others, there is usually a deeper issue concerning whether one is loved by God. This feeling can be traced back to many different situations, such as being raised by critical, perfectionist parents who give the child negative messages. It can also go back to prenatal or birth issues, such as not being wanted by the parents or being "the wrong sex."

The woman described above who was given away by her birth mother mostly felt resentment and rage, which covered up the deep unworthiness she also experienced. Her Heart Center was closed down to everyone she loved, even to her own children. She instinctively knew that something was wrong, but she didn't know what it was or how to change it.

When she began releasing her anger about being rejected at birth, her Heart Center started to open. She could feel the love she knew was there for her family but that she previously couldn't access. She was able, through hypnotherapy, to accept and feel unconditional love for her inner child. She was able to "re-parent" that child that was rejected by her birth mother and begin to release the unworthiness.

Often, unworthiness issues have been experienced lifetime after lifetime. There are many cultures where it was or is shameful to be born a girl or to be in the wrong caste. Many people have had to hide their culture and/or religion, pretending to be something they're not in order to avoid persecution. Deep existential shame issues will usually lead to feeling unworthy of love, especially of God's love. This often closes down the Heart Center and blocks the giving and receiving of love.

Only when these layers upon layers of shame, resentment, and unworthiness are worked through in hypnotherapy can an individual move out of the ego and personality issues and begin to claim her individual spiritual connection. Since the Heart Center is the "spiritual gateway" from the lower to the higher centers, when it opens up, the kundalini energy really begins to flow. People then begin to experience a feeling of bliss and unconditional love. For many, this is a very new experience and they may even begin to cry without knowing why. The tears are tears of joy rather than sadness, and the deep emotions are usually about "coming home" to a connection with the soul.

It's useful to note, here, that the fourth chakra strongly influences the functioning of the thymus gland, located in the center of the chest just behind the upper breastbone. Because this gland directly influences the functioning of our immune system, fourth chakra balancing and energizing can also have a profound effect on our overall health and resistance to disease.

The Fifth Chakra

Name:	Throat Chakra (*visuddha*)
Location:	Throat
Color:	Blue
Element:	Ether
Gland:	Thyroid
Maslow Needs:	Aesthetics (symmetry, order, and beauty)
Spiritual stage:	The fifth stage of spiritual unfoldment brings a degree of self-liberation from the limitations of physical matter and circumstances, and authentic expression of one's essence regardless of the outside world: "The world has my body but not my soul."
Developmental stage:	Approximately 7 to 12 years of age

The fifth or Throat chakra represents one's place of expression and creativity. The corresponding developmental stage is the latency stage of sever to twelve years. This is when a child needs to learn how to discover who she is and to express that true self.

This is often impossible, especially in families that believe that "children should be seen and not heard," or where the *parents* want to decide who the child should be instead of discovering *who the child is*. These scenarios often cause the child to adapt and to repress the true self. This involves repressing emotions, thoughts, and creative expression, all of which can close down the Throat Center.

In families where there is a "family secret," children are conditioned from a very young age not to express themselves. For example, the woman who was abused by her stepfather was conditioned by her abuser not to speak about it. Often an abuser will use guilt, shame and fear to get the child to keep quiet. In this case, the stepfather told his young victim that if she told her mother, the mother would go crazy and end up in a mental hospital. Then he would be put in jail which would leave the girl (the victim) an orphan to live in an orphanage. This frightened her enough to never speak her truth and, as a result, her Throat chakra shut tight. In fact, she often had sore throats as a child, indicating some type of chronic disease in this area of her body.

Past life issues may also play an important part here. For example, people who were killed or tortured for being healers often have Throat chakra blockages. When expression of your true authentic self was a crime punishable by death, that ancient fear and shame is carried in the body's cellular memory.

The individual who hasn't worked through these issues often experiences being "an imposter" and never feeling real. As these issues are worked through, however, the person begins speaking the truth, expressing feelings, and discovering the creative expression within. The voice opens up and the individual is free to truly express who she is. It is a beautiful process, like watching the petals of a flower gently unfold.

The Sixth Chakra

Name:	Third Eye Chakra (*ajna*)
Location:	Forehead, Brow (Between the Eyes)
Color:	Purple/Violet
Element:	Spirit
Gland:	Pituitary
Maslow Needs:	Self-actualization (finding self-fulfillment and realizing one's potential)
Spiritual stage:	The sixth stage of spiritual unfoldment heralds an approaching blend of personal consciousness with the universal: "Not my will but Thine be done."
Developmental stage:	Approximately 12 to 18 years of age

The sixth chakra (the "Third Eye") is located in the forehead and is often referred to as the intuitive or psychic center. This is the seat of true wisdom, where the thinking mind comes into contact with the intuitive mind. This is where, if one is listening during meditation, God speaks directly.

The corresponding developmental age is the adolescent years from ages twelve to eighteen. This is when the child is exploring identity vs. roles and either gains clarity of vision or learns to project his own experience of fear, shame, and confusion onto other people and the world. If the adolescent is not clear about his identity, confusion sets in and the projections turn into intense judgments where one is so caught up in thinking, analyzing, and debating that she has cut off the intuition and feelings. This happens when the lower chakras are energetically blocked, usually because people have not done therapeutic work in these areas. It is difficult to experience true clarity in life if you are filled with shame, fear, guilt, and rage.

Personal clarity is something that develops more profoundly as you begin to do Heart-Centered therapy. During a hypnotherapy or breathwork session, you begin to get very clear about a certain situation in your life. It's almost as if we walk around with a protective film over our eyes, analogous to cataracts. As you do the work, the obscuring film lifts and you can see people and situations more clearly. You recognize your own issues as well as those of others. If you're a therapist, it's amazing how much more perceptive you are with clients.

The film, however, will return if you don't continue to do the energetic release that is necessary. In the same way that cataracts often grow back, we have to keep our vision clear by keeping the energy flowing through the chakras. And when our vision opens up, the ultimate clarity is to see our own spiritual connection. Some people begin by seeing auras or energy around others. Eventually we may have "a vision" of Jesus or the Divine Mother or white light. This is the state of self-actualization or true Personal Transformation. It's important in these moments not to judge, censor, or try to change what comes to you, but to simply receive it, feel the grace, and let it be.

The Seventh Chakra

Name:	Crown Chakra (*sahasrara*)
Location:	Crown of the Head, Fontanel of the Skull
Color:	White or gold or violet
Element:	Spirit
Gland:	Pineal
Maslow Needs:	Transcendence (moving beyond the personal and the interpersonal to the transpersonal; enhancing one's sphere of influence by helping others find self-fulfillment and realize their potential as well)
Spiritual stage:	The seventh stage of spiritual unfoldment is the culmination of what has come before, yet ironically reveals the great illusion that there is a final destination in the Eternal Dance of Life: from every newfound peak comes into view a challenging new and distant horizon.
Developmental stage:	Adult years

The seventh (Crown) chakra is, as its name suggests, the crown of the entire chakra system. Its expression represents the greatest attainment for a human being, and it is the gateway from ordinary human experience to the higher, transpersonal realms of consciousness.

The corresponding developmental stage for this chakra is the adult years ... *if*, of course, the other chakras are brought into balance in order to activate this highest chakra. If they are not, a person may become fixated at one of the earlier stages and will remain an "adult/child," stuck in earlier ego issues.

When people dwell in their egos, they may think they are enlightened and try to convince others of it. They may brag and blow their own horns, and this is the grandiosity of the crown chakra. When you work through many of the lower chakra issues, however, the energy will flow through those chakras and the crown will open up.

This is when one's spiritual connection can develop, and when one can really think clearly and make wise decisions based on an infallible inner guidance system. We call this *discernment*, and it transcends identification with a personality, personal history, and the lifetime accumulation of limiting self-beliefs. Certainly it is the goal of any spiritually-oriented therapy to help people find their way to this experience.

Transformational Work in Terms of Chakras

As you can see, the chakras are really tied to a person's development. If someone progresses ideally, all of the chakras can become activated and that person shines as brightly as she has developed in spirit. She becomes peaceful, passionate, powerful, loving, creative, intuitive, and wise as the chakras open, and will experience any one of these to the degree that her soul has evolved through many lives.

But no matter how much a soul has evolved and *wishes* to shine brightly through the chakras, it can be hindered by personality and ego issues that block its spiritual force from coming in through the chakras. In order to attain the higher states of consciousness, that force must be able to flow freely through all of these energy points.

Again, those issues come up when circumstances keep someone from developing as she's meant to: a young girl abandoned or kept from ever expressing herself or made to feel shame about her sexuality or put through anything else that's harmful to ideal development shuts down the chakras associated with any of these hindrances.

Repressed emotions or traumas arising from challenges like these are stored in the body's cells, and once we have taught our cells to repress certain stimuli, they are more likely to repress similar stimuli in the future. This is what Freud referred to as the repetition compulsion. But we can reverse this trend by releasing whatever has been repressed. In order to do so, we need to access the state a person was in at the time of the repression (developmental stage and chakra experience) and provide therapy from there. The Personal Transformation techniques of hypnotherapy, breathwork, Energetic Psychodrama, Kundalini meditation, and interpersonal clearings all work together to move the energy that has been repressed in order to open up the chakras.

Once we help someone enter into the state where repressions took place and where the developmental stages were derailed, we take them through a re-parenting process. By installing a loving, healthy, nurturing parent into the unconscious, the developmental tasks can be rehearsed and replayed until completed. As these stages are healed, the individual moves out of the ego issues and into spiritual expression.

Communication with the Soul

So long as someone is blocked by personality and ego issues, she cannot access the wisdom and insights of her higher self. What is the higher self? It is, in a sense, the phone wire between the personality and the soul — it is the means by which they communicate. When the higher self is blocked, the soul is silent ... at least to the ears of the personality. This is bad news for anyone, because allowing the messages of the soul to come through means that we can know our purpose, draw the people and circumstances into our lives that can help us to fulfill that purpose, and determine how to best fulfill that purpose. So opening up to the higher self gives one plenty of extra power.

This kind of power is important for everyone, and it's certainly important for therapists and counselors — our work, after all, is not as simple as getting answers from a book. Often we need to have real insight into another person's issues in order to help her navigate through them. If we do not have clear communication with our own souls, we are less effective in our work, and of course may not feel fulfilled because we may not be fulfilling our real purpose here on Earth.

When inner issues *have* been cleared away, then we need to learn how to pay attention to the guidance we receive from our higher selves and how to keep this means of communication clear. And the number one key to understanding your own guidance is through *feelings* or *emotions*.

When we block our emotions, the energy coming in from our souls becomes distorted and can cause physical disease. But when we're open, our emotions help us to know what our soul wants for us. This shouldn't be confused with the desires of the body or personality. The soul's expressions will be those based in love both for ourselves *and* for the world around us at the same time.

Since emotions are our windows to the soul's guidance, this also means that we need to keep our emotional channels clear. This means that we shouldn't ever suppress an emotion, but if we know that it's an emotion of the personality rather than of the soul, then we should work to transmute it or let it out in a way that harms no one. For example, if we feel anger toward someone for cutting us off on the highway, we can try to transmute that into compassion by trying to understand the other driver's experience. Perhaps they are on the way to the hospital. Perhaps they didn't see us. And perhaps they've experienced the things we've talked about in this book that need healing. The important thing is not to take it personally and to realize that it is almost certainly not about us.

Expression of negative emotions (those of the personality — i.e., fear, shame, hatred) such as yelling them into a pillow or hitting a punching bag helps one to release the energy of the emotion without harming another person. It can be made productive in this way, or at least neutral, and keeps the emotional channels open to soul guidance. It's important to keep in mind that old marriage adage of never going to bed angry — advice that we should follow whether we're married or not. The more we're able to keep the emotional channels clear, the more open we become to the intuition and the closer we come to a place of expressing unconditional love for all people.

Another way of listening to the soul is to look at the circumstances of your life and the people that are most important to you. Again, once we've cleared the way for the soul to speak with us, it begins drawing in people and circumstances that will help us to more easily recognize and fulfill our soul's purpose.

Prior to clearing the way, the soul often speaks to us through painful experiences that help us to *get* to the point of clearing. Once we are clear and the soul can start implementing its plan, it is still possible for painful experiences to help us on our way; but we'll often find doors opening, people presenting opportunities or resources, and coincidences that confirm what we think we're meant to be doing. Taking note of all of this and considering it a form of communication allows us to better hear our souls.

We need to be careful, though. If we get a very distinct sense about something we need to accomplish, we may create in our minds how that will be accomplished. If we become so determined, we may stop listening to the soul, which might have a different idea about how to accomplish the goal. Suddenly, we can find ourselves fighting to reach a point that should be easy to reach … and would have been if we had just kept listening to the voice within. Keeping our eyes and ears open to what automatically comes into our path can tell us a great deal about what steps to take, and this gives us even more power.

These are the steps you can use to improve your own intuition and — for those of us who counsel others — to better receive insights for working with clients. And of course these are steps that we can share with clients so that they can hear their voices for themselves. When the personality and ego issues are cleared away, you simply need to ask for guidance, then meditate on the answers. We've found that they will come, especially when your motives are set to helping others. Trust that the universe wants you to do just that.

Drumming, like chanting, is in my soul

Opening the Chakras

When the root and sexual chakras open, a person experiences life force energy and passion opening up within. She has released the fears and shame that block these vital energy channels.

As she goes through transformational work and releases the codependency, powerlessness, and victimization held within the third chakra, she begins to experience power coming from within. This is not the abusive power that comes from overpowering, but the gentle power that comes from a deep level of self-confidence and accountability.

As this lower chakra work is completed, the heart chakra opens and love begins to pour forth. This comes from valuing the true self and feeling a deep sense of worthiness within.

There is a strong connection between the third chakra and the fifth. As the seeker claims her power in the solar plexus and discovers the unconditional love in the heart, she can then release the repression held within the throat chakra and fully express its power of creativity. She begins to speak her truth without feeling shame; can sing more clearly; and/or writes with words that flow from within. The fifth chakra opens up to allow the individual to be transformed through all forms of creative expression.

The sixth chakra energy opens up when the transformational seeker is willing to see clearly, when the conscious choice is made to lift the veils of illusion and to invite spiritual presence to be fully viewed. Often the individual will experience a visit from Jesus, the Divine Mother, a guru, Buddha, Great Spirit, angels, or other spiritual guides and helpers. The intuition opens up and the person begins to truly trust her inner knowing.

The seventh chakra is the crown and opens up as the individual grows into self-actualization or God-Realization. This does not happen until the lower chakra work is well on its way to completion. The lower chakras are portals to the upper ones. Each door that is opened allows the next to open as well. They don't always open in order, however, but open according to urgency.

Chapter 7
Spiritual Connection Questionnaire

I mainly see myself as
    ❏ A religious person
    ❏ A spiritual person
    ❏ An atheist
    ❏ A spiritual seeker
    ❏ Other _____
    ❏ Not sure

Religiously, I identify myself as
    ❏ Christian
    ❏ Jewish
    ❏ Buddhist
    ❏ Hindu
    ❏ Muslim
    ❏ Native American Church
    ❏ Unaffiliated
    ❏ Other _____
    ❏ Not sure

My relationship with God is:
    ❏ I am connected and comfortable with God
    ❏ I feel disconnected from God
    ❏ I feel unworthy of God's love
    ❏ I feel angry at God
    ❏ I don't trust God
    ❏ God scares me
    ❏ Other _____
    ❏ Not sure

I believe in: (check all that apply)
    ❏ Angels
    ❏ Spirit guides
    ❏ Shamanism
    ❏ Other _____
    ❏ Not sure

On a regular basis, I:
- ❏ Attend church/ synagogue/ mosque
- ❏ Pray
- ❏ Meditate
- ❏ Chant
- ❏ Worship God in my own way
- ❏ Pray in Native American sweat lodge
- ❏ Other _____

I have had these spiritual experiences:
- ❏ Seeing angels
- ❏ Connecting with God from within or experiencing Jesus within
- ❏ Hearing messages from my Spirit Guides
- ❏ "Knowing things" before they happen
- ❏ Experiencing the White Light within
- ❏ Seeing "auras" around some people
- ❏ Miracles
- ❏ "Healing Hands"
- ❏ Other_____

Spiritual authority issues
- ❏ I distrust priests, ministers, rabbis, imams, or nuns
- ❏ I don't trust authorities and God falls into that category
- ❏ I am angry at authority figures, including God
- ❏ The issues I have with God are the ones I've had with my own father (I am repelled by the concept "God the Father")
- ❏ I cannot accept God as the ultimate authority ("Thy will be done")
- ❏ Other _____

What spiritual practices do you find fulfilling or are you attracted to? After each one, name the values from the Chapter 1 Questionnaire involved.

A. _____   _____

B. _____   _____

C. _____   _____

Your Project: Send a letter to God
Write a letter to God about what is working and what isn't in your relationship. Be honest and focus on what practices you do or want to do to strengthen your connection.

Chapter 7
Authority Issues Questionnaire

Which of the following situations "trigger" a response within you, and/or do you attract into your life? Prioritize the top five (giving each a number).

T   1-5

❑ ❑ A. Policemen: getting a ticket or getting arrested
❑ ❑ B. 'The system' such as the IRS, state or county officials, or school officials, Deans
❑ ❑ C. The Church, priests, ministers, rabbis, imams, nuns, God
❑ ❑ D. Bosses or supervisors
❑ ❑ E. Teachers or instructors
❑ ❑ F. Lawsuits: initiating against others or others initiating them against you

Which of the following possible underlying causes for authority issues apply to you?

❑ ❑ A. Strict religious authority
❑ ❑ B. Caregivers were controlling/inflexible, domineering, critical
❑ ❑ C. Caregivers were shaming or they were always "right" and you were always "wrong"
❑ ❑ D. Caregivers were abusive physically, emotionally or sexually
❑ ❑ E. Caregivers were fearful and anxious
❑ ❑ F. Inconsistent caregivers (broken promises, rules change without warning, hypocritical)
❑ ❑ G. Rigid military or sanctimonious ministers' families (on display, have to look good)
❑ ❑ H. 'Rebellious parents' who had not grown up themselves
❑ ❑ I. Caregivers kept children powerless (expressing feelings was "disrespectful")
❑ ❑ J. Physical or emotional abandonment by caregivers, teachers, religious figures

How do authorities carry their power in a way that you can accept gracefully? After each one, name the values from the Chapter 1 Questionnaire which those characteristics address.

A. _____   _____

B. _____   _____

C. _____   _____

D. _____   _____

What are your customary tactics with the authorities in your life? Name someone that fits each.

❑ Adaptive smiling and agreeing, then not keeping agreements, being late, not showing up at all, having excuses

_____

❑ People-pleasing and then nasty gossip behind the authority's back

_____

❑ Smiling to face and then "stabbing in the back"

_____

❑ Actively rebelling through insubordination

_____

❑ Organizing others to get them on your side

_____

❑ Saying yes when you want to say no

_____

Your Project: Practice Non-reactivity with Authority

Deliberately seek out at least five authority figures to interact with, practicing not getting "triggered" by them in ways that you have in the past. Then write about your experience and how you can avoid being triggered through understanding the underlying causes for your authority issues.

Chapter 8
The Death Experience

"Healthy children will not fear life if their elders have integrity enough not to fear death."[101]

So far, we've looked at all of the developmental stages that a person passes through from the interlife to the womb to childhood and all the way into the adult years. There is, however, a final stage of development as one enters his later years and approaches death itself.

Of course death is not so permanent as we've made it seem. It only leads back into that first stage we discussed, the interlife. Nevertheless, many people fear death for a number of reasons. They may not know what lies on the other side. They may not want to leave behind what they have here. They may not want to suffer for the sins they've committed while here on Earth. They may not want to die before making amends with family and friends. And these name just a few of the many possible reasons.

For therapists, it can be an honor to help people through this final stage of Earth life without that kind of fear, ideally guiding them through several healing processes and ultimately to a conscious transition when possible. This can be a powerful experience for the therapist and for those who are close to the departing person, in addition to the one leaving our world. As an example, I think of Ingrid.

Ingrid had been a healer and spiritual teacher for many years prior to my meeting her. She had also been diagnosed with cancer and underwent a mastectomy — and her cancer had metastasized — shortly before we met. When she came to us, she told us that she didn't have long to live, but that she wanted to do some work with us before she died. We told her that her cancer was to become her teacher, and that it would pave the way for a conscious death. She was evolved enough to know that to be true, and so we began our work together.

One way that Ingrid prepared for a conscious death was to create some extra time for completing as many of her unfinished relationships as possible. Also, for her cancer to truly become her teacher, she needed to fully get the message of what it was about. And she became clear that she needed to do two years of healing work. When she gave us her money for the two-year advanced training, she said, "This was going to be my dying money. But I am giving it to you so it can become my *living money*." She continued, "I now realize that I have more living and growing to do so that, when I die, I can do it from a place of peace and full consciousness."

In one of her hypnotherapy sessions, Ingrid recognized that, because the cancer was in her breast, it symbolized her maternal nurturing. We asked her "to give her breast a voice," which is a gestalt projective technique. The cancerous breast responded, "I'm tired of giving, giving, and more giving. Too many people want too much from me. When will there be time for me?" This awareness led her into her main life issue, which was rescuing and feeling responsible for others in her life to her own detriment. She began to see how her own needs never got met as she spent all her time, money, and energy on others. She saw why she had to get cancer, the most serious of illnesses, in order to wake up and begin taking care of herself.

Because Ingrid was a powerful healer in her own right, it was much easier to accomplish healing work with her. And because she knew that her time on Earth was limited, she made the most of every precious moment. One group healing session was particularly powerful, and all those present could actually feel her spiritual angels all around her participating in the process. After we went through the emotional connection work, we energetically cleansed the body of the cancer. After the session, we all felt that a physical healing had taken place.

And indeed, Ingrid did have a remarkable healing that weekend. As it turned out, her tumors shrank considerably, almost overnight! This gave her the additional time she knew she needed in order to heal unresolved misconceptions about herself and others in her life. The cancer and those in her support group "held her feet to the fire" about fulfilling her own needs and making conscious choices about how to use her valuable time.

She made amazing changes in her life, told her truth where it needed to be told, and completed many relationships in the ensuing two years of her training. The final meeting of her group consisted of a powerful Native American Vision Quest. Her group mates were all going into the wilderness for four days and nights without food or water to seek a clear vision. She wanted to go with them but knew that, physically, she was deteriorating. She knew that she wouldn't be able to complete the quest, but she wished to support her classmates with prayer.

Ingrid was able to walk all the way out to "the sacred land," a nearby forest where the vision questers were each put in their individual spaces for the four days and nights. As the vision quest supporters sat around the campfire during those four days, Ingrid used the time not only to pray for her friends, but to get clear about her own upcoming journey of transition.

After the vision quest was completed, Ingrid headed in to see her oncologist and was told her that the cancer had spread to her bones and that death was now imminent.

Ingrid's spiritual name — revealed to me immediately and clearly through meditation — was *Mataji*, which means "Revered Mother." As she moved into her transition phase, she asked that her friends only use that name. When the doctor told Mataji that she was "terminal," she said, "That's not possible when one realizes that one is eternal." Mataji knew she was eternal and that her consciousness would not end when she separated from her body. She was also aware that her state of consciousness at the end of her physical life would determine where and how her existence would continue into the next life.

Mataji asked a close friend and fellow Wellness student for assistance in her transition. She was also supported by one of our energy workers, especially during a brief period when she experienced many dark entities and horrific visions. Our energy worker assisted Mataji to release these demons, which were based in fear. Once the demons/fears were released, Mataji was fully ready to make her transition. Her body then became extremely ill, and she entered residential Hospice care a few days later. Mataji asked only to remain God-conscious at the moment of her death.

Her friends and family told us that conscious connected Breathwork and the clearing process taught by The Wellness Institute were invaluable during her death process. As they sat with her during her transition, they practiced our model of Kundalini meditation, especially filling each chakra with light. The energy around Mataji was recalled as indescribably pure and etheric. She even spoke in her fitful sleep one night, concerned that she needed to remember who she was and where she was going.

Mataji's request for minimal medication was honored, as she wished to remain as clear-minded and conscious as possible during her transition. Even though her physical body was in pain, she was able to rise above it because of her strong desire to be as clear as possible during the experience of her own death.

Mataji continued to do energy work on herself throughout the process, moving energy from each chakra as needed. Her friend anointed her with rose and frankincense oils as she requested. There was one final chakra meditation — in which she recounted all that she had loved in this life — shortly before she would drop the physical body. The room filled with a light that was visible and palpable to her friends and she began breathing in the breathwork pattern, listening to the CD *Returning* by Jennifer Berezan. The music and her breath carried Mataji into the light and she deliberately slipped out of the body with her last exhalation at noon on Christmas day. The air was filled with spirit and her companions realized what a great gift it was to be present to share this experience with her.

Mataji's daughter, her sister, and her friend sat with her for the next hour, supporting her complete release. They then washed her body in rose water. As had been pre-arranged, Mataji's body remained undisturbed for three days and then she was cremated. During the three days following her transition, a group of her loved ones, students, and friends gathered, read the *Tibetan Book of Living and Dying*, meditated, and prayed that Mataji would remain God-conscious as she had requested.

Mataji asked that we not call on her for a period of one year after her transition, and to be sure that — when we *did* call on her — we call for Mataji and not Ingrid. A group gathered the following Christmas to meditate together and call on their friend and teacher, Mataji. And over the years since her passing, she has come to many in the Wellness family to give guidance and support.

Mataji's transition is a powerful example of what this last phase of life can mean in a person's spiritual growth. It's impossible to say that any stage of life is the most important, because each is critical in the sense of making a person whole. When early stages in a person's life are successfully navigated, there is greater potential for him to become self-actualized to the degree that his soul has developed, and he can really fulfill his life's purpose. At the same time, much that has "gone wrong" in a person's life can be addressed and corrected, in a sense, in the final years.

What's more, we say that the earliest stages are a child's first years, and that maturity is a person's last. But that is because we speak of a person's life as having a beginning and an ending. This is true as far as the personality is concerned (although even *that* can be tricky when, for instance, a soul becomes confused and hangs on to a personality after its earthly life has ended). But as far as the soul is concerned, the stage of maturity and preparation for death precedes the interlife and a new life as much as it follows the adult years.

In other words, as Mataji knew, there is nothing terminal about death. When we look at things more cyclically, understanding the process of reincarnation and the interlife more fully, death takes on a vastly new meaning. And for those of us working as therapists, keeping this perspective can help us better assist our clients in a holistic sense, keeping in mind *all* of the factors in their struggles and growth. What follows is a process that therapists can use when helping clients through this transition, which I hope that any reader will find useful by knowing what can be done for those preparing to leave this world. And because the kind of therapy we're discussing in this book is really about healing, I'll refer to therapists as healers as we go through these details.

Preparing for Physical Death

Ultimately, we must all face death of the body. Those who have fulfilled their dreams and accepted themselves completely, who have achieved wisdom, ego integrity, and self-actualization, are prepared to meet death with dignity and readiness. Those who have been afraid to dream, to excel, and to accept themselves completely, live in fear of death. Healers have the opportunity to help make the most of the transition in either case in the following ways:

1) Helping the dying to tie up loose ends. This involves helping people to conclude personal relationships in a healthy way and to achieve a whole and peaceful reality within themselves. This way, they can be in the most appropriate personal space for stepping from this world.

2) Helping the dying to release any fear around death. Most people are confused and afraid about what lies on the other side of physical death. They don't know what will become of themselves or their relationship with their loved ones. Even those who believe in a spiritual afterlife tend to have very skewed notions about what waits for them, especially if they have been indoctrinated with teachings of a fiery hell and heinous judgments. There are plenty of ways to help them release this fear and replace it with ideas they can look forward to.

3) Helping family and friends to assist the one who is dying, and to find healing and growth for themselves through the process. As important as it is for the dying to tie up loose ends with the living, it is just as important for the living to tie up loose ends with the dying. This fact is emphasized in the song *In The Living Years* (by Mike and the Mechanics), which tells about a son's wish to have told his father all the connections he realized they had; but it was too late to make this connection because the father died before the son took the chance to tell him. There are ways to help people share everything they need to with those who are dying, and to show them how their prayers and meditations can assist their loved ones after death occurs. It is also possible to turn the death into a rich learning experience for all who are left behind in this world, in turn making the person's life even more valuable and honored, and making the most of who they were.

Each of these paths for helping with the death experience is important for the spiritual health of everyone involved, and often for the mental and emotional health of those still living. Of course a lot of this work can be done any time in a person's life, but if things haven't been addressed earlier, they should certainly be addressed as someone prepares for physical death.

Using Heart-Centered Therapy to Assist the Dying

Completing Unfinished Business

If we happen to be good at communicating our thoughts and feelings, it can be easy to forget how many people lack the tools, skills, or even the confidence to do the same. Especially in the case of our high-speed society, people living beneath the same roof seem to see less and less of one another. They may watch TV during dinner, if they even have dinner together. School activities keep kids away from home for much of the day, and heavy homework loads keep many students locked away through the evening hours. This means that even very social and/or educated children are growing up without much family interaction, and may suffer from harbored but unexpressed thoughts and feelings about those they are living with.

This says nothing about those who have grown up in unstable families and have buried many of their emotions; those who were bullied by parents and never had a fighting chance to express themselves; and those in so many other situations where healthy communication was simply not taught or encouraged. As much as anyone, though, people in these situations are touched by death, and most will want to remedy the pain and suffering of the years now far behind them.

Whatever the reason for things unsaid, the time of approaching death is the time for things to be said. This can be done even if it isn't possible to reach the necessary friends and family, or if there is reason for things not to actually be said to a person. For example, using the "pillow technique," one can talk out all the circumstances, all the anger and frustration, all of *anything* they are holding on to without fear of hurting another person's feelings. This can allow for a tremendous release, even to the point that the dying person takes on a whole new forgiving experience of the person in question — and in that case, they may then want to invite the person in to talk face to face; having said all the hurtful things already, they can feel free to tie up all other loose ends with that person without the fear of hurting them.

Another technique is to actually use hypnosis so that the dying can enter a trance state and release their inhibitions about what they can and cannot say to or about other people. Again, a healer can determine with the client whether things should be said in the presence of family and friends, or if the work should take place just between the two of them. Once in the trance state, the client can verbalize all the pain being held inside, and through the process, release it. What's more, he can discuss all the positive things about a person — things he may have been too embarrassed to say for social reasons or just because of his own insecurities.

All of this can bring things to the surface and set a person free. So often, when these things are not yet let go, they are what hold a person prisoner in the body — it is as if the soul gives the personality a chance to clean up old business by letting the body hold on, so that the soul can release karmic ties with the people they have loved or not loved. When that business is cleared, the soul knows that it's time. And so often, that is when we see a beautiful departure from this world.

Asking for Forgiveness

As the end of one's life approaches — especially if illness forewarns that they'll soon pass from this world — thoughts often become intensely reflective. During this period, people often see things they have done in a new way. They understand how they have hurt others, either intentionally or unintentionally. With that understanding often comes guilt.

This kind of guilt may or may not be valid. People may blame themselves for things they had little or no control over, or for injuries they never intended. They may blame themselves for a pain someone else chose to feel due to simple misunderstandings. Or they may blame themselves because they realize that their distinct and even conscious selfishness simply caused suffering in others. But the value of guilt is really only to spur reconciliation and to encourage good relations between people. It is not a valuable thing to hold on to, and certainly not to die with. Holding on to guilt through the death process means carrying karmic ties. It ends up making for an unpleasant passing, and added work for future lives.

By using hypnosis with the dying, however, one can help people access those feelings of guilt on the deepest levels of their minds. After all, no matter how aware they are of these feelings, the roots of self-blame are always stored on the subconscious level. As you know, weeds always need to be removed by their roots. When healers help people to do this, they help to relieve their suffering. Potentially, guilt like this can manifest as suffering in the afterlife as well, and with help, a person can avoid that experience of a self-inflicted hell.

This process of hypnosis should involve asking for forgiveness, even if the injured are not physically present during the session(s). Forgiveness should also be asked of God, because on a very deep level, patients will recognize that their entire journey as a soul comes back to their relationship with God. And finally, they should ask forgiveness of themselves. They need to recognize themselves as humans on a journey; to know that whatever faults they had were part of that journey, and that now it's time to leave all of that behind. When they forgive themselves, the last remnants of self-blame can be released.

Releasing Pent-up Emotions

Guilt is only part of what can eat away at a person inside. Humans have an uncanny knack for burying emotions as a survival tactic. The problem is that this mechanism focuses on survival of people in the outer world while confusing much of their inner world. If these buried or pent-up emotions are ever released in an uncontrolled setting, they can drive a person to outrageous acts or to a total break-down, after which they can no longer function in the world. If they are *never* released, then they are carried on in the person's emotional body, even after he has left the physical world. This can lead to a great deal of turmoil and pain in the interlife.

Helping people to release their emotions in a controlled way allows them to avoid either of these problems, and it often helps them to see more clearly what they need to communicate with others before they depart this world. It also helps to unblock a person's supply of life energy; this can mean increased health and vitality for someone not yet leaving the world, and it can mean a cleaner departure for those in the process of death.

Releasing Attachments

I mentioned that people often need to finish communication with others in their lives before they can leave this world. Anything unspoken can cause a sort of attachment that needs to be let go. But there are other attachments as well, and it's important that every kind be released before death.

Someone can be attached to both things and people — perhaps it's not just something unsaid, but undone. Do they feel a need to complete an unfinished project? Do they need to make changes to their will? Do they want to do just a little more to help with a nephew's business? Are they simply so in love with their spouse that they cannot bear the thought of moving on alone?

Any attachments like these can keep people in ailing bodies far longer than they ought to be there. One can help them to release all of these in a number of ways: perhaps helping them to see all that they have already given; helping them to wrap up issues; helping them to see that love and other relationships are of the soul and not the body. Healers can help people to escape unnecessary, extended pain.

Integrating Disowned Parts of the Self — Soul Retrieval

Many or even *most* individuals will deal with the issues above to some extent. Something we call "soul retrieval" is not as frequent an issue — but when it *is* an issue, it is absolutely critical to the client's well-being. All indigenous healers around the world practice soul retrieval as an important part of the completion process.

I mentioned early in this book that babies experiencing some form of birth trauma may dissociate during the trauma in order to avoid the pain of that event. In other words, they have quite literally left a subconscious part of themselves back with that event. (I specifically mentioned circumcision, but feeling unwanted in the womb, experiencing an abortion attempt, early separation, or other traumatic birth events can trigger this as well.) Dissociation may be a useful, short-term mechanism, but isn't healthy in the long-term.

Of course life holds many potential traumas in the forms of abuse, accidents, natural disasters, major illnesses, and personal loss. Any one of these can cause people to dissociate and to leave part of their subconscious selves behind. When part of a person has split off like this, he will generally have a feeling of being empty inside. He may say things like, "Ever since that time, I just haven't felt like myself."

Another common experience of this phenomenon is described by a familiar song, which laments, "I left my heart in San Francisco." Those who are close to the person needing soul retrieval will often feel that it's hard to reach the person; indeed, the healer may find this person drifts off and is hard to contact. This may especially occur when entering into the subject of whatever caused their soul to fragment.

If someone doesn't deal with this prior to death, then he will literally be in a scattered state in the afterlife, and will have to "pick up the pieces" there. At that time, the experience of the lost self will be much more conscious and disturbing.

This creates a need for soul retrieval, which is a method for taking a client back to the moment of dissociation and splitting through hypnosis so that he can consciously deal with the event and retrieve and integrate the missing parts of his inner self. This process is often a powerful spiritual and emotional healing for the person, and of course offers him a more satisfying afterlife experience.

Strengthening Spiritual Connections

One of the more unique aspects of Heart-Centered Hypnotherapy is the way it can guide people into discovering or sensing their spiritual state of being. For patients passing into the next world, this is by far the most important part of the preparation and healing process, simply because it deals with those issues that they will very soon encounter face-to-face.

Individuals will really fall into one of three categories on this issue. The first group is made up of those people who already have a clear connection with who they are spiritually, and the trance work will simply enable them to strengthen that connection.

The next group is of those for whom spirituality was possibly a background issue. Maybe they were religious or loved God in their own way, but they never made this their life focus. They never had a chance to clarify the connection with their own spirit. This becomes the time, then, for them to really develop that connection and to address spiritual issues regarding their relationships with others, but also regarding their own motivations and what — spiritually speaking — they wish to accomplish next, in the spiritual world or in future lives.

Heart-Centered Hypnotherapy will assist them in discovering their spiritual connection through visualization and often direct experience with the connection itself. Clients may see or feel Jesus, the Divine Mother, Buddha, White Light, the Great Spirit, or the spirit of Unconditional Love. It's important that healers feel comfortable with spirituality in all its forms so that they don't impose any specific religious doctrine onto the client. This work isn't about religion, but about helping the client discover what feels right for him. This is the only way to make sure that he finds *his* connection with the Divine.

The third kind of client is the one who has denounced God, religion, and spirituality in general. Maybe he saw the corruption of certain religions and associated all things spiritual with this corruption, or perhaps he carries issues from past lives. Whatever his reason for being in this place, as death draws near, he most will reconsider his relationship or connection to the Divine. Through Heart-Centered Hypnotherapy, he can be gently guided back into that connection. He may even have spiritual experiences during the process, and it's important to support his experience and assure him that it's never too late to develop a relationship with Spirit.

Using Heart-Centered Therapy to Resolve the Fear of Death

After healers have helped people to resolve all these issues prior to death, they may find that their clients still harbor fears around death. That fear in itself can cause a last attachment that needs to be let go — an attachment to this world. But more than that, why should someone have to experience this beautiful transition in a state of fear?

In the next world, like attracts like much more quickly than in this world. Someone leaving this world in a state of fear is likely to draw a fearful experience around them as they wake up into the next world, which means they face an unpleasant obstacle that they wouldn't otherwise need to face. And of course, speaking strictly in terms of their earthly experience, someone afraid of death will spend his or her last hours, days, even months unhappily rather than peacefully and in celebration of what they have accomplished.

A healer can help them to eliminate this fear of death on both the conscious and subconscious levels. There is a great deal of information about Near Death Experiences (NDE) that one can share to help persuade clients about the glory that awaits them. People who have had these experiences often report a blissful death experience, and find that the return to Earth (after all they didn't ultimately die) is disappointing and an emotional letdown.

The most commonly known element to NDE stories is the experience of a bright light. During the death process, the personality and kundalini rise up through the *sushumna* (the chakra column, or silver cord) and out through the "birth canal" opening, which is the crown chakra. On this path, they strike the pituitary and pineal centers in the brain, which causes the third eye to open. It is at this moment that the clear light of God is seen. This is the well-known light of the NDE, and it is into this light that people must direct themselves.

Another method for removing the fear of death is to have a client experience the transition through hypnosis. Alexander Levitan[102] presents a technique called Hypnotic Death Rehearsal, wherein a client in trance is asked to project himself into the future, visualizing his or her own death. This experience often occurs spontaneously in past-life regressions. Once past the dying and into the death, clients nearly always experience the other side as calm, peaceful, illuminating, and transcendent.

By describing what is known or leading them to even experience it themselves in a safe, clinical setting, one can help clients to actually look forward to their next step — after all, it is part of a long and continuing journey that gets better with every stage. With these techniques, the healer can also assist clients past religious dogma that may hold them in fear, and emphasize how important it is that they enter the light on the other side. They must be clear on this because, during the death process, a person's consciousness will pass through the subtle energy field in which all the emotional memories of that lifetime are stored. If he has experienced many hardships, passing through this field can be difficult, and it will become more of a challenge for him to keep focused on the light. Armed with the knowledge that he needs to enter that light, he will find it easier to do so.

Helping Family and Friends to Assist and Heal

The final step to making one's passing as smooth and beneficial as possible does not take place directly between healer and client, but between the healer and the family and friends. One reason for this step is that attachments are not just a one-way street. After the dying person has released attachments to people and things of this world, it's important that family and friends "let go" of the dying person so that they don't unintentionally keep the person in an ailing body longer than necessary. If we haven't experienced it ourselves, many of us have heard stories that sound like an incredible coincidence — for instance, someone dies *just* after their last family member made it to their bedside to say goodbye. The soul is aware of things that need to be finished, so friends and family need to feel finished too, to make sure the passing is not inappropriately delayed.

This step is also important because, by the strength of family and friends, one can actually have an easier transition out of this body and through the various initial stages of the next life. By praying and even visualizing the departed moving into the light, friends and family can help raise the energy necessary for the transition to take place. This work also helps to keep them focused on helping the person along rather than calling them back for selfish reasons. For example, it is appropriate for people to grieve the loss of a loved one; but it's important that their grief not turn into a calling back of the departed. This is especially of concern shortly after the passing. Having friends and family focus on sending energy for the departed to continue on the necessary path is a good way to avoid this challenge.

Finally, the process of working with friends and family can be extremely healing for them as well. In many cases, this will be a first instance in a long time that this group has come together with a single purpose, sometimes because life gets in the way and sometimes because there is ill-will between them. The passing of a mutually-loved person can bring groups together and create a great deal of healing between them. It can also give them a chance to try understanding, together, the message left behind by their loved one's life, and in turn, they can perhaps give more attention to the meaning of their lives as individuals and as a group. If the passing of one person can affect many others in this way, then that passing gives one final meaning to that person's life — she becomes immortal not only because her soul lives on, but because her effect lives on in others, and there is no greater way to honor a person's life than this.

Chapter 8
Leaving Relationships Questionnaire

There is a great variety of the ways to leave a relationship (with a person, a group, a job, an aspect of your life) when ending it becomes necessary (through divorce, geographical relocation, death, resigning or being fired, completion of a time-limited commitment). Check those that apply (or have applied in the past):

❏ 1. Make the relationship so painful that it becomes easy to end it
❏ 2. Blame the other person/people ("Your problem is . . .")
❏ 3. Build in a loophole ("Well, if this doesn't work out, I'll be back.")
❏ 4. Idealizing yourself or others, i.e., glossing over any real problems and pretending everything has been "just fine"
❏ 5. Playing the martyr, becoming the hero ("I am doing this for your benefit.")
❏ 6. Wait for them to leave you
❏ 7. Don't let them leave you ("I'll leave you before you leave me.")
❏ 8. Withdraw emotionally by being too busy, unavailable, forgetting meetings
❏ 9. "Slip out the back, Jack," and "Don't look back."
❏ 10. Play the self-sufficiency card ("I don't need anybody. I can do it myself.")
❏ 11. Denial: Hang on too long, ignoring any problems and the reality that it is ending
❏ 12. Have a stash of alternative relationships waiting to cushion the pain of leaving
❏ 13. Become preoccupied with a diversion to avoid the feelings
❏ 14. Spiritual bypass ("My relationship with God is all I need.")
❏ 15. Cut your losses ("I don't need a loser like you in my life.")
❏ 16. Pre-grieving the loss in secret so you can simply announce you are leaving as a done deal, all very logical with no messy feelings
❏ 17. Pretend that it doesn't affect you ("I'm cool with it.")
❏ 18. Numb and go through the motions like an emotional zombie
❏ 19. Turn the grief into anger and strike out at the other(s)
❏ 20. Turn the grief into guilt and strike out at yourself ("I'm so stupid. What's wrong with me")
❏ Other _____

❏ Other _____

What is your style of grieving?

❑ Healthy grieving - Working through the feelings toward acceptance.

❑ Inhibited mourning - Refusing to show feelings (e.g., not viewing the body).

❑ Delayed grieving - Medicating feelings with drugs, work or other escape activities.

❑ Transferred grieving - Feelings transferred onto others or inanimate objects, most commonly with anger since it is often difficult to express anger to a loved one who has died.

❑ Resistance to change - Fear of unknown may prevent the person from accepting the change.

❑ Failure to come to terms with our ultimate destiny - Denial of death, fear that our life may count for nothing and other spiritual issues need to be addressed. Even focusing on the hope of living forever ("I've lived many past lives before, so I'm not really sad") can inhibit our grief work in the here and now.

❑ Other _____

❑ Other _____

Your Project: Make a list

Make a list of all the people, jobs, towns, memories, or aspects of your life that you have lost and how you dealt with (or didn't deal with) the grief. What pattern do you observe? And what sense do you have of the connection between your style of grieving and your prenatal and birth issues

Chapter 9
Tools for Healing

My own path of both healing and discovery of my purpose began its first stage when I was young and asked my parents to take me to temple. Another important connection came with my trip to India those many years ago. It continued when I returned to the States and — unrealized by me at the time — began fulfilling Maharaji's prediction that I would teach certain healing methods to thousands of people over time.

Those healing methods have come to be known as Heart-Centered therapies, for while we use several techniques — such as hypnotherapy, psychodrama, and breathwork — all are indeed centered around the heart.

Why is that so important? First of all, because science is showing us that the heart's rhythms reflect the state of discord or harmony within, physically, emotionally, and spiritually. Other bodily systems — i.e., neural, hormonal and biochemical — sync to this heart rhythm. It is the master switch setting the pace for one's state of being. When one feels appreciation or happiness, the body and brain experience order and coherence, reflected in a highly resilient heart rhythm. When one experiences hostility or frustration, the body's and brain's experiences are disordered and erratic, reflected in a heart rhythm vulnerable to stress.[103] So work that heals the heart heals a person on all levels.

Our underlying interest with all individuals is discovering the needs of their soul, helping to heal it, and assisting them as they transform into people pursuing their soul purposes. This is spiritual work indeed, making it a realm of work that many therapists sadly ignore or avoid, to the neglect of their patients' optimal well-being.

Nearly every instance of work we have done with clients and students could illustrate this. One comes to mind. A woman named Samantha came in once with a weight problem and, through our hypnotherapy work with her, she realized that she ate to fill up an extreme feeling of emptiness. She described her emptiness as pervasive and something she had experienced throughout her life. As a result, she had tried to fill the emptiness with food, sex, drugs, and relationships … none of which had worked.

We used hypnotherapy to go back to the source of this pervasive feeling of emptiness, and Samantha entered a toddler state when she was told that her mother had died. Only 18 months old, she had no concept of what happened to her mother, especially because the adults around her didn't know what or how to tell her. They were trying to pretend that nothing had happened and that Samantha's mother would be back. But even as a small child, she felt the pain and isolation of abandonment with the loss of her mother, compounded by the feigned ignorance of her caregivers.

The next scenes in her hypnotic regression had to do with being placed in a Catholic orphanage with no contact, warmth, or physical affection. She felt herself disappearing and dissociating – going into shock – as her pain increased and the love dissolved from her life. At this point in the therapy, I asked Samantha where the pieces of her soul were. "They're gone," she replied. "They're not here."

I instructed her to go and find these soul pieces, wherever they were. She reported that she could see some above her bed in the orphanage, hovering around, but that they were definitely disconnected from her body. So I directed her to go and retrieve as many as she could and together we would bring them back into her body. As she did this, I worked energetically at the same time to help reconnect the soul pieces with the appropriate chakras. Soon she began to feel a warmth move into her feet and legs. A sublime smile came across her face as she experienced her soul filling her up. This was a whole new experience for her and she could even feel the energy moving into her fingertips! After her session, Samantha was amazed and ecstatic as she finally started putting the pieces of her life together, at last working in harmony with her soul instead of only experiencing the emptiness of its absence.

This story shows how important the soul is in terms of true, transformational healing, and it is why you could really say that Heart-Centered therapy is a way of assisting the soul through therapy. But we can also get more detailed about what our therapies hold in common. No matter what form they take, Heart-Centered therapies:

1. Include an enlarged perspective of **life-long, existential and often karmic patterns**.

2. Incorporate a **corrective emotional experience** and new major life decisions.

3. Are designed so that sessions complete with self-acceptance, **heart-centered love,** and a healing experience.

4. Involve **trance management** as a key to healing. This means gently putting a client into the state of relaxation, resolving issues in the subconscious mind, and then clearly bringing them back to a strong, conscious mind state for integration.

5. Usually include some physical **energy release** to remove blocks to the flow of subtle, emotional, and psychic energies. We encourage physical and cathartic release of emotions that are held in the body as body armor.[104]

6. Uncover, identify, express, and **release emotions** (catharsis), and teach how to effectively contain the release of intense feelings through appropriate and acceptable channels. This reduces clients' avoidance or fear of their own intense emotions.

7. Combine a **balance** between expansive abstraction (the "wide-angle lens" state that allows for recognizing lifelong patterns and overarching themes) and focused concreteness (the "telephoto lens" state that allows the unconscious mind to follow the trail of current experience back to relevant source traumas earlier in life).

8. Incorporate a **dual level of awareness** (the "doer" and the transcendent "observer") to help create more objectivity, allowing less defensive examinations of and experiments with variations of behavior or belief, and generating more compassionate self-acceptance (of the blamed inner child).

9. Include a regression to the state in which any self-limiting belief was initially established, identifying it explicitly, releasing it, and **creating a new decision or belief** to replace the old one.

10. **Reduce the transference complication** of psychoanalytic or talk therapy since each session goes back to the source of any reaction the client may have to the therapist in order to resolve these issues on the subconscious level. This encourages clients to take responsibility for their own issues rather than to blame their reactions on others.

11. **Strengthen the ego** (empower the client) so that new building blocks can be put in place to do the deeper work. This comes first from self-compassion and self-forgiveness, and then from recognizing personal talents and strengths that have always been available but were too often hidden by self-sabotage.

12. **Confront existential issues** — those overarching patterns in one's life that are present from the beginning and consume so much of one's energy — such as unworthiness, confused identity, or powerlessness. We know that healing from trauma and going on to really thrive requires confronting the lessons to be learned from adversity and ultimately one's purpose in life ("Why am I here?").[105]

13. Incorporate, when appropriate, a **spiritual connection** determined by the client, not proselytized or judged by the therapist.

14. Include a **positive healing experience** at the end so that each session becomes a powerful resource state on which new decisions and behaviors can be built.

Transformational Results

By working in this way with a person's soul, we're able to help her transform, which Carl Jung believed was the entire goal of psychotherapy. And according to Jung, this kind of transformation is really about progressively moving away from a narrow identification with the ego and towards the Self, from the personal to the transpersonal — or, in popular terms of today, from the lower self to the higher self. We can see progress toward (or into) such an advanced state when we:

1. **Are fully present in every moment, refraining from ego dissociation or distraction.** When the ego is less and less fettered by childhood wounds of abuse, shame, and abandonment, addictive behavior and dissociation are unneeded. The individual has extinguished the deep, underlying fear of nonbeing and feels existentially complete, choosing to remain present in each moment. This allows the process of reclaiming the real self to unfold. It means that the individual has permission to feel and express the deepest emotions and thus to release the patterns of dissociation and shock.

2. **Make daily choices based on intuitive knowledge, wisdom, and love rather than on ego-state fear, fabrication, and rationalization.** When the person's deepest motives change from fear or avoiding anticipated pain to an intuitive *inner knowing*, decisions will serve the highest good of everyone involved.

3. **Identify and manage positive energy and avoid "taking on" negative energy.** As people become free of internal ego preoccupation, they become aware of the impact of subtle energy and the importance of managing it. They are also able to identify healthy and unhealthy energy patterns in every interaction — in themselves, in others, and even in groups.

4. **Live in integrity.** Integrity is the natural result of full cooperation between the Self and ego, where the Self is guiding one's actions. In this case, the "private self" and the "public self" are alike; they exhibit

the real self. Living as an integrated person eliminates self-consciousness, anxiety about approval, defensiveness, and secrets, resulting in honesty, keeping commitments, courage to speak the truth, and thus complete trustworthiness.

5. **Spiritually manifest what they say they want.** A measure of ego surrender is manifestation of the goals someone is clear about. In this case, the person has eliminated deep, unconscious feelings of unworthiness or unconscious beliefs that are contrary to what is desired, both of which are obstacles to manifestation. For example, if one is asking for money, she no longer unconsciously holds the belief that money is evil or that she doesn't deserve to flourish in life.

6. **Accept ourselves for who we are, acknowledging the continued growth we desire.** The *life path* of transformational work replaces the ego's tendency to judge by performance and offer only conditional love, instead accepting oneself as a "work in progress." Surrendering the ego is a continuing, lifelong process rather than a single event.

7. **Heal and resolve unhealthy relationships while attracting healthy ones.** Every relationship we have reflects our deepest beliefs about ourselves. Healing a "victim consciousness" pattern in the unconscious mind releases the *repetition compulsion* to repeat those imprinted, unhealthy relationships, and allows new, healthy relationships to develop.

8. **Freely express our emotions spontaneously through healthy release.** In transformational work, people learn to identify emotions through being aware of the bodily sensations that accompany a feeling, and to release these emotions in a way that doesn't hurt another person or property, freeing them from projecting unacknowledged or repressed feelings onto others.

9. **Are current, not unfinished, in every interaction of every relationship.** Ending the repression of feelings eliminates projection, and thus unfinished business in relationships. Jungian analyst Marilyn Nagy[106] says, "Whatever qualities we have that are unknown to us we experience first of all in projection." That is, whatever issues remain unacknowledged and unresolved in me, I will see and struggle against in you. Forgiveness is vitally important in the process of completing this kind of business.

Staying current in relationships is also important when we are speaking of a conscious death. Unfinished business in this process will be painful. If we are unable to *forgive on the soul level*, then we may karmically attract this person back into our next lifetime to replay the relationship again in another, perhaps even more painful version.

10. **Are prepared for a conscious death, no matter how unexpectedly it may come.** Socrates said that "true philosophers make dying their profession, and to them of all men death is least alarming."[107] A conscious death is one that is accepted with emotional composure and spiritual confidence. One of the best examples of this principle happened in India. When Mahatma Gandhi was unexpectedly shot in a crowd by an assassin, he was so prepared for a conscious death that he immediately said God's name three times — "Ram, Ram, Ram" — in his very last breath.

11. **Recognize the karmic patterns being fulfilled, and stop creating new karma. (We accept that we are 100% responsible for our life experience.)** A powerful way to work through karmic issues is to become aware of your individual karmic lessons in this lifetime. This gives the deepest spiritual meaning to the concept of "I am 100% responsible for what I create and experience in my life." It is only by seeing the bigger picture of our lives that we *heal* and *release* the old karmic patterns. Once we get the lesson, we no longer need to keep repeating these painful experiences. We then devote our energies to serving the transformation of others, helping them to transmute their fear, anxiety, negativity, addictions, and illnesses into love, power, and oneness.

Again, Heart-Centered therapies take many forms, but in the end, they all address the deepest issues of a human being in order to help people make the most of their lives. But if transformation is the goal, and true transformation involves following the dictates of the higher self rather than the lower, how do we help to inspire that transition to a soul-guided lifestyle?

Ego Work in Heart-Centered Hypnotherapy

In Heart-Centered Hypnotherapy, it's important for a healer to begin by developing a healthy, adult ego state in the client. An unhealthy or undeveloped adult ego state will fight against any transition toward the higher self taking control. The ego needs to be strong in order to allow for this transition.

So in our hypnotherapy, we start by asking the client what age the internal "adult" seems to be. This is a most interesting question in terms of developmental issues. At times, the developmentally arrested client will answer that there is no adult within. Other clients may describe the adult as age twelve or fourteen. This should be a red flag to the therapist who can then recognize this state of fixation and implant an adult ego state if possible. If there is only an adolescent present, we may ask if this youngster could grow up — an internal maturation process.

If it doesn't seem possible to implant an adult, then ego-strengthening of the ego that *is* available needs to take place before any deep inner work is suggested. Again, the ego must be well established before the process of surrender can begin. Part of the strengthening process involves the release of shame and fear, the 'glues' of repression and grandiosity. This release loosens the possessiveness of the ego-identity because the ego no longer needs to hide, defend, or promote itself. The ego thus moves toward surrender, so long as it's in a place of true confidence and deep inner security.

Granted, some people will not get to the point of surrender in this lifetime. In other words, their task may be just to heal from a lifetime of wounds and develop a strong enough ego to survive this lifetime. For them, that is simply yet importantly a first step toward transformation, because it sets them up for a future time when they *will* be able to surrender that ego.

Meanwhile, there are plenty of people who seek therapy who already have a good, strong adult ego within. These clients will easily find the adult within and the age will be very close to their present age. They may still have many complexes that require treatment and that are holding them hostage so to speak with self-defeating behavior, but they are the people who can more likely release their defenses enough to eventually surrender the ego and reach transformational healing.

Even in this case, a person's competent adult ego state is deliberately strengthened to create the vehicle for safe self-exploration, using generalized supportive suggestions to increase the client's confidence and minimize anxiety. This adult ego state is reinforced as a resource state with an anchor so that it is readily accessible whenever needed by using the implanted reminder, such as recalling a relevant image, a powerful word, or a positive memory. This is especially important if the client regresses to a childhood trauma where no competent adult was present. We now remind her that, in this corrective experience, there is an adult ego state present where there wasn't before. The strengthened adult ego state, of course, becomes generalized in the person's life.

Exploring and expressing feelings strengthens the ego. When someone reacts strongly to a current situation, it's because there is some unresolved issue from the past getting activated by the situation. We use Gestalt techniques to help the person focus on and follow the feeling. Their inner guidance can then take them to the initial cause or causes of this feeling. There may be, for instance, several instances throughout a person's life, perhaps each in a different ego state, where some sort of trauma occurred and stunted the development of that ego state.

Once the person reaches an ego state in its developmental stage (e.g., bonding, separation, or latency) that underlies the feeling, we help them to experience the causative incident in a new and healing way. We give them permission to speak up and tell their truth, if necessary, as they may not have been able to when the event first occurred. As they're able to express themselves adequately in this early ego state and heal themselves of the incident, they remove the cause for strong emotional reactions to certain trigger events in their current lives.

The corrective experience of this approach may take the form of incorporating one's own shadow side; of a deep sense of forgiveness; of the release of some repressed emotion (grief, anger, etc.) through expression; of "making new decisions" to replace neurotic, self-destructive habits; or of "extinguishing" anxiety, fear, or shame using behavior modification techniques of flooding and desensitization. These corrective experiences are powerful because they are experienced on the unconscious and transpersonal levels and at the exact developmental stage in which the *source trauma* was experienced.

The process of "making new decisions" is similar to the model established by James Goulding for redecision therapy, a combination of transactional analysis and Gestalt therapy. "The steps in redecision are: Enter a scene as a child, explore it, experience it, and discover a way to redo the scene so that you are a victor rather than a victim."[108] In redecision therapy, however, the deeper subconscious state is not specifically accessed. We take someone to the actual place and time where these decisions were made, and in this age-regressed ego state, the self-defeating beliefs and behavior decisions can be changed most effectively. This is called *state dependent learning.*[109]

The extinguishing or desensitization technique is commonly used in behavior therapy, providing a way for an individual to become free of debilitating fears, guilt, compulsions, or anxieties. This technique is powerfully effective when combined with the hypnotic state.[110] The executive adult ego state is strengthened in the process of experiencing control over previously compulsive behavioral choices or intrusive thoughts.

Ego-strengthening is also enhanced when the body's energy is engaged, identifying and addressing blocks in specific areas of the body. The body carries memories of early trauma and abuse in the form of sensations specific to the site of invasive trauma (e.g., sensitivity in the temple area of the head caused by use of forceps at birth, or tendency to gag or experience choking or suffocation caused by oral sexual abuse). When in the course of hypnotherapy these "body memories" come to an individual's attention, they can be powerful reminders from the unconscious mind of what happened that was repressed from the consciousness, to be held in the body instead.

This forgetfulness due to storing memories in the body is called *traumatic amnesia* and is the basis for the symptoms of post traumatic stress disorder (PTSD). To the amazement of most people, we have consistently found that the body remembers what happened when someone was even too young to put the experience into words and concepts — that is, when he or she was *preverbal*. This is well documented by others in the field such as William Emerson, Arthur Janov, David Chamberlain, and Thomas Verney.

In the same way, the body or body parts can also carry *disconnection* from feeling, numbness, shock, or withdrawal. Rather than having sensitivity in the temples or a gag response — as in the examples above — there is an absence of sensation or physical feeling. Awareness of such a somatic dissociation is just as much a reminder to the conscious mind as body memories are. Knowing where such energy blockages are in the body provides a clear communication that "*X* marks the spot: trauma happened here." Wilhelm Reich called this process 'body armoring'.[111]

These reminders from the body, whether in the form of active memories or of passive dissociation, are more than bookmarks of trauma, frozen in place. They also provide access to the resolution of that trauma. We work psychologically to strengthen ego states to resolve old, dysfunctional patterns and make the ego states empowered, resilient, self-accepting. In a similar way, we work somatically to strengthen the body (the nervous system, the hormonal system, the posture, the breath, and even the cells) to thaw out what has become frozen and to empower the body to return to a state of natural, unrestricted flow.

Often, survivors of early abuse or trauma have come to believe that their body and its functions betray them. The body's response of shedding tears in a sad circumstance is seen as an unacceptable weakness, is hidden from others, and eventually the tears dry up. The body's sexual response of excitement, believed to leave one too vulnerable and therefore open to be attacked and abused, is shut down and eventually leaves the person non-orgasmic or incapable of enjoying orgasm. Achieving body awareness within an accepting, therapeutic environment can help restore a healthy sense of the body and allow one to experience its sensations as friend, not foe.[112]

Finally, activating physical energy during hypnotherapy *in the powerless ego state in which the trauma originally occurred* is immensely empowering for the client. Ego states, particularly those created in moments of trauma, may be predominantly somatic. For example, the child physically shuts down to become totally still as a means of defense against the terror of abuse, and creates a "somatic ego state" of pervasive shock and immobilization.

Following the somatic bridge (body memory) of immobilization back in regression may lead to conscious access of the source trauma memory which created that ego state — the incident of terrifying abuse. That wounded ego state can be dramatically healed by retrieving it for re-experience in age regression, abreacting the experience, and allowing a means of reintegration and transformation of the trauma experience into a *physically* corrected experience of empowerment. A physical corrective experience activates resources in a client's body (somatic as well as emotional resources) that had been previously immobilized by fear and helplessness. The regressed person is allowed to actually experience the originally immobilized voice yelling for help, and the originally immobilized muscles kicking and hitting for protection. These somatic and emotional corrective experiences *reassociate* the individual's originally dissociated body and emotion in positive ways to positive outcomes.[113]

During hypnosis, clients also may spontaneously experience competing aspects of themselves — substructures of the personality that have relatively autonomous existences and which need integration. This experience is similar to the sub-personalities described in Psychosynthesis, developed by Italian psychoanalyst Roberto Assagioli.[114] In the regressed trance state, clients are easily able to fully experience and identify with the "needy child" part of themselves that's in conflict with the "competent adult" part. The ability in the hypnotic, expanded consciousness to embrace both aspects of the psyche simultaneously allows for integration and self-acceptance, and facilitates the ego surrender process.

Finally, every Heart-Centered Hypnotherapy session ends with self-accepting identification with the most loving part of oneself, and a reunion of forgiveness between any estranged ego states. Thus, one begins to love the inner child who has been blamed for abuse and rejected as bad, or the adolescent who made serious mistakes and has been blamed ever since. One of the most reliable barometers for progress in healing childhood trauma is the adult's ability to accept and love that inner child. Almost every woman we have worked with who was sexually abused as a child initially rejected the girl at the age of abuse in her hypnotherapy session. There is a feeling that this girl "is dirty and stupid." Gradually, the adult comes to have compassion for that little girl, placing the blame on the perpetrator where it belongs, rather than on the child.

Illustration of a Hypnotherapy Session

The following is an example of how a hypnotherapist might help a client reach issues of an ego state in the developmental stages that he failed to adequately complete:

A husband and wife are arguing. The woman wants to go to another city on a weekend shopping trip with two of her girlfriends, and her husband doesn't want her to go. He feels threatened by her independence, scared that she might meet a man and begin an affair, and jealous of his wife's girlfriends. He wants to keep his wife close where he can — if not control her — at least keep an eye on her.

In a hypnotherapy session the next day to address this issue, the man's therapist begins the session (after hypnotizing him) by bringing his attention to the fight that he had with his wife the night before. "Get in touch with the emotions you have, and where in your body you feel them." He feels angry, scared, and ashamed of having those feelings. He experiences the angry feelings as restlessness in his fists and his throat; the scared feelings as a sinking feeling in his stomach; and the shameful feelings as a desire to crawl into a corner and disappear.

"Good," says the therapist as he describes all of this. "Now go back to another time when you felt these same or similar feelings. Now I'm going to tap your forehead and take you back to the source of this feeling or pattern in your life. As I count down from ten to one, feel yourself getting younger and younger, back to the source of this feeling of anger and scared and ashamed in your life.

"Ten: going back to one of the first times where you had this same or similar feeling. Nine: all the way back to the source of these feelings or emotions. Eight: all the way back to the source of those angry feelings of restlessness in your fists and throat. Seven: feel yourself getting smaller and smaller; littler and littler. Six: just allow yourself to go back to one of the first times in your life when you felt that scared, sinking feeling in your stomach. Five: back to the source. Four: feel yourself moving on back, all the way back to one of the first times in your life when you felt the shameful feelings of wanting to crawl into a corner and disappear. Three: all the way back to the source. Two: moving back, feel yourself going back to your childhood. And one: all the way back to the source of these feelings of anger, fright, and shame. When something comes to you — a time, a place, a feeling, a person — just raise your finger."

The man raises his finger. "Okay, now put your finger down," instructs the therapist.

The man finds himself in a situation at the age of twelve when he is leaving home for a two-day music camp with some other kids in his seventh grade class. He is scared to be gone from home, partly because of his uncertainty and lack of confidence, but even more so because he believes his single mother needs him at home. Having been told so often, "Dear, you know you are the man of the house now that your father is gone," he doesn't trust her enough to leave her alone. He is angry at his mother, scared to have such a heavy burden of responsibility at the age of twelve, and ashamed of his predicament.

Following those same feelings back a second time, he finds himself at age four, in a situation in which his mother is leaving the home for a weeklong training for her new job. He is angry that she is leaving him, feels abandoned, and feels that he doesn't matter. He is scared because his father has arranged for his grandmother to come take care of him for the week, and he feels smothered and suffocated by her. He is ashamed to have these feelings because both his parents told him, "You should be ashamed. Your grandmother is taking a whole week out of her life just to take care of you. Is this how you show your appreciation?"

Through reliving these experiences, he discovers the intricate pattern of development of his over-reaction to his wife's independence. The experience at age twelve, the beginning of adolescence, was focused on his need for belonging and the contrary need to achieve independence. Another developmental task at that age is reconciling with authority. His predicament at age twelve resulted in inadequate completion of those tasks, resulting in self-doubt and self-judgment rather than competence and independence. The self-doubt created a fear of vulnerability and a fear of intimacy. He began a life-long pattern of abandoning himself to avoid separation, which he interpreted as failure.

Actually, that pattern did not begin at twelve. The regression to age four showed him that he was already doubting his self-worth and at the same time questioning the trustworthiness of others. In developmental psychology, the child of three to four years of age is called the *Existential Child* because of the sudden awareness that he is not in total control and, in fact, may have very little control of his life. With serious self-doubt, this child also becomes distrustful of others who make decisions that the child doesn't like. Deeply in need of social inclusion, he imposes exclusion on himself as the only way out of the dilemma.

As this man pursues his hypnotherapy further, experiencing regressions to even earlier situations, it becomes clear that the original source of the pattern lies very early in his personal history during the prenatal womb time. This may be a situation where his parents were not married and, upon discovering the pregnancy, reacted with feelings of wanting to discontinue the pregnancy. In any case, this man now understands that when he reacts to his wife's independence, it is really the twelve-year-old, and the four-year-old, and even the prenate reacting to the perceived threat of abandonment. He never conceived that a part of him was stuck in what is called *arrested development* at ages twelve, four, and even younger. Each of these "inner children," a part of him stuck at an unfinished developmental task, is what we call an ego state.

Energetic Psychodrama

Another technique we use in Heart-Centered therapies is called psychodrama. As with hypnosis, psychodrama is not a method that we developed; but as any Heart-Centered therapy, our primary concern is for the client's soul progression and hopeful transformation. We call our form of this process "energetic psychodrama." The difference between traditional psychodrama and energetic psychodrama is profound. Ours is completely done while the client is in a trance state with others in the group acting out life characters as well as shadow parts of the protagonist (the client whose story is being reenacted).

Energetic Psychodrama is a technique in which we represent *externally* our internal psyche, where we can observe that psyche more objectively and complete unresolved conflicts by re-experiencing them with a corrective reframe. Many Heart-Centered students and clients find energetic psychodrama to be the most effective and quickest method of healing.

Traditional psychodrama was originally created as a treatment modality by Jacob Levy Moreno in the 1920s in Vienna. He was a psychiatrist who later immigrated to the United States. He said that psychodrama represented the turning point from treating individuals in isolation to treating individuals in groups, and from treatment by verbal methods to treatment by action methods.[115]

Classical psychodrama provides an opportunity for clients, in a group therapy setting, to structure their internal psychic reality externally and interact with the representation created. The *protagonist* (the person whose story is being enacted) selects other group members (*auxiliary egos*) to play the roles of characters in the psychodrama. The *director* (the professional who leads the group) sets the stage and directs the psychodramatic action based on the intentions of the protagonist. A *double* (the supportive inner voice of the protagonist) can play the role for the client if it is too traumatic for the client herself to re-enact the scene. The group members are referred to as the *audience*. Traditional psychodrama is not done in a trance state and often takes several hours to complete.

In our work, the protagonist enters a trance state, similar to a dream state, surrounded by the manifestation of her psyche. Through the trance state, she has deeper and deeper access to memories, feelings, and spiritual helpers. We encourage her to go where she needs to in order to get the deepest healing. This work can often be accomplished in ninety minutes.

Psychodrama is a method of treatment that follows people into their inner reality, allowing them to describe their inner experience of any life situation and work with it as they see and feel it. Through dramatic action, the psychodramatist brings long-buried situations to the surface to relieve emotional pressure; creates a 'holding' environment through sharing, support, and acceptance; and then allows the natural healing forces of the psyche and the emotional self to continue working.[116] Energetic psychodrama is highly effective because it is experiential and taps deeply into unconscious material; it is corrective; and it is a group process.

Energetic Psychodrama is Experiential

Energetic psychodrama is experiential because it allows an internal experience to be externalized and experienced from a new perspective. It does so by making everything from relationships to life stress to untouchable feelings *concrete*, bringing them to life from the people and environment in the group therapy session. As some 60% of people learn best kinesthetically, and others learn visually, this can be immeasurably more powerful than other techniques for many clients, as they're able to make what's inside them come to life in a visual and physical way, rather than merely discussing and cognitively *knowing* what's inside. In fact, it is well known that experiential learning is much more effective and has longer lasting benefits than cognitive learning alone.

Certainly it is an important technique for use with preteens, since we know that children under the age of twelve think concretely rather than conceptually.[117] Even adults attempt, usually unsuccessfully, to access and correct various internal states simply by thinking about them. But by engaging all the senses, we have more access to and more outlets for past experiences ... some of which (especially pre-verbal memories, for example) are perhaps *only* accessible through such means.

For example, a "family sculpture" — with family members placed physically in relation to each other — could demonstrate visually how distant the antisocial brother is and how clinging the over-solicitous mother is. "A picture is worth a thousand words." As another example, experiencing the opposite pulls of one's spouse and job — physically, kinesthetically — is often more helpful than any amount of talk regarding these conflicting responsibilities. During an energetic psychodrama session, we may use a blanket and have it tied around the protagonists' waist. Someone representing her boss and job responsibilities are pulling at her on the left while husband, home, and children are pulling on the right side. This conflict and the actual internal, visceral feeling that is aroused when the senses are engaged in this manner adds a great deal to the treatment process, as this can activate body memories, taking someone like sonar to early traumatic experiences or other deeply-held, unconscious material. In the end, the protagonist is encouraged to find her internal power to solve this situation, rather than to just let herself remain in this ongoing conflict. The group encourages her to take her power, speak her truth, and stand up for herself.

An interesting point about this form of psychodrama is that it is so spontaneously engaging that people experience some degree of "suspended disbelief." The client and those playing roles "get into the action" to the extent that it becomes the foreground reality, and the fact of being a spectator recedes. This occurs mostly for the client since she is induced into an altered state of consciousness, and other group members are not formally induced. They do, however, often slip into a light trance state as they play their roles, especially when the roles trigger something familiar to them.

Energetic Psychodrama is Corrective

Energetic psychodrama is also effective because it is inherently corrective. With psychodrama, we can re-write history. We can react differently than we did originally, say what we couldn't then, protect what we couldn't then, and set new boundaries. A client can look on her past as an abused child (for example) with empathy rather than with the judgments and shame that have filled her self-experience ever since. This correction often takes the form of reworking missed developmental stages.

As I've explained throughout the book, there are certain lessons for a child to learn in each stage of life. For example, from zero to six months of age, infants need to learn trust, safety, and bonding and to know that their needs will be met. If an infant, for whatever reason, did not learn to trust, then we can go back to those scenes in the energetic psychodrama and begin to implant trust and bonding for that infant. During this psychodrama, the client playing out this baby stage can be loved, held, rocked, and told all the positive things she needed to hear before. This is what we call the corrective experience.

The corrective experience can come from having a change of heart about the characters in the drama or from having a new realization about a previously abusive situation. An example of this is a woman who was very angry about her physically abusive father, and about her mother who didn't protect the children. During her psychodrama and several regressions, she suddenly saw her parents as young children who were in the Holocaust. They were terrified and separated from their parents, who were later killed. The woman then began to cry for her parents and held them in her arms. She told them how much she loved them and, even though she also had been hurt, she was able to forgive them. She saw how they had no role models for good parenting and most of their reactions came from their own desperate fear and rage engendered in the Nazi concentration camps. A powerful corrective experience like this is life changing and often brings about deep understanding, forgiveness, and healing on the physical, psychological, and soul levels. This example also illustrates the plasticity, or flexibility, of an individual's ego states. The client needed to be in an altered state, in her own age-regressed child ego state, in order to find this compassion for her parents. And yet of course that dispassionate letting go of her customary resentment, blame, and judgment of them could only come with the *simultaneous* presence of a mature adult ego state.

Energetic Psychodrama is a Group Process

Finally, energetic psychodrama is often more effective than other techniques simply by virtue of being a group process. Certain issues — particularly those involving shame — are most readily treated in a group rather than individually. The ultimate release of shame requires that one acknowledge shameful behavior to a group of peers, release the feeling of judgment (by self and by others), and receive loving acceptance in spite of any reason for shame — the original mistake or bad deed. Regardless of the issue, however, the loving support of a group with healthy norms is invaluable to healing many issues, and provides the ongoing reinforcement necessary to making behavioral change permanent. There is great healing in just having one's history and feelings witnessed by others. There is also great healing in being loved and accepted even when the truth is known.

Advantages of group work also include the efficiency of benefits to multiple group members from one member's session. Often, the participants who play roles in a session, or even those in the non-participating audience, find their own issues triggered during someone else's session. This provides them with not only a direction for their own work, but potentially with some immediate resolution as well.

One example of this was a student whose father had been physically and sexually abusive to him as a child and had recently and suddenly died. The student had been unable to grieve because of all the repressed feelings of anger, fear, and shame. In the psychodrama, everyone in the group played a different family member as he continued to regress to younger and younger scenes with his father and family. As he described the scenes, they were re-enacted so that he could actually express his true feelings that he was never able to express directly in his family. As he worked through these feelings with each family member — his father with the punishing rage, his mother who never protected him, his twin sister who was the favorite, and his older brother who was much like the father — things became clearer and clearer for him. He discovered that underneath all these feelings was a little boy who just wanted to be loved and appreciated by his father. This is when he was finally able to feel the true grief for the loss of his dad. He was able to cry, and so did many of the group members along with him, especially at the end when we played the song by Luther Vandross, "Dance with Your Father Again."

This session, as in most energetic psychodrama sessions, touched off the pain, sorrow, and grief that was in the hearts of many participants who longed for the love and intimacy they never had with their family members. People who have previously been shut down to emotions, who use laughter to cover their pain, or who suffer from shock and trauma that brings numbness in the form of addictions, find energetic psychodrama one of the most powerful techniques to help them reconnect to themselves and bond with others at the same time.

Preparing for an Energetic Psychodrama Session

Choosing the Focus Member

An energetic psychodrama session begins, of course, with one person from within the group as the focus of the session. Although her therapeutic needs will be addressed directly, the needs of everyone else within the group will also be addressed.

Selection of this focus member involves several criteria. One is choosing someone who is most ready to work, who is closest to her feelings or most "plugged in." Another is choosing someone who feels isolated from the group and needs to be brought into the center of the group's energy. Another is choosing someone whose issues are particularly relevant to the majority of group members. Everyone present can benefit from the work of one person through their identification and transference with the client.

One clear example of this was a time when, in a group of thirty people, three of the female members happened to be in a relationship with other women outside of the group. One of the members, Jennifer, began to feel more and more unsafe in the group because of these three women. Even though there are very strict rules about not having sexual relationships with group members or teachers, Jennifer began to fantasize that they were all three having sex together. When I spoke with her about her fears, she became very upset and screamed that she was against homosexuality.

A few weeks after the group session, Jennifer called and said she was not coming back to the group. She blamed it on "the lack of morals" in the group. I told her that she was completely fantasizing this behavior and encouraged her to check it out with the other members. When she did, she began realizing that her reaction was irrational. Then, in talking about it with another group member, it gradually dawned on her that the whole situation reminded her (unconsciously) of her mother's emotionally incestuous engulfment. Jennifer returned to the next group meeting, and explored her mother's abusive presence throughout her childhood in an energetic psychodrama. Everyone in the group felt immense compassion for Jennifer, who had been such a challenge to everyone previously. And

Jennifer experienced, perhaps for the first time in her life, a healthy loving sense of sisterhood with all the women in the group.

Once the focus member is selected, she will need to develop what's called a *sociogram* of family and other significant people in her life. This diagram provides a map of the cast of characters with whom the client is emotionally engaged for reference during the energetic psychodrama. This is helpful for identifying relevant roles to be played in the scenes created. Also, when the subject identifies a fellow student to play her mother, for example, this also identifies some projection that she may be unconsciously displaying to this group member.

To create a sociogram, the member draws a circle to represent herself in the middle of a piece of paper. Then she locates her significant relationships in circles on the paper, as close or distant from her circle as she feels them to be in real life, and as big or small compared to her as she feels them to be. She then draws lines between herself and each of the others, labeling the line with a description of her emotional relationships.

Setting the Stage, Filling the Roles

Once the sociogram is drawn, the focus member shares it with the group. This helps everyone to better understand who the drama involves and how to best bring those people to life for the focus member. It also helps to determine what roles may need to be filled for work on a particular issue or story in this person's life.

Members of the group are then selected to fill each of those roles, either by the focus member, or the facilitator can designate people for those roles. For instance, if a group member's husband has had an affair and she needs to deal with this therapeutically, she could be put in the place of "the other woman" in someone else's energetic psychodrama, helping to give her a new perspective on her own scenario.

As roles are filled, each group member can be given the chance to ask for clarification about how to best dramatize a given person. The focus member can then give feedback so as to make the whole effort as real as possible for her.

Finally, the focus member will talk for a few minutes about what she is feeling and wanting to work on. The facilitator will be carefully listening for key phrases such as "stuck," "trapped," "left out," "abandoned," or "angry" in order to get a visual image of how this scene could be acted out.

Keep in mind that energetic psychodramas can be created around dream material as well, with drama characters being the most vivid elements of the dream. They can also be created around sub-personalities.

Drama characters might include "the shadow side" (e.g., a self-destructive or violent part of oneself), inner children of various ages, idealized characters (spouse, boss, children, self), etc.

The Induction: Rock and Breathe

"Rocking and breathing" is a technique that looks a good deal like a tantrum, and is a means of getting the focus member in touch with her feelings and into an appropriate trance for the psychodrama. It is also a more physical type of induction to the deeper trance state. It begins with the person rocking back and forth on her hands and knees, then going down to lay on her stomach — arms pounding, legs kicking up and down — while yelling. The purpose is to get her absorbed in her bodily experience and out of the mental and cognitive experience that can keep her from the trance state. Specifically, this pattern activates the energy of the umbilical area, the belly button, which is primally connected with our most deeply-embedded, existential issues. By observing and listening carefully during this process, a practitioner may be able to pick up emotional cues that can help in planning out and running the energetic psychodrama to follow.

Returning to the Source

Age regression to the source of dysfunctional life patterns is the hallmark of Heart-Centered work, so energetic psychodrama facilitates the client in going back to the source of the issue she's chosen to work on. This may or may not be what she consciously *thinks* the source is, which is why it's important to have her in the trance state, where she is more open to inner guidance about what to address in her journey.

Remember that the source could be something well beyond conscious memory, such as birth issues. For example, "I don't deserve to exist" is a common belief that comes from pregnancy or birth issues. So during a session, for example, the client may feel a tightness in the chest and a sense of dread. Encouraging her to stay connected to the feelings in her body, the practitioner can then ask the question, "Where are you?" She may report that she is "in her mother's womb." And so, with sufficient time to explore the realities of her predicament, it may become clear that she has issues of anxiety about moving forward in life, and a deep unconscious sense of unworthiness from this period.

Now she naturally moves forward in time to other situations and relationships in which she also feels anxious and unworthy. The group can bring these relationships to life through playing their roles, and the focus member is then able to experience the psychodrama with the new awareness of *why* she feels anxious in her life in the first place.

Concluding a Psychodrama Session

When the action of the energetic psychodrama comes to an end, every group member — role-player or not — shares the experiences they had during the session. This is validating for the client and important for the members, as long as sharing is the expression of their own vulnerable feelings rather than analysis or advice for the focus member.

Finally, as with all Heart-Centered therapies, the session ends with heart-centered love, in which the focus member experiences empowerment and self-acceptance with an enlarged perspective. She feels nurtured by the corrective experience, has clarity for new life decisions, and feels safe and supported when making future, healthy choices.

Illustration of an Energetic Psychodrama Session

Once the session begins, it generally takes place in three or four stages: 1) acting out the current situation; 2) learning who the drama is really about (often pointing to someone in the family of origin); 3) pushing through old feelings in order to take personal power; and 4) finding closure and "de-roling" the role-playing group members.

Sometimes the current situation will be about issues that are opened by a co-worker, a group member, or even the therapist. In this case, the drama begins in the current situation and, when feelings reach a peak level, the focus member identifies who this is really about. Often this is when a family of origin member is identified. Whoever it is, the scene then shifts over to that person, helping the focus member push through the issue and come through with more personal power on the other end.

To help the client gain this power, she first must break through the old pattern. Usually something physical is helpful for this — something that she couldn't do as a child, such as saying "No!" or yelling for help or kicking and fighting against the perpetrator of her abuse. This gives her a sense of power where there was none before. In any case, there is always what we call a "corrective emotional experience" for the client, preferably in the age-regressed state.

For instance, if she goes back to cowering on her bed, pretending to be asleep while her father sexually molests her, it is vital that she experience — *as that six-year-old girl* — sitting up and confronting her father (i.e., the group member playing the role of her father), yelling for help, hitting and kicking to make him stop, getting up and running to get help (from mother, or a trusted uncle, or the police, etc.). *Physically* experiencing these "alternate realities" actually changes the way in which these memories are stored in the brain (specifically in the hippocampus) and creates a new template, or "meta-experience" upon which new choices (beliefs about self as well as behavior) begin to be based.

There's an important point to understand about creating an "alternate reality" as described above. It is counterproductive to change the behavior of anyone other than the client, because that would discount her actual experience. In other words, having the abusive father suddenly stop the abuse and become repentant and loving and nurturing toward his daughter would be crazy-making for her in the energetic psychodrama. It would cause her to question her already tentative belief in her own perception of reality. As much as we may wish we could change him, we can't. And even if he is now, thirty years later, no longer abusing his daughter, to go back and attempt to change the history of what was *done to her* can only be confusing. It is valuable, clarifying, and empowering, however, to change *what she did* by bringing to bear all the resources that are available to her now as an adult that were not available to that terrified, isolated child.

What we are describing here is actually changing the pattern of *repressing* feelings into one of *expressing* them.[118] An example is the expression of anger through the use of a bataka, tennis racket, or better yet an "energy release hose". The hose is a heavy duty 18 inch long rubber hose which makes a loud sound when hit down on a punching bag laid on the floor. It produces a powerful feeling for the person, who very often was conditioned as a child to never express loud or angry feelings. We learned this technique in the 1980s from Elisabeth Kübler-Ross (the death and dying expert). The dark cloud of unexpressed anger is often actually a mechanism for holding down other more vulnerable emotions, such as sadness, hurt, guilt, grief, or loneliness. Once the dam breaks to allow the expression of the anger, these other feelings underneath become more accessible. Also, the hypnotic trance state allows easier access to those painful feelings.

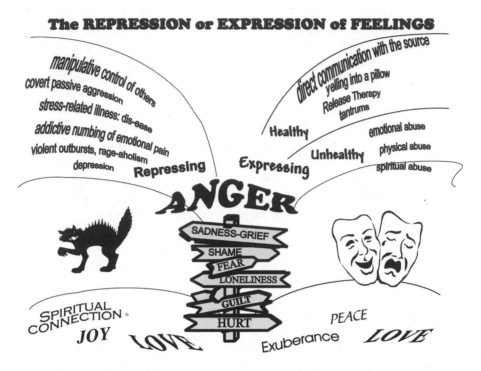

The REPRESSION or EXPRESSION of FEELINGS

manipulative control of others
covert passive aggression
stress-related illness: dis-ease
addictive numbing of emotional pain
violent outbursts, rage-aholism
depression   **Repressing**

direct communication with the source
yelling into a pillow
Release Therapy
tantrums

Healthy

Expressing

Unhealthy

emotional abuse
physical abuse
spiritual abuse

ANGER

SADNESS-GRIEF
SHAME
FEAR
LONELINESS
GUILT
HURT

SPIRITUAL CONNECTION

JOY   *LOVE*   *Exuberance*   *PEACE*   *LOVE*

Before we leave this topic, it's worth noting that sometimes there will be an "energy vampire" in a group — someone who feels empty inside and tries to fill that void by sucking energy from others. This isn't something that the person does consciously, so it's not vicious. Instead, it is a desperate attempt to feel connected. From the work that I have done, I feel that these are often people who have substantially lost the connection to their own souls and that is why they feel so empty. They may also be people who didn't experience the critical early bonding with their mothers, so they have chronic feelings of emptiness.

Energy vampires sometimes have personality disorders as well — often borderline personality disorder tendencies — and they will constantly try to engage you in rescuing them. They are experts at playing the victim role, and they disperse a great deal of energy in attracting catastrophes so that they can gain sympathy from others. Sometimes the number of victim situations they can attract is just uncanny. If you feel drained by someone who constantly tries getting you to rescue her, she is probably an energy vampire.

Some of these vampires are incessant talkers. They ramble on and on and continually go off on tangents. Sometimes they don't even take a breath between words and you can't seem to find a space where you can break in to excuse yourself. This person is actually in a dissociated state, disconnected from her emotions and experience, but the form of her dissociation is active not passive. We call this excitable form *sympathetic shock dissociation* to differentiate it from the daydreamy form, called *parasympathetic shock dissociation.*

So in group settings, it's important that the leader learn to recognize these folks and set boundaries on them by treating their shock. If the leader fails in this, they will end up taking over the group. Everyone will become annoyed with them and with the situation, and will feel too drained to get the necessary work done.

Heart-Centered Breathwork

The third major modality used in Heart-Centered therapies is breathwork, or breath therapy, which allows us to work on the physical, emotional, psychological, and spiritual levels of a client.

This is a powerful form of therapy because breath itself straddles the fence between conscious and unconscious activity. We can easily breathe without being conscious of it. However, we can also consciously control our breath. And the breath is an accurate barometer for the emotional state: by observing our breathing at a given moment in time, we can discover the degree of excitement, fear, anxiety, grief, calm, etc. that is being felt. For example, let yourself notice how you are breathing the next time you experience fear, or anxiety, or embarrassment. It will almost certainly be shallow and timid. On the other hand, most of us know the value of "taking a deep breath" in moments of stress or fear, which can immediately bring us to a state of calm and a more rational perspective.

On the physical level, breathwork actually begins to change the structure and functioning of the body. As we bring the breath under conscious control, we begin to understand the subtle energy that we are composed of and learn to manage it for optimal health and growth. We gain conscious influence over many of the processes once believed to be autonomic, such as our sleep cycle, recovery from injury and illness, and the functioning of the immune system.

Because of its profound effect on our physical bodies, breath therapy can bring us to the edge of decisive moments in our history by accessing body memories. Consciously, we have a number of defenses that keep us from accessing those "turning point" moments — for instance, shame, fear, loneliness, unworthiness, pain, abandonment, and spiritual isolation. But because breathwork operates directly through the body on the unconscious, these defenses are less effective than in cognitive, verbal therapy.

Many of these moments accessed through breath therapy occur in utero or during birth. Through it, we can release the traumas of birth and, in a sense, become "reborn" in terms of how our birth affects the rest of our life. The therapy, however, is not limited to releasing traumas in these earliest stages of our lives, but in *any* developmental stage. This is how it affects us on our deepest emotional and psychological levels.

Just as there are defenses against accessing the lower aspects of the unconscious (repressing the fear, suppressing the rage, rationalizing the guilt, or denying the abandonment), there are defenses against accessing the higher aspects (intimacy, spiritual surrender, or artistic creativity), and these are known as *transpersonal defenses* — mainly the fear of letting go and trusting, or surrendering. These defenses, built into the body itself as character armor[119], provide the greatest challenge to the client in breathwork. For the process to be effective, one *must* let go and surrender … physically, emotionally, and spiritually. Doing so can lead to experiences of transcendent unity with nature, with life, and with God's creatures; a sense of God's embrace itself; or an expansion beyond the everyday identification with our narrow and limited self-concept. Such transcendent experience, common in the resolution phase of breathwork, is really the same as the enlightenment experiences I encountered in India.

How Breath Therapy Works

In breathwork, the client deliberately breathes more quickly and deeply than normal in a cyclical fashion so that there is no pause between breaths, between inhalation and exhalation. We call this breathing pattern *conscious connected breathing*. The two primary physical effects are to super-oxygenate the body and to enhance the discharge of toxins from the body. During breath therapy, clients may experience any of the following:

- **Tingling all over,** which may become more intense as they continue breathing. This is the release of blocked energy. When it comes from their hands, this is healing energy.
- **Pressure on the top of the head.** This may mean they are "crowning" or coming out of the birth canal. The practitioner can get a pillow and place it by the wall so the client can push against it with her legs. The therapist can place their hands on top of the client's head so she can feel the pressure that she is attempting to

push through. The sensation of pressure can be instead the Kundalini energy rising up to the crown chakra.

- **A tight band around the head** which may slowly move down into the chest. This is the baby's experience of going through the birth canal. It is usually accompanied by rapid breathing.

- **Tight or rapid breathing.** This is usually connected with the experience of coming through the birth canal. Clients will experience this breathing until they complete the birth process and are finally "born."

- **Breath release,** which may be like a total, energetic orgasm. The breathing opens up and it is automatic — without any effort. The therapist should make sure the client keeps breathing after the breath release; there are more spiritual awakenings to come.

- **Change in body temperature.** A blanket should always be handy for warmth if requested.

- *Tetne* is an experience of tightening or cramping in the hands, fingers, or the jaw, and often comes when the client is forcing the air out or in some way trying to control the breath. Slowing down the breathing and relaxing the exhalation will generally lessen this experience.

- **A pause in breathing and the sense of leaving the body.** This is okay as long as it is near the end. Otherwise, it usually indicates drifting into a dissociated disconnection from the body, and the therapist should gently instruct the client to keep breathing.

- **Going into shock.** This can happen in breathwork or hypnotherapy, or in any experience that's perceived as threatening or that activates a body memory of an earlier threat. In this case, the person leaves her body, loses self-awareness, feels no emotion, and usually is numb. This dissociation, again, can take an activated form (agitated, anxious, panic) or a passive form (lethargic, sleepy, depressed). Shock is a deeper state of withdrawal than what we usually call dissociation, which is similar to daydreaming, or "spacing out." If someone is dissociated, you can bring her back into her body and into self-awareness simply by reminding her to breathe, or with a gentle touch as you would wake someone from a light sleep. However, the individual who has descended into defensive shock has withdrawn not just her connection to the body, and not just self-awareness, but her actual essence. That essence (the soul) has gone into internal exile, or what we call the "witness protection program." Resolution requires coaxing a re-connection through providing a deep level of reassurance of safety.

- **Spiritual experiences.** Breathwork provides an opportunity to quiet the incessant chatter of the mind, to enter an intimate alliance with the wisdom of the body, and to loosen the customary limiting ego identifications and boundaries. These are conditions within which spiritual connections flourish. Usually these higher states occur in the session only after initially contacting and clearing residual emotional baggage, such as guilt, shame, anxieties, the grief of loss, the hurt of betrayal, or the rage at injustices. That is why it is so important for the client to keep breathing if she stops, thinking that the process is over once she has experienced her birth or some other dramatic event. She can be invited to continue to breathe until she has a clear spiritual experience.

Afterwards, the client is likely to experience increased relaxation; a sense of expansion and well-being; a loosening of psychological defenses; an acceptance of ecstatic experiences; a vision or some form of enlightenment; and a sense of the purpose for her existence.

I have many people say to me, "You mean to tell me that just laying there and breathing for an hour and a half does all that?" Yes, and virtually everyone who tries it finds that it works. But why and how? Let's look into this briefly.

Arthur Janov has researched extensively into the process of primal therapy. He defines a primal experience as "a vivid psychophysiological reexperiencing of a painful event from infancy or childhood."[120] In this experience, the vital signs first rise to a peak and then fall during a parasympathetic recovery phase, characterized by crying. Janov recounts a unique "locomotive breathing" (heavy, deep, rapid breathing) which accompanies certain birth or other primal episodes[121], and says that this breathing pattern, organized deep in the brainstem by the medulla, is triggered by traumatic memory. Through my clinical experience, I've found that the process works the other way as well — in other words, that simulating the breathing pattern can trigger the traumatic memories to be released, and that is the approach we use in breath therapy.

Stan Grof has used the breathwork process for self-exploration and healing, and he has observed that as clients breathe in the prescribed manner, tensions in the body tend to collect in a uniquely individual pattern of muscular armoring. The bands of constriction that develop tend to occur approximately at the chakra energy centers: in the forehead or the eyes, the throat, chest, navel, and lower abdomen. Then these tensions eventually release as the breathing pattern continues, parallel to Janov's observations. Grof, however, recognizes that, frequently, the final outcome is a deep mystical state.[122]

What both researchers are describing is a gradually increasing activation of the sympathetic nervous system, the body's way of stimulating proactive response to stress or excitement, followed by a parasympathetic recovery phase, the body's entry into rest and relaxation. This sequence can be repeated in multiple cycles in a given breathwork session. Arousal of the sympathetic nervous system is known to cause emotionality and excitement, while the quieting effect of the parasympathetic system is more conducive to reflection, reverie, and meditative calm. These two systems, the SNS "arousal" and PNS "quiescent" systems, normally act in an antagonistic fashion — that is, increased activity of one tends to produce decreased activity in the other. Studies have shown that maximal stimulation of either component can induce a "spillover" effect that — rather than inhibiting the activation of the other — results in the simultaneous activation of both systems.[123] Such a simultaneous activation of both systems can result in various forms of peak experience, such as spiritual or mystical experiences or "near-death" experiences.[124]

Similar breathing techniques, called pranayama (pronounced prah-nah-yama), have been used from ancient times up into the present by yogis and spiritual masters from India and around the world. All those years ago in India, Maharaji had taught me to use the pranayama technique to promote my spiritual awakening. What a surprise it is to me that I am now teaching people to use a similar technique, the conscious connected breathing, to heal emotionally *and* to advance spiritually. As you can see, this makes breathwork an integral tool in Heart-Centered therapy, because it is soul work — it allows one to tap into spiritual experiences while at the same time releasing past traumas in the physical and emotional bodies that keep the soul from accomplishing its work here on Earth.

The Medicine Wheel

While hypnotherapy, psychodrama, and breathwork are perhaps the three *primary* tools we use in Heart-Centered therapy, they are by no means the *only* ones. As an example, we use the medicine wheel as a metaphor for successfully navigating many of life's challenges, and in particular the grief process.

The shamanic traditions of many cultures teach the medicine wheel as a way to connect with spirit and to affirm our place in the universe. In general, the medicine wheel teaches that each of the four directions has specific tasks for us to attend to in the process of living on the planet and in carrying out our growth process. In addition to east, south, west, and north, there is the direction below (Mother Earth), the direction above (Father Sky), and the center of the universe (the Creator). There are power spirits for each direction, and there are special sounds and specific types of meditation advised for the passage around the medicine wheel. This is an exciting structure through which to do internal work, and we'll talk here about its usefulness for dealing with grief.[125]

The South

The sun rises in the East, but it shines most brightly and abundantly in the South, bringing its warm breath of compassion to soften hearts that have grown cold. The southern portion of the medicine wheel is the place of *the Inner Child of the Past, the Healer,* and the spirit of the *Serpent.* Here we learn how to shed our past, to erase any limiting and negative vestiges of our personal history (the way the serpent sheds its skin), and to learn at the same time to walk with our bellies against Mother Earth, to be close to the earth again.

By calling on the spirits of the winds of the South, we can face our family-of-origin experiences and release our grief, abandonment, separation, and loss issues from the Inner Child part of our personality.

It is traditionally from the South also that teachers and healers bring salvation in the form of ceremonies, rituals, and sacraments. This is the challenge of faith: to maintain a full heart, an open heart, a strong heart, and a clear heart.

The Mode of Healing here is Storytelling.

The West

The sun sets in the West, bringing an end to every day, and yet the full circle of daily life is only half complete with the sun's retreat. Darkness descends on one half of the world while the other half comes to life. The western portion of the medicine wheel is the place of *the Warrior.* In this direction, we are called upon to face our deepest fears and our mortality.

In the West, the spirits of the *Jaguar* and the *Grizzly Bear* come to teach us about overcoming and facing our fears. It is in the West that we deal with the grief about giving up our illusions. We deal with our loneliness and our deep terror about the suffering in the world and the degree of our impotence in the face of the great forces at work in the universe. Those forces include failures, death, annihilation of our illusions, and the requirement that we leave the known in order to ever encounter new, richer, and more complex experiences.

This is the place where you come to meet your death, where you come to lose fear through symbolic death in a place of power. For example, according to the traditions of the ancient Incas, you could not enter Machu Picchu, the sacred City of Light, until you had died, till you were already dead and thus had no fear of death. There's a death stone outside the city, shaped like a canoe, pointing to the west that the shamans would come and lie on. The Jaguar would come and take them, rip the energy body from the physical body, and take them through a complete circle around the earth before bringing them back from the East. Such is the symbolic journey taken by all who use the medicine of the West.

The Mode of Healing in the West is Silence.

The North

The northern portion of the medicine wheel is the place of *the Visionary* or *the Leader*. The work of the North is to come into a direct communion with the masters, with the divine, settling for nothing short of that immanent experience. It is only in the darkness of the north, in the nighttime that follows the descent of the light in the West, that dreamtime comes alive. Dreamtime offers a loosening of rationality, a freedom from the tyranny of mundane concerns, and that brings contact with spirit world, the archetypes that inhabit the Underworld. That allows for visions.

The spirit guides of the North are the *Bison* and the *Horse*. Bison reminds us that we can achieve nothing without the aid of the Great Spirit, and that we receive what we humbly ask for. Horse represents power: not only physical power, but especially unearthly power, the power to journey to far off lands and return safely. In this direction we face our deepest rage about being here on Earth again. To come into direct communion with the divine, we must first face our fundamental rebellion at being separated from God, acknowledging any anger at God/Goddess or anger at having to take responsibility for being alive.

In addressing this archaic grief, we are called upon to forgive all of our family members, and ultimately to forgive ourselves. In dealing with current grief issues, we deal with the forgiveness of the person or people who have left us, and forgive the aspects of any situation that is causing us grief.

Here the Mode of Healing is Dancing, movement.

The East

Finally, the eastern portion of the medicine wheel is the place where we are offered the task of *Mastery*. We are assisted here by the spirit of the *Eagle*, who gives the capacity to see far and wide, and yet to observe the smallest details. It is here that we remove our old masks of fear, anger, shame, and illusion and step into the fullness of our being, which represents our vision of all that is possible once liberated from the harness of repeating the past.

It is this vision that we are then asked to hold for ourselves and our communities in order to turn it into a reality with the dawning of each new day. We are also given the opportunity to share our knowledge with others. Of course these opportunities bring with them challenges to overcome, as we must avoid disappointment or discouragement about the process of turning a vision into a reality. We need to avoid arrogance and complacency, yet accept that which we're able to accomplish and the time that it takes to get things done.

Since the medicine wheel is a circle, we must also note that the East is no more the end of our journey than death is the end of our journey on Earth. Each stage moves into another as we move through the Spiral of Life. There is a cycle of beginning, of shedding the past and learning new ways, of ending, and of envisioning new beginnings in each day, in every task, in every relationship, and in every life.

The Mode of Healing in the East is Inner vision, intuition, wisdom.

Sweat Lodge Ceremony

Related to the medicine wheel work is the work we accomplish by means of the sweat lodge. We have been introduced to the sweat lodge by our Native American friends. We often complete our workshops of deep healing work with a sweat lodge, which represents the womb of mother earth. The lodge is built in the shape of an igloo, constructed with a frame made of willow saplings. Blankets are then arranged over the frame to keep it warm, dark, and moist inside. A fire is built outside the lodge and volcanic rocks are placed inside the fire to heat for several hours until they glow red-hot. People begin to gather outside the lodge and then go in one by one after being smudged (purified) with burning sage.

We enter from the door in the east and walk around clockwise inside in a circle to the edge of the door. Each person sits close to the next until the whole lodge is filled with people. The person who "pours the water" is the

Native leader who may sit in the west facing the door and the fire outside, or in the east. There is also an altar outside the door with sacred artifacts, feathers, pipes, and herbs such as sweet grass, cedar, and sage to put on the rocks.

The sweat lodge is a sacred place to sing and pray and celebrate life. There are four rounds, each one beginning and ending with Native prayer songs to open the heart and call in helpful spirits. Between rounds the door is opened for air and to bring in more hot rocks. This continues until all have prayed and are spiritually cleansed. When the door is opened for the last time, each person files out and forms "a receiving line" around the fire. We go around and greet and hug each person to welcome them from their incubation in the lodge back into the world again. This is usually a very profound experience for everyone.

Soul Retrieval

Soul retrieval is another important tool in our approach to healing. It's one that I've mentioned elsewhere in the book, and of course fits into our model because it addresses one's healing from the level of soul integration.

In our language we have expressions such as "lost soul" or parents who have "broken their child's spirit." But do these actually refer to something? They can indeed, because any traumatic experience of abuse or assault — whether physical, emotional, or psychological — can lead to a period of dissociation or shock, which is a mechanism for avoiding the pain of the event. At this time, one or more "pieces" of a person's soul can essentially break apart from the rest of the soul and leave the person. This disconnection from parts of the soul can lead to feelings of emptiness or of "something missing," or a sense from others that this person "is a lost soul."

Physical beatings or sexual abuse are obvious instances when this type of dissociation can occur, but the criticism, shame, and threats of abandonment that parents often dump onto their children can lead to the same sort of thing. They may not look like much on the outside, but inside they can have similar results, even though the child may not even be aware of the pain.

Modern psychology often refers to dissociated parts of the self and explains that integration is an important part of therapy. And more than that, we've learned from both ancient and modern shamans that soul retrieval has always been recognized as one of the main functions of the shaman or healer. This spiritual work is accomplished in the "trance state," and therefore naturally fits in with hypnotherapy work involving the soul as ours does. When we bring someone into the trance state and have her visit an event in which pieces of the soul have been disconnected, we can have her literally look for and retrieve those pieces. After sessions like these, people will tell us that they feel "whole" or "complete" for the first time since the event, which often means "since before they can remember."

An interesting point related to soul retrieval is the fact that, when people *lose* pieces of their soul, they can also have pieces of *other people's souls* enter their bodies and essentially become a part of them. Often, another soul will enter when someone is on her deathbed; in hospitals and cemeteries; or in a home or building where someone has died. Physical signs of having taken on another's pain (a "split soul," not multiple personality) include:

- Breathing problems, asthma (choking or drowning death)
- Chest pains, headaches (heart attack or stroke death)
- Headaches (brain tumor death)
- Smoking, drinking, drug use (substance abuse death)
- Anxiety or fear (a fearful death, e.g., a disaster, violent assault, or accident)
- Grief (death of a broken heart)
- Fighting or anger (violent death)

In the parentheses, we see what the other person may have gone through for their soul to split apart, sending them into the recipient body.

Another related piece to this topic is the matter of spiritual attachments. Extensive clinical evidence suggests that disincarnate beings — the spirits of deceased humans — can influence living people by forming a physical or mental connection (or attachment) which can be detrimental in various ways. I gave an example of this in chapter 3, in which Molly's father had "latched onto her after his physical death." This condition is referred to as Spirit Possession Disorder.

Earthbound spirits are the most prevalent possessing entities to be found. A disembodied consciousness seems to attach itself and merge fully or partially with the subconscious mind of a living person, thus exerting some degree of influence on thoughts, emotions, behavior, and the physical body. The entity becomes a parasite in the mind and energy field of the host.

A spirit can be bound to the earth plane by emotions and feelings connected with a sudden traumatic death. Emotions such as anger, fear, shame, jealousy, guilt, remorse, and even strong ties of love can keep the spirit tied to the earth. Erroneous beliefs or lack of education about the afterlife can also keep the spirit earthbound.

Following death by drug overdose, a newly deceased spirit maintains a strong appetite for the drug and this hunger can not be satisfied in the non-physical realm. This hunger can only be satisfied through a parasitic attachment to a person. As a result, many drug users are actually controlled by the attached spirit of a deceased drug addict.

Many spirits also remain in the earth plane due to lack of awareness of their passing. An attachment can be neutral, totally self-serving, malevolent in nature, or benevolent. Regardless of how benevolent their intentions, however, they still cause an energy drain on their host.

Finally, attachment can be random and completely accidental, simply occurring because of physical proximity to a dying person such as in a hospital or accident scene. In about half of the clinical cases, it is a random choice with no prior connection. In the remaining cases, it involves some unfinished business from this or another lifetime. Even if there is some prior interaction, the attachment only perpetuates the conflict and carries little possibility for resolution. Some investigators estimate that 70–100% of the population is affected by one or more disincarnate beings during the course of their lifetimes.

As you can see, then, there's plenty of reason not only to work with a person's soul in therapy work, but to ensure that her soul is complete and unencumbered with the presence of other souls or soul fragments. The healing work of integration needs us working with a person's entire soul … and *only* her soul.

Energy Work in Heart-Centered Therapies

By now we've looked at the major techniques used in Heart-Centered therapies, along with some of our specific approaches of applying them: the medicine wheel, sweat lodge, and soul retrieval methods featured in this chapter. None of these techniques, of course, can be *taught* in a book, but only introduced, not only because there is so much information involved in each, but also because there are so many subtleties that can only be appreciated through more personal training.

Energy work is a good example of this. You may have noticed that I frequently talk about the use of energy in the process of working with clients, and this is such a central part of our work that it's important to talk about it here.

The type of energy we're discussing is that subtle, "universal life energy" mentioned in chapter seven under the discussion on chakras. This energy is known and studied in many walks of life, often under different names. For instance, mystics have "studied" it through meditation for eons; practitioners of Chinese medicine have worked with it as "Chi" for that long in acupuncture; quantum physicists are studying it today as they explore the subatomic world, where certain elements like photons are considered to have no mass, and where energy and mass often become one another; others work with this energy for healing through techniques like Reiki; and we can even use it for experimental, diagnostic purposes through devices such as an aura camera that utilizes Kirlian photography.

In fact, we specifically use aura cameras to assess the changes a person undergoes after passing through therapy. The images below show a woman who came to us shortly after having surgery with general anesthesia and, as you can see, her aura was literally missing from the top of her head down, representing all the chakras below the crown. This indicates that the soul has withdrawn, which is indicative of anesthesia or shock. After two days of personal healing work and morning meditations, her aura was bright, full, and vibrant. This demonstrates both the success of her therapy and provides technological validation of our work with subtle energies.

Since working with this energy is so integral to what we do, we begin teaching how to do so in our first levels of training when we meditate as a group in a circle, holding hands, and showing how to pass energy around the circle through the hands and heart. This is rudimentary work in "energy transfer," and we get into more advanced levels of it as students pursue higher levels of training.

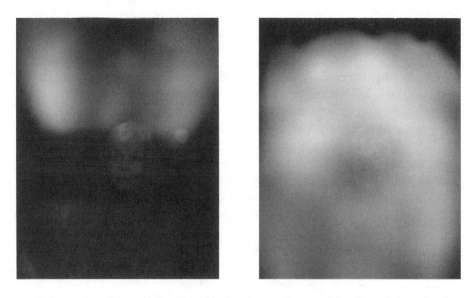

Left: a woman's aura shortly after having surgery with general anesthesia
Right: after two days of personal healing work and meditations

This gives a good overview of the techniques we use and, I think, of how Heart-Centered therapies differ from other forms of therapy available. But all of our discussions so far have focused on the health and healing of people as individuals. If one thing gives our lives meaning most of all, however, it is our relationships. Thus, healing relationships is an important part of healing people too. Like any "last but not least," that brings us right into the final topic we need to cover: healing through relationships.

Chapter 9
Mind-Body Questionnaire

Check off what is true for you. Then prioritize the top five (give each a number).

✔ 1-5

❑ ❑ A. I tend to abandon my health and medical needs.
❑ ❑ B. I sometimes ignore somatic signs and symptoms.
❑ ❑ C. I often have accidents due to inattention.
❑ ❑ D. Self-care is a foreign concept to me.
❑ ❑ E. I consistently numb my feelings. What pain am I attempting to numb? _____
❑ ❑ F. I feel very self-conscious about my body.
❑ ❑ G. I obsess on what clothes to wear, what size I am, or how I look.
❑ ❑ H. I know I self-punish (such as illness, disease or accidents).
❑ ❑ I. I tend to hold in my feelings, especially anger and grief.
❑ ❑ J. I often take care of others and ignore my own needs.
❑ ❑ K. I use alcohol, food, marijuana or pills to numb my feelings.
❑ ❑ L. I take out my feelings on others.
❑ ❑ M. I tend to somaticize feelings (turn them into an illness or pain).

1. When I get sick or have pain, the parts of my body most often affected are (check all that apply):

   1) Lungs   4) Intestine   7) Heart   10) Skin   13) Spine/back
   2) Throat   5) Sex organs   8) Head   11) Eyes   14) Thyroid
   3) Pancreas 6) Liver   9) Ears   12)
   Other_____

2. These illnesses affected my body (*where?*)

_____

3. These illnesses affected my life (*how?*)

_____

4. The accidents I have had affected me (*where in body?*)

_____

5. If your body could speak, what might it say? "I feel …."

_____

6. If there was a gift or lesson in my illness, injury or accident, it would be:

_____

_____

_____

_____

_____

_____

_____

Your Project: Ask your body for a consultation. Ask each part of your body (especially those checked in 1. above) what it wants to communicate to you about what care it needs from you.

_____

_____

_____

_____

_____

_____

_____

_____

Chapter 9
Prosperity Issues Questionnaire

What are your attitudes about prosperity?

1. **Money**

   Positive _____

   Negative _____

2. **What do you say about money?**

   Positive _____

   Negative _____

3. **How do you use money?**

   Positive _____

   Negative _____

4. **Rich people are** _____

   _____

5. **Poverty is** _____

   _____

6. **Money represents** _____

   _____

Where did you get your attitudes about money? Who have you passed them on to?

A. **Guilt**
   1. Who made you feel guilty about having, sharing or giving away money? _____
   2. Who have you made to feel guilty?
      _____

B. **Shame**
   1. Who shamed you about having, or not having enough money?
      _____
   2. Who have you shamed?
      _____

C. **Blame, resentment and anger**
1. Who blamed you about your lacks?

    _____

2. Who have you blamed?

    _____

D. **Fear**
1. Who made you feel fear about money?

    _____

2. Who have you taught fear to?

    _____

E. **Hurt, sadness and grief**
1. Who made you feel hurt or sad about money?

    _____

2. Who have you made to feel hurt or sad?

    _____

Your Project: Make three lists

Make three lists: (1) everything you are grateful for in your life; (2) everything you are ready and willing to let go of and give away; and (3) anything you don't have and feel that you really need in order to be fulfilled in your life.

Chapter 10
Healing through Relationships

By now, we've covered all the stages of life, looking at the various traumas that can affect people and how those traumas can be resolved with Heart-Centered techniques. But you might have noticed along the way that there's an important theme running through all of life's stages, and that is the theme of relationships.

Unhealthy relationships, after all, are very often the things that cause traumas; likewise, healthy relationships can keep us strong and even help us to overcome past traumas as we learn that we *can* trust and *can* rely on others to support us. We remember the old saying that "no man is an island," and this is true. Our life experience isn't just made up by our own choices, but by everyone's choices — especially by those who are closest to us.

Another old saying tells us that we teach what we most need to know, and that was certainly true as I began teaching hypnotherapy in Los Angeles. There were just about six people in the class, and the way that I taught that class was the beginning of the model that we still use to train thousands of therapists all over the world. And as I started teaching, I found myself covering this very topic of relationships.

What Is a Healthy Relationship?

Once I began to teach about codependency, it was clear that I had a book inside my heart and soul that was yearning to come out. When I taught about the victim triangle, there was a passion underneath the teaching that gave me a clue that this was a personal issue for me. I began to write my book, *Breaking Free from the Victim Trap: Reclaiming Your Personal Power*, and many of my own family members as well as David's family members seemed to fit very neatly into it. I was curious how two people such as David and me— who had come from codependent, dysfunctional, and addicted families — could come together and create such a healthy relationship.

I began to see the value in the relationship with David that I had never had before with anyone. The difference was that it was the first non-codependent relationship I had ever had with a man. He was the first man I had ever been with who was not threatened by my success or by my power. I never felt the desire to hold myself back in order to rescue him. I could fully be myself in all areas of my life, and that only intrigued him more.

And it worked both ways. I was not threatened by his success or independence. I enjoyed the fact that he had other things in his life besides me, and that made him more interesting to me. Neither one of us minded being alone if the other one had plans that didn't include us. This was very different from other relationships I had been in.

We let the relationship grow slowly. Neither one of us was in a hurry to remarry since we had both been divorced and each of us had a child. We let the trust, the respect, and the romance develop at its own pace. There was no pushing, manipulation, or hidden agendas. The love grew day by day, week by week, month by month, and year by year. The best way we avoided power struggles was to always keep our money separate. That way we each maintained our own independence, with neither one controlling the other's money. We avoided the authority issues that most people get into when they have to ask the other if they can spend money on something.

Having a relationship without codependency at first felt like something was missing. It seemed to be slightly … *boring*. But what I finally realized was missing was the drama. Or as Stephen Karpman called it, The Drama Triangle.[126] That is the victim, rescuer, and persecutor games that we had both played in our previous relationships, and that most people play in most of their relationships. Since we were both successful, independent adults, no one needed to be rescued. Neither one of us played the victim, so the triangle was a moot point. We then had to learn to relate to each other as real people rather than as the roles we had played in our previous relationships. The challenge to do this is what brought excitement into the relationship.

Some people bring out the worst in each other and some bring out the best. David and I seem to bring out the best in each other because of the mutual respect we share. And because of this deep respect, we have never tried to change each other. The love that has grown between us is truly unconditional. It isn't based on, "I'll love you if you change," or, "I'll love you if you'll fit yourself into my image of what I think you *should* be." But rather, it's always been characterized by the word, *Namaste*, which means, "I honor the place in you in which the entire Universe dwells. I honor the place in you which is of love, of truth, of light, and of peace. When you are in that place in you, and I am in that place in me, we are one." A healthy relationship is a Divine meeting of Souls.

As we carved out our lives together, we did a lot of personal and spiritual growing. What made our lives interesting was not empty drama but the process of discovering what our mission was together. Through many past life sessions, we realized that another reason there was no drama was that we had no unfinished past lives together. What had brought us together was our past karmic relationships of spiritual service on the path of enlightenment. Neither one of us had ever had a relationship like ours, which is built on a strong spiritual foundation. And to me, that is the glue that holds us together. Above all else, we both know that we are here to serve God through the service and healing of humanity. Every opportunity we are given to bring healing to others from different communities and different cultures brings us closer together as a couple, and it brings us closer to God as well.

The first ten years of our relationship were spent gathering the tools for our spiritual journey together. We each contributed and shared our gifts as we explored which way our paths would unfold and come together. When I met David, he was a financial planner and was doing business. He was also a social worker and was active on the community mental health center board of directors. He brought all those skills to me as I shared my healing tools with him. At the beginning, we had no idea how our paths would fulfill our karmic purpose together.

Since then, our years have been spent fulfilling that karmic purpose. Our work is one with our spiritual path. There is no separation. Every training and class that we teach is an integral part of our growth toward enlightenment. Each time we participate in the healing of a soul, our souls' purpose is fulfilled. Each time we participate in a Heart-Centered Hypnotherapy session, meditation, energetic psychodrama, or breathwork session, we experience our souls dancing together in joy.

Now I have learned that a healthy relationship is one in which both people feel fulfilled on the very deepest soul level. It is beyond the *maya* (illusion) of personality, the fleeting pleasures of the body, or the superficialities of social contacts. A healthy relationship inspires each partner to fully explore and discover the true self as expressed through the soul.

How Healing Happens

During that first ten years, the teaching of the Heart-Centered therapies really took form. It all began to flow and emerge from the creative source which is inside all of us. It felt like I had so many teachers and so much knowledge from which to draw: the humanistic Gestalt therapy of Fritz Perls, the Transactional Analysis of Eric Berne, the bioenergetics of Wilhelm Reich and Alexander Lowen, the hypnotherapy of Donald

Keppner and Charles Tebbitts, and the spiritual practices that I had learned in India.

Things were really coming together personally, professionally, and spiritually until a big crash occurred. My relationship with David felt very good and solid until an old boyfriend contacted me after twenty years. He had made it big in show business and I was really happy for him. I had no romantic intentions but I did want to connect with him as I was excited about his success.

David was not clear about my intentions and was somewhat threatened by my excitement to meet with my old friend and lover. He took this as a message that it was okay for both of us to have an extra-marital affair, and he proceeded to do just that. He never lied and immediately told me all about it. He expected that it would be okay with me since he thought that was what I wanted with my friend. He told me the complete truth since our relationship was very open and non-possessive.

But I freaked out! I was extremely hurt, angry, and devastated. In fact, I was surprised that my reaction was so strong. It is only in hindsight, after much emotional work, that I truly realized what this was all about for me. The affair triggered my deepest abandonment issues going back to my father leaving for World War II when I was six months old. It also triggered my sexual abuse issues of feeling betrayed by those I trusted and loved the most.

I began drinking wine to deal with the pain and stress of the situation, especially because the woman with whom he had the affair lived in our community. David assured me that it had been very brief, that it was me that he loved, and that he would never do this again. He told me over and over again how sorry he was and that he never would have done this if he had realized how much it would hurt me.

None of his words could take away the deep pain that I was feeling. Before I knew it, I was unable to stop drinking wine. I knew I needed help, so I entered Sierra Tucson, a wonderful in-patient treatment center for all types of addictive behavior.

This experience became another "blessing in disguise." It facilitated my working through these issues on an even deeper level than I had been able to previously. Professionally, I learned a great deal about the field of addictions from the program at Sierra Tucson. When I returned home, I began to incorporate what I had learned into the Heart-Centered therapies. It became clear that hypnotherapy was a powerful tool with which to treat all of the addictive behaviors.

After completing Sierra Tucson's thirty day program, I thought the majority of my treatment was over. I soon realized that it was just beginning. Some weeks later, I began to have severe pain down my left leg. I went to the doctor, had an MRI, and was diagnosed with a herniated disc that was pinching the sciatic nerve in my lower back. The doctor wanted to immediately sign me up for surgery. I was about to do that when I got a clear message from my inner guides that this was not the thing to do. "No surgery" was the message. So I cancelled my surgery date and began using the hypnotherapy tools that I had developed in order to heal the pain in my back and leg.

In therapy, it turned out that the pain was actually a body memory of being raped by my seventeen-year-old uncle when I was about two years old. A medical doctor told me that it is the sciatic nerve that would be pinched by a grown man having intercourse with a child. So this sciatic pain going down my leg was a message telling me what had happened, reminding me through a "body memory" about the pain that I had experienced so many years ago. Retrieving this memory helped my therapy progress.

As we've discussed in earlier chapters, the psyche has a method called "dissociation" for dealing with severe pain. This is a way in which young children can "leave their bodies" to avoid severe physical or psychological pain. We are now learning about shock and how that plays a big part in leaving the body. If a child is being raped, beaten, or even shamed, he may begin to have the experience of "floating on the ceiling" or "getting lost in the wallpaper." This is a powerful, protective mechanism that has been documented with children as well as with women delivering babies and World War II and Viet Nam veterans. It is called Traumatic Amnesia. Even though the conscious mind has repressed the traumatic memory through dissociation, the body remembers. The muscles, nerves, and tissues remember. There is scientific evidence that even the cells remember.

I had never consciously remembered the rape by my uncle, until now. But as I reviewed the "evidence" of my life, it all made sense. It made sense that in my psychotherapy practice I had specialized with children and adult women who had been sexually abused. It explained why I had become a "child advocate" and had fought so hard for children to have "rights" and for their voices to be heard in the court system. As I worked through the anger, fear, shame, and grief, I began to feel much lighter in my life. I no longer seemed so angry at men, nor did I have such a strong desire to rescue women and children. David and I did a lot of healing in our relationship and it became stronger and clearer than ever.

As I allowed the sexual abuse memories to come through, the sciatic pain down my leg diminished. After about six months of releasing the emotions through intense hypnotherapy, I was able to find forgiveness in my heart for my uncle. I then got a clear message that I was ready to receive healing and that it was time to ask God directly for this healing. The next day, my back was pain free and there was no more pain in the sciatic nerve. It is now more than twenty years later and it has not returned.

Healing is a basic ingredient of personal transformation work and it comes in many forms. It sometimes occurs spontaneously and immediately. But most often it occurs in stages and layers. As the layers of pain, hurt, shame, fear, and anger are released, the body begins to heal and the immune system strengthens. I continue to get the lesson of "the gifts in adversity." There were so many healing gifts in this entire experience for me. It did, however, take me several years to fully appreciate those gifts.

Founding Our Community

David and I held a mutual vision of having a healing retreat center where we could live and do our trainings. We envisioned a beautiful place among the trees in the Pacific Northwest. We used all the principles we knew of creative visualization, as well as the prosperity principles, in order to manifest it. We also envisioned teaching all over the world and having more classes and students. We attended an inspirational program called The Pursuit of Excellence, created by Randy Revell, where we wrote out our visions and life goals.

As we began looking for the place we had visualized, we were having a difficult time. Living in metropolitan Seattle, the realtors really did not have the correct picture of what we wanted. David and I looked at numerous possible locations near Seattle, but were unsatisfied. We were getting discouraged. We found ourselves drawn deeper and deeper into the Cascade Mountains of the Pacific Northwest. The mountains always felt like home to me. One day a friend told us about a retreat center thirty minutes from the city that was for sale. As we drove there, up into the woods, along a magnificent winding tree-lined road to get there, I began to feel more and more excited. When we pulled up and saw this beautiful retreat center nestled in the forest, I knew I was home. We knew that this was the place for us, and everyday it became clearer.

After seeing the magnificent house and retreat center, we were taken for a walk on the trail down to the salmon spawning creek on the property. This is when I began to have some past life memories of living on this land and surviving on the salmon, greens and berries that grow naturally here.

When we were told the price of the place, we went into shock because we knew we could never qualify for a loan to buy it. When I meditated on the property, I knew deep in my soul that I had lived there before in another lifetime and that we would be living there for many more years to come. By this time we had learned about the laws of manifestation and we decided to put them to work. We didn't know how we would possibly get the money, but we knew we had to. We continued to visualize all the steps necessary to purchase the retreat center and could visually see ourselves living there while doing our healing work. But how?

The Divine Mother Connection

It had been over ten years since I'd been to India and found God within myself. Since that time, however, I had always continued to pray, meditate, and chant. But I had felt that I didn't need a "guru" or spiritual master in the flesh during that time. So when a friend of mine told me that the Divine Mother would be visiting Seattle and holding a retreat, I responded by saying that I was not interested. He showed me her picture and told me to let him know if I changed my mind. That night, I went to sleep and the Divine Mother — Amritanandamayi, known as Ammachi — came to me very clearly in my dream. She said it was time for me to "come home." I woke up and asked David if he would like to join me in attending a spiritual retreat the next weekend. He was happy to accompany me, since he had always wanted to meet one of the saints I had spoken about.

When we went to the retreat, I knew that this was an important connection in my life. I remembered wondering if I would ever again want or need another guru in the flesh. It became clear to me that I had been attracted to Ammachi for a reason, and that reason would become clearer in time. I showed her the picture of the land and the place we had been looking at. I asked her if this was "our place." She said it definitely was. I told her that we could not qualify for the loan, nor did we have the money it would take to purchase it. She said that we needed to "let go of our attachment" to the place and pray, and that she would help us.

We were not sure how to let go of the attachment. We went through a whole process of learning how to "let go" on one level, the ego level, and yet maintain our vision on a deeper level, the spiritual level. That pesky ego level got tested over and over again. Every week we heard about different people who were looking at "our" property and who wanted to use it for different purposes. One was a wealthy doctor who wanted to tear down the buildings and construct a very modern home. Another was a group who wanted it as a retreat center. Each time we heard one of these stories, we had to "let go" and say to ourselves, "Well, if we are supposed to be there, we will. Let God's will be done."

One day we got a call from the seventy-year-old woman who owned the property. She said that she and her children would like to meet with us up at the property. We were excited and nervous at the same time since we had no idea what to expect. We all sat around the dining room table and she told us that they had several offers from folks who could pay the full price, some in cash! We were holding our breath by that time and just looking at her. But then she went on to tell us that those people had wanted to do something that wasn't in line with her family's spiritual vision for the property. She said they had heard about our Wellness Institute and they would feel much more spiritually in alignment with the type of work that we do. They wanted their place to continue on as a spiritual healing center where people would come to learn, heal, meditate and grow personally.

As she spoke, I began to feel a very strong spiritual presence in the house and I slowly began to get the lesson about letting go on the ego level to open up to God's will. It was all happening in that moment, but there were no words to describe it. The woman made us an offer that we could afford and we were able to work out an agreement that worked for all of us. We knew that this was a miracle, since it is quite unusual for anyone to sell prime real estate for less than the market value just to preserve the integrity of the land and their vision for its best use. It was quite mind boggling to know that we had attracted someone like Louise, who was listening to her inner voice and her spiritual guides. At that moment, I saw that Louise and I had been connected in many other lifetimes and our souls recognized each other.

We were incredibly grateful for the gift brought to us by the Divine Mother and the Universe. This is often referred to as Divine Intervention.

As I write this story, I am amazed to truly understand how manifestation and attraction work. The most important thing is to be very clear about what we want and to hold on to our dreams even when they seem impossible. There are so many possibilities in life, most of which we are unable to fathom with our conscious minds. Here again it is vital that we learn to "let go" on the ego level, the conscious level, and yet maintain our vision on the deeper spiritual level, the unconscious intuitive level. This is another subtle reminder of the "I body no" lesson.

Past Lives Return

We moved onto the new property and began planning our first Heart-Centered training at our new place. We were so excited to be able to have our class in this beautiful, mountain-forest location with a magical, salmon-spawning stream running through it. A few days before the first training, I was playing and planting in my new garden. As I stood out there and surveyed the property, I began having a substantial déjà vu experience. I felt as though I had lived on this land before and that it was all completely familiar to me. This feeling gave way to actual visions, where I saw myself as a Native American there — a medicine man. Suddenly all the buildings and fences disappeared. I saw many people coming on foot and horseback from all over to receive medicine and healing from me. I used the natural herbs that are plentiful in these mountains as well as other healing methods. In our garden, we grew many of the healing herbs to make teas for various illnesses. We often danced and did drumming circles. My soul was completely connected through the drums which seemed to be a way of sending messages to other tribes as well as to Mother earth. We also went on long canoe trips up and down the coast to visit other villages in the summer. When it was time for me to die, I was very old and was buried on this land down by the creek. I went down there to sit in the forest by three majestic cedar trees when I knew my time had come. It was very peaceful and I felt like my soul remained here after my body was long gone. I saw that I had been buried in a sacred space next to the creek under one of the cedar trees.

A few days later, we began our first training on that land. One of the women in the class turned out to be a Native American who felt very connected with the location. She asked if her husband, who was a medicine man, could come and bless the land for us. We agreed to have him come. As I was still teaching the class, the medicine man arrived and David walked him around the ten acre property. The medicine man offered blessings and put feathers around in the four directions. David told him nothing about my past life experience.

After a time, the medicine man said that he was picking up some "spirits" down by the creek. They were telling him that a highly revered medicine man had lived on this property long ago, that people from all around these parts would gather here for ceremonies and healing, and that this land had always been used for healing, ceremonies, and communal gatherings. David was amazed and couldn't wait for the class to be over so he could tell me what "the spirits" had said. He still did not tell the medicine man about my déjà vu or visions that completely coincided with what he had picked up.

It was around this time that the curriculum for our very first Internship program came to me to teach. Several of my students had said that they wanted to learn more, so these requests gave birth to the Internship Advanced Training Course. During this program, I felt drawn to Native American music and drumming, but I really knew very little about it. I played some tapes and we all tried to drum and sing with it the best we could. I remember feeling very connected as we chanted around the fire with the music. I wanted to learn more, and so did several of my students.

One day I received correspondence in the mail from one of my first healing teachers. His name was Brough Joy and he had a healing/retreat center outside of Sedona, Arizona. He asked if I ever worked with groups and whether we'd be interested in visiting there. In meditation, it came to me that this was an important reconnection and that we needed to go to Brough's place. I scheduled one of our Internship advanced training meetings there.

In Sedona, we found a Native American guide to take us around and show us the power vortexes that are so prevalent in Sedona. It was a beautiful sunny day and we were feeling very happy as we began to climb up to one of the vortexes called Bell Rock. I remember looking out over the whole valley and suddenly was overcome with grief. I began weeping and couldn't stop for quite a while. Our guide left me alone until I felt better and approached him. I told him of the vision I had of many people being massacred and that somehow I felt I had been there. What came to me was that I had been a tribal elder and that hundreds in my tribe had been massacred and there was nothing I could do. I felt that

I had then taken my own life there in despair, with the intention to be reunited with my people.

The Native guide then shared with us that this was the exact spot where there actually had been a great battle and that most of the tribal people had been killed. He said that I was "picking up" on the many grieving spirits that continue to inhabit the land, especially in this area. I knew deep in my soul that this was an important connection for David and me to make and that coming to Sedona was the right thing to do.

That whole week was spent exploring the energy vortexes around Sedona and the ancient caves that contained hieroglyphs or pictures of the prehistoric Anasazi, ancestors of modern Pueblo Indians. The pictures were clearly of animals, tools, and symbols important to their communication. As I stood there, many more past life memories came flooding in. I felt more and more connected to the land and the ancient people in this area, and the experience helped to explain why I had always been fascinated by caves and have always loved to explore them.

Learning the Sweat Lodge Ceremony

In the last chapter, I talked about our sweat lodge ceremonies, and it was there in Sedona that we first learned all about them. When we met at the retreat center in Sedona, magical things happened in our group. It was amazing. One of them was that they asked us if we wanted to do a traditional Native American sweat lodge. I told them that we did, even though we knew little about it. The Native, named Daniel, taught us that the sweat lodge was a sacred ceremony for the Native Americans and that he was willing to share it with us. We all put on shorts or bathing suits, brought towels, and left our shoes and jewelry outside. We entered into a small, igloo-shaped structure that had been built with bent tree branches and blankets thrown over for the walls.

In the center of the sweat lodge was an open pit, and outside there was a big fire for heating up rocks. We all filed into the lodge and sat close together, gathered around the pit in a double file circle. Daniel told us that this represented the womb of the Mother and that we would be reborn. We watched as his helper, the rock man, brought in the rocks on a pitch fork, one by one. As each rock was brought in, we began to feel warmer and warmer. But that was nothing compared to what we felt when Daniel closed the "door" of the lodge and began pouring water on the hot rocks. Hot steam filled the lodge and nearly took my breath away. Daniel then took out his drum and sang a native chant. I was totally blown away. His voice, the words, and all of us being in there together became a powerful and moving experience for me. It brought back so much, especially the sacredness of the sweat lodge ceremony.

After the beginning songs, Daniel taught us how to pray. We each had a turn to say our deepest and most private prayers in the dark and yet be "witnessed" by all the others present. I had many past life experiences as we sat there. The songs and the experience were familiar to me, and I felt like I had "come home." I found myself longing to drum with Daniel. I asked permission to do so and he gave it. A drum was passed around the circle to me and I began to sing and drum along with Daniel. Even though the songs were in a Native language that I had never heard before in this lifetime, I found that they just rolled off my tongue. The words did not pass through my mind, but just seemed to be coming from a deeper place inside me. I felt a powerful sense of fulfillment and connection as I sang with Daniel. The music, and especially the drumming, touched a deep level of my soul.

In the sweat lodge, there were four "rounds." Each round was dedicated to a different purpose. At the completion of each round, we were given the opportunity to get out if we felt too hot or needed to stretch. Several people got out for that purpose. I felt compelled to stay in and often was the only woman in there between the rounds. In the lodge that day, however, I did not experience being a woman but rather a warrior. As I drummed and sang, my life as a warrior became clear to me. I knew that I had to be strong for the younger ones to set the example. I knew that I was their "elder," which also meant I was their teacher in the past life, just as I was in this life.

This experience in the lodge was the beginning for all of us in discovering our ancient roots. The Native American rituals of drumming, singing, and praying together became an integral part of our community throughout the years to come. We attracted many different shamans, medicine people, and indigenous people to teach us and remind us of our history together.

It had been our custom to always sit in a circle on the floor in low seats called "backjacks" for the Internship Advanced Training Program. Sitting in the circle and "sharing" was actually another Native custom where they would pass the "talking stick" to each person whose turn it was to share their feelings or thoughts. We always passed a small wireless microphone to amplify voices. I realized that this microphone was our modern re-creation of passing the talking stick.

Community

There are so many types of relationships in our lives. As children, our relationships with our parents are especially powerful, but as adults, we often look for a "significant other." This is where we can spend years, or lifetimes, playing games as I talked about earlier. Or, this is where we can mutually support one another's spiritual goals and walk a magnificent path together, as David and I have been fortunate to do.

But our friends and extended families have a lot of influence on us as well. As we're growing up, we have less choice about who is in our lives (though we no doubt chose them prior to incarnation), and I've talked a great deal already about the impact parents can have, for instance, on children as they grow up. The older we get, though, the more we choose our personal groups and communities. The people in these groups continue influencing the growth patterns of our lives, which is why choosing any kind of relationship is a choice we shouldn't take lightly.

Poor choices can lead us into places we really wish we'd never gone. On the other hand, gathering supportive people into your life can lead to a healthy, interdependent growth pattern for everyone involved, the way it did in the case of our Internship group. I've included this chapter at the end of the book because relationships don't impact just one stage of our development, but every stage.

There are two ways that groups can hinder our transformation, but many ways in which they can expedite it. The first hindrance comes from the fact that transformative experience can be group-dependent, what Carl Jung called the collective experience of transformation. Unfortunately, this transformation is temporary and conditional, limited by being created and experienced within the group. It takes place on a lower level of consciousness than an individual experience because the collective psyche of the group sinks to mob psychology. The group experience is easier to achieve, because many people united and identified with each other, sharing a common emotional experience, exert great suggestive force. The individual becomes dependent on the group for creating the experience, rather than developing the personal capability of autonomously experiencing it.[127]

The second hindrance is the support we may receive *not* to change. The process of transformation often results in estrangement from those who have been our companions in ordinary life. As we develop new insights, new interests, and new life scripts and goals, those in our companionship circle who haven't changed in a similar way are no longer able to effectively support us. Seeing that can be frightening for them when they feel that they are losing us, or that the life they're "comfortable" with (no matter how uncomfortable it might really be) will change in some way. As a result, they may even try to sabotage our growth in new directions, trying to draw us back to our old ways. This is especially common with relationships that have involved addictions or other behaviors designed to keep us numb and asleep. There may be no more effective support (not healthy, not desirable, but powerfully effective) than an addict encouraging a fellow addict to "use."

Despite the possible hindrances, we always have the opportunity to gather a *healthy community* around us, a network of new companions and like-minded friends who are supportive of our newly expanded perspectives. This is a community of seekers on the same path who value consciousness over unconsciousness. After spending time with people who share their souls on the deepest levels, it is difficult to go back to superficial cocktail parties and idle chit-chat. It becomes boring to spend time with people who are not honest about their feelings and are still highly involved in feeding their hungry egos.

Such a community is what Abraham Maslow called a *eupsychian* environment, one that maximizes healthy psychological growth. "Socially, this means sharing the company of people who value transpersonal growth, who undertake practices to foster it, and who provide an atmosphere of interpersonal safety that allows for defenselessness and experimentation".[128] What this group can best provide to a transforming individual is "a courage, a bearing, and a dignity which may easily get lost in isolation".[129]

According to Jung, the process of individuation "brings to birth a consciousness of human community precisely because it makes us aware of the unconscious, which unites and is common to all mankind".[130] It is the final step in transformed consciousness: serving the suffering humanity with compassion. Joseph Campbell spoke of this final phase as "the hero's return."

> The transition from the state of consciousness where we feel trapped or entangled in a net, to the state of consciousness where we are consciously and intentionally participating in a network, is one aspect of the process of liberation through transformation. The question is ... how can the limiting net be changed into a liberating network?[131]

One of the great gifts of discovering the work of Heart-Centered therapies is that we have learned how to create and maintain a healthy, supportive community. We also learned the Clearing Process from Elaine Childs-Gowell, a Transactional analyst in Seattle. It is a technique that assists each person in an interaction to own his or her own projections. We have learned over twenty-five years of working with professionals that they very often do not have a safe, confidential community in which they can do their own personal growth work. But more than that, we have seen over the years the importance of healing within relationships. That applies to sessions with a therapist as well as every other relationship. And if the therapist hasn't done his own consciousness work, he will have too much counter-transference to really help the client. Most therapists have really not healed their own codependency, raising the magnitude of necessity for this work, as each therapist touches the lives of so many others in need.

Considering, then, the importance of relationships, we'll take a look at some of the relationships we all have, including those that are healthy as well as those that are unhealthy.

Relationships with Spouse/Partner/Children/Family Members

These intimate relationships offer opportunities to uncover deeply hidden wounds, and also to heal those wounds. One area of concern is power struggles or control issues (usually related to the 2nd & 3rd chakras). The developmental stage most commonly triggered with control issues is security, the 18-36 month-old child. Sometimes a family member who is insisting that you submit to his demands is quite literally reenacting his "terrible twos." These struggles can be played out in the realms of money (1st chakra — fear of not having enough), sex (2nd chakra — shame/abuse), or time (1st chakra — again, fear of not having enough).

Birth trauma may also play a role in control issues in relationships, and we refer to these as authority issues (usually related to the 1st & 3rd chakras). For example, people who had a forceps delivery may resent being told what to do. Those who had an anesthetic birth often find it difficult to assert themselves in times of high stress. If abortion was discussed or considered by the mother, there may well be huge mistrust and anger at authorities. Twins often grow up with difficulty having equality in relationships.

Worthiness/unworthiness is another common theme, like control. The developmental stage usually triggered here is that from birth to 6 months (survival) and 18-36 months (security). Examples of how birth issues can influence later relationships include: never feeling good enough (the birth issue of being unwanted or the "wrong" sex), never feeling that you belong, or putting others down to make yourself feel better.

Intimacy issues are another basic area of relationship conflict. The developmental stage triggered here is usually birth to 6 months, where survival depends on the caregiver's ability to bond. Inadequate caregiver bonding results in the experience that one's survival is threatened, and can show up later in life as an overpowering fear of abandonment, or an inability to trust, or a tendency to abandon others physically or emotionally. This can also be created by a premature birth that requires placing the baby in an incubator or isolette. Another intimacy issue is feeling suffocated in relationships and needing to keep distance, or excessive "personal space." This may be caused by a birth trauma of being stuck in the birth canal, or having a delayed birth such as when the doctor is not available and the mother is told to "keep your legs together until he gets here."

We have already become very familiar with the victim / rescuer / persecutor patterns in relationships, often resulting from conflict in the 18-36 month developmental stage. The victim pattern usually is focused in the 2nd chakra, exhibited as powerlessness, manipulation, getting approval through pity, and control through helplessness. The rescuer pattern concentrates in the 3rd chakra, exhibited as taking power through caretaking and getting approval through meeting everyone else's needs. The persecutor pattern is also focused in the 3rd chakra, where power is captured through abuse and manipulation.

Another center of relationship unease is sexuality / shame / passion, usually resulting from inadequate completion of the 6-18 month developmental stage of exploration and nurturance. An individual who grows up to be sexually inhibited has probably experienced shame and fear regarding passion and aliveness, repressing the 2nd chakra energy. Someone who acts out sexually or is sexually compulsive also likely experienced fear and shame in the context of abuse, identifying with the powerful abuser and having uncontained activation of the 2nd chakra energy.

Integrity issues underlie many relationship problems, originating in the18-36 months developmental stage of security and separation. When people feel powerless, they tend to not tell the truth as much and to not ask directly for what they want. Manipulation puts people out of integrity, especially in relationships. Lack of personal power, a blockage in the flow of 3rd chakra energy, usually leads to manipulation and need for approval.

Commitment is, of course, a common relationship issue. Fear of commitment is usually caused by an early and deep-seated fear of abandonment or fear of annihilation, going back to the developmental stage of conception to 6 months and a mistrust of parents or caregivers. Their love may have been unpredictable or conditional, or they may have considered abortion or giving the baby up for adoption, leading to difficulty for the individual in trusting relationships later in life.

The Body

Of course our relationships with our parents, partners, friends, and family are not our only relationships. How we relate with anything in this world constitutes a relationship that is important to us in the moment and in our growth.

For instance, as mental/emotional beings, we have a relationship with our bodies. As with any relationship, this one can be healthy or unhealthy. The relationship would be unhealthy, of course, if you failed to maintain the body with adequate food, exercise, and sleep, or if you failed to practice preventive health by seeing the dentist and perhaps the doctor on a regular basis. And this may in fact tell you about other relationship issues; for example, you might actually *make* such choices because you were abandoned emotionally or physically at an early age and thus grow up abandoning yourself.

Likewise, you might associate so highly with your body that you feel about your inner self the way you feel about your body. The body, of course, is simply a means of expression for who you really are, but that doesn't mean everyone makes the distinction. We look in the mirror and we see too fat or too thin, too many pimples or wrinkles, or just plain ugly, even though there are millions of other people with these same issues. It's not that these are inherently negative looks, but that our response to these things speaks about our lack of confidence or lack of support others have shown us.

Some people will take care of others to the point of neglecting their own bodies (and other personal needs) and become physically, emotionally, and/or mentally ill. Some wound their bodies, others starve their bodies or overfeed them. Some become addicted to substances. And others, of course, have positive relationships with their bodies, feeding and caring for them well. In each case, we are not just seeing a relationship with the body, but all of that person's relationships manifesting in the physical form. These relationships can stem from past sexual abuse, childhood abandonment, fear of one's parents, and so on … right on up to more ideal experiences, such as receiving encouragement and love from others.

Life's Work, or Calling

Another important relationship one has is with his work. Observing this relationship — in ourselves or in others — can give us a big clue about how one views the world. Do they owe something to the world, to others, to their children? Does the world owe them? Do they owe from a sense of obligation, or from a place of gratitude and happiness to share and serve?

Often, if someone believes the world owes him, or if someone works only because he must, and he only brings resentment into his job, we can look once more to his past experiences — either in this life or another — in which these attitudes were instilled in him. At the same time, the more someone rises above his past circumstances and begins to take a delight in serving others with passion and creativity — regardless of his career — the more we see someone connecting with his soul.

Of course there are many grades of these distinctions. Many people go to work only because they expect something in return. We call this service. Some work completely from the heart, expecting nothing in return. We call this *seva*. Most people fall between the two extremes, experiencing various benefits from their work — such as a sense of accomplishment or recognition from others — and experiencing moments of honest bliss when they see that they have helped someone else. In fact, some will experience outright transcendence or unity when serving another, finding that the actor (oneself), the act, and the recipient are all One in God. We call this *Karma Yoga*.

Some will take delight in serving others regardless of their careers while some will follow their passion into work that they were "born to do." Both are positive pathways on the road to enlightenment. We call the first of these "right livelihood," in which you realize that any job can become a spiritual practice when the ego is removed. The more one becomes in touch with the soul, however, the more often a pathway will open up allowing one to do the thing he's passionate about. In doing so, he finds that money comes as money is needed. But to reach this path, it's important to stay open to the signals we're sent by the soul about the choices we need to make.

Of course all of this really underscores the difference between a job, a career, and life's work. A job is something you do every day mostly to earn money. You often wonder what you're doing there and may feel bored, restless, and increasingly unhappy. A career is daily work that moves you toward a goal and feels more meaningful than a job. It also makes use of your skills and education, and allows you to continue building both. The money you earn seems to be an important part of it, though, and you seem to need raises in order to continue feeling successful.

Life's work, however, is what the soul is trying to accomplish through each incarnation, and the more we connect with the soul, the more we can reach that goal. This kind of work is spiritually, emotionally, and mentally fulfilling. Each day, you look forward to this kind of work. You feel challenged, excited, and stimulated by what you're doing. It is wonderful if you can earn money doing your life's work, but you would continue to do it even if you didn't have the need to earn money. It is activity that excites and delights you.

Money / Abundance

Another relationship that's core to many people is money ... or the apparent lack of it. Again, this relationship shows us a great deal about people and where they are in terms of personal growth. For instance, one who doesn't feel worthy of having money on some level may need to develop the 1st and 4th chakras, while those who have poor integrity around money (perhaps failing to pay bills or cheating on taxes) may need to develop the 3rd chakra.

We spoke about the developmental stages of life throughout this book, and people's relationships with money can help us to see what stages they may be stuck in, giving us some direction in how to work them through their issues. Those who were physically or emotionally abandoned in the first six months of life, for instance, may fear that there will never be enough and their needs won't be met. This feeling covers not only money but all material possessions and becomes a belief in lack or scarcity.

There can be several birth issues surrounding money as well, for those who never overcame these traumas. We summarize them in the following way:

- **Caesarian births take the easy way out.** This trauma leads to those who aren't very good at overcoming obstacles. They often expect to be rescued. This generalizes to having difficulty being assertive in asking or in pursuing material goals.
- **Anesthetic births often feel powerless.** Anesthesia of course inhibits a baby from having any power in the birth process, and this translates into those who feel powerless about finding jobs, making money, or achieving their goals.
- **Forceps delivery often causes rebellion to authority.** And since those with money are often in authority positions, this type of

delivery trauma can lead to those who rebel against those with money. This can create power struggles between those who have and those who want. The forceps adult, however, may just give up in anger and resentment.

- **Breech birth people often struggle and create obstacles that don't even need to be there.** They make earning and receiving money much harder than it needs to be. Breech birth people also feel guilty and take on responsibility for other people's pain. So financially, they tend to rescue others and give away what they do have and end up resenting it.
- **Inhibited births, from being stuck in the birth canal, often lead to those who feel "stuck"** in business, their careers, and their earnings. They don't seem to know how to move forward in their lives.
- **Those whose parents considered aborting them often feel hopeless about life** in general and powerless about having anything more than bare subsistence. Underneath they don't feel they deserve to thrive or even to be alive.
- **People who were born the "wrong sex" usually feel hopelessly inadequate and are always trying to prove themselves.** As a result, they usually become work-a-holics. Although they work very hard, they never seem to have enough.
- **"Un-affordables" — or those whose parents feared they couldn't afford them — often incorporate money fears.** They tend to think that they cannot afford things in life. They may settle into "Depression thinking."
- **Births involving the risk of death can lead to those who hold themselves back.** Whether the risk was for the mother, the child, or both, the child may grow up holding back so as not to be the "cause of death" in any situation, including those involving career and money.

God and Spirituality

In terms of soul-based work in therapy, one of the most important relationships we can look at is a person's relationship with God and spirituality in general.

There is nothing like a brush with death — your own or that of someone close to you — to focus the mind on God, the afterlife, and spirituality. This also applies on a deeply unconscious level to experiences of separation from the familiar, from loved ones, or from support. An individual who tends to feel abandonment in such situations usually feels, unconsciously, separated from God. And feeling abandoned by God leads to great fear and also immense anger. These forbidden emotions usually only surface to conscious awareness, where they can be expressed and released, in an altered therapeutic state. And developing the capacity for healthy separation and completion in our relationships is vital to healthy spirituality and, of course, to approaching death with serenity.

The areas of conflict in relationships in general apply to our relationship with God as well. While seldom acknowledged, power struggles and authority issues are common, since God is the ultimate authority ("Why did you make this happen in my life?" or "You can't force me to love those bastard parents of mine"). Unworthiness ("sinful") and the resulting shame are likely to be triggered, and forgiveness can only be accepted to the extent that one feels intimacy and security about not being abandoned.

Integrity issues underlie our spiritual relationships, too. When people feel powerless, they tend to not tell the truth as much and to try to bargain and manipulate to get their needs met ("God, if you will just get me out of this predicament, I promise it will never happen again").

Commitment and fear of commitment is a hallmark of any spiritual journey, and can be observed in people's devotion to their daily practices, such as prayer, meditation, mindfulness, ceremonies, confession, or sacred activities. Commitment, or faith, also is the basis for trusting God ("becoming as a child"), and letting go of control ("Not my will but Thine be done").

The aspect of healing that we designate as "soul retrieval" is itself preparation for a deeper spiritual connection and the step of assuming the mantle of Child of God.

Healing through Relationships

The first step in healing through relationships is understanding their true purpose. Many people believe that each relationship — whether with a person, our bodies, money, work, God, etc. — is about meeting their emotional needs, and they get frustrated when this doesn't happen. In these cases, they're failing to grasp why the relationship exists in the first place.

Keep in mind that, during the interlife process, we choose for ourselves the relationships that can come into our life. Not all of these relationships will manifest, because we have free will, and through our choices, we may outgrow the purpose of a potential relationship. In that case, we may end up never choosing the circumstances that would bring the relationship into being. In other words, we create for ourselves both a carrot and a stick as motivations to grow. The pain of unhealthy choices is the stick, and that stick gets bigger and more painful if we ignore the initial lessons. Some of us have experienced the stick becoming a two-by-four that we could no longer ignore. Fortunately, there is always the carrot out in front of us, the healthy choice, waiting to be taken.

Someone's soul may choose several potential relationships with other people that will almost certainly set up the problems of codependence. If this person learns the soul lessons inherent in this kind of relationship, however, and learns how to become a strong, independent individual pursuing his soul purpose, then he may turn to a different set of potential relationships that the soul *also* put in place — those that could manifest once he learned this lesson. In this case, his choices take him away from encounters with additional codependent relationships, and into healthier, interdependent relationships. For some, their second marriage (or workplace or place of worship) is everything positive that their first wasn't; for others, subsequent marriages are duplications of the first, repeating the same mistake over and over again.

As another example, a person's soul may choose a family situation where abundance is a problem, and may complicate the problem by going through a birth where the mother chooses to use anesthesia. In this case, the person born may feel powerless in terms of attracting wealth, and this may be an ongoing issue for years. He may feel frustrated about this lack of money and keep wishing for more money to get by, never considering the lessons inherent in the situation. Once he *does* recognize and address the lessons the soul wanted to learn, however, then these issues with money no longer have a *purpose* for the soul, and money can begin to flow.

In other words, the relationships we find ourselves in aren't accidental, and they aren't there to simply make us happy ... or miserable. We get frustrated with them because we think they *are* supposed to make us happy, and this just makes the problem worse because — all too often — we end up blaming our partners, our families, our jobs, money, God, etc. for our problems. In the end, though, each of these relationships is in place to help us grow toward the Light and to realize who we really are as souls. That's why we call the challenges of relationships "Gifts of Adversity." Approval, security, material possessions, status, power, and other earthly desires are illusions that keep us from finding God and achieving our purpose. These are illusions that need to fall away through our growth in relationships.

The value of relationships is that they act so well as a mirror, showing us what it is that needs to change in *us*, and not in the other parties involved. As a result, we often attract people into our lives who encourage our shadow side — what we said we'd never become — either bringing us to act it out or to confront and overcome it.

For example, if some past trauma — from this life or another — has created a tendency to distrust others, you're likely to draw people into your life people who are worthy of not being trusted, those who will betray you. Not until you start reflecting on life and looking at it in new ways can you break from that pattern.

Likewise, those who feel they are unworthy are likely to attract those who will criticize them. Those who fear intimacy will attract those who reject or abandon them. Those who feel powerless will attract others who rescue or persecute them. In each case, a shift needs to take place to break the pattern. And of course when these issues stem from the past and are lodged in the unconscious, it can take a process like Heart-Centered Hypnotherapy to take someone back to the core events and recreate them within the person, *allowing* them to reframe their perspective, their feelings, and their visceral responses to the issue.

Whether the changed perspective comes from Heart-Centered therapies or other forms of reflection on the situation, that new perspective can often help us to see others in a new light. We can perhaps better understand *why* someone treated us in some way, and while we may not condone what happened, we can at last forgive. And forgiveness heals. It cleanses our own energy field (aura), and it releases karmic bonds that have connected us with another person. When this happens, we are free to create new, karma-free relationships with them if they are still with us; or we may move on in our lives without simply running from our problems.

When we understand that relationships are here for our growth rather than for our happiness (even if many *do* bring us happiness), then rather than becoming frustrated with some of them, we can begin to look for their purpose in our lives. And they're always ready to yield us clues. For instance, family themes help us see what we're here to heal. These themes can include:

- Addictions
- Suicide, depression, self-destructiveness
- Power struggles

- Violence
- Grief, loss
- Maintaining an image at the expense of authenticity
- Abandonment, either physical or emotional
- Abuse, either physical, sexual, or emotional
- Codependence
- Fear, anxiety, phobias
- Bankruptcy, cheating, dishonesty

In any type of relationship, the bottom line to remember is that it's in our life to help us gain experience, knowledge, and wisdom and to create the necessary pressure to encourage personal transformation. When we remember that, then the healing can begin.

Now there are three important things to recognize about the healing process: first, that healing comes in stages. We do not become unwell overnight, so we shouldn't expect to become whole overnight either. The healing of one relationship may simply be the key to exploring and healing others, or to seeing a pattern among several relationships that guides us to see the deeper, underlying issue at hand. As each layer is peeled back, we are freer than before, and more able to hear the whispers of our souls and to come a little closer to following that still, small voice within.

That brings us to the second truth about healing: that it is never just about physical or even about emotional healing. It is about healing the entire individual and connecting a person with his soul. In fact, many instances of healing are little more than changes in consciousness, because healing need not always imply a correction of the physical body. Sometimes the body is too far gone, or too far damaged, for a full recuperation, or even any recuperation at all. But the body is here for a short time only, no matter how long we live; to the soul, a single incarnation passes quickly, and the hope in that time is that consciousness will expand.

And that brings us to the last point about healing: since healing is really about expanding consciousness, the whole process becomes more beautiful still. Because as any person's consciousness expands, he more potently affects everyone else on the planet, and encourages their healing as well. We are all linked in this way, so that the steps we take to heal ourselves and those around us are steps taken to heal the pain felt throughout the world. And in the end, that is what we're all really here to do.

Chapter 10
Relationship Issues Questionnaire

[Give each statement any number from 0-5: 0 for never true, 1 for rarely, 2 occasionally, 3 sometimes, 4 usually, and 5 for almost always true.]

1. ____ I find myself in power struggles with the people closest to me.
2. ____ I find myself in power struggles with authority figures such as policemen, the IRS, teachers, priests, ministers, or rabbis.
3. ____ I notice that I find myself arguing with others about money.
4. ____ I notice that I argue about sex (when, where and how to have it or not have it.)
5. ____ I realize that I enjoy being in control of people and situations.
6. ____ I feel powerless in my relationships with others.
7. ____ In my relationships I enjoy being "one-up."
8. ____ I can clearly see the faults in others.
9. ____ I am aware that I compare myself to others and I come out on the short end.
10. ____ No matter how prepared I am for something, I feel like I should have done better.
11. ____ I strive to be accepted by others, but I don't feel that I am.
12. ____ I know if I could just do better, certain people would like me a lot more.
13. ____ If I could just keep my weight down, I know people would like me more.
14. ____ I get upset when my spouse, children, or friends are later than they said they'd be.
15. ____ It's easy to cut off a relationship, especially if I think the other person rejected me.
16. ____ I find that other people reject me, especially in personal relationships.
17. ____ I am smart enough to know that you really can't trust what other people tell you.
18. ____ I know that others don't usually do what they say they will do.
19. ____ Other people are so needy that it is difficult to be in relationships with them.
20. ____ I feel sorry for others and try to help them as much as I can.
21. ____ I don't like to hurt people's feelings, so I often don't tell them how I really feel.
22. ____ I help people so much that I have little time left for myself.

23. _____ It makes me feel good to take care of other people's needs.
24. _____ I don't understand why the people I help the most are often the meanest to me.
25. _____ I have so many of my own problems; I am unable to help anyone else.
26. _____ Bad things seem to happen to me.
27. _____ I have lost my temper and physically hit someone else.
28. _____ I have the ability to say very cruel things to others, and sometimes I do.
29. _____ I don't get angry, I get even.
30. _____ When I'm angry, I get very quiet.
31. _____ I know how to get my way in situations and I usually do.
32. _____ I don't enjoy sex and would rather not have to do it.
33. _____ I don't seem to have any passion.
34. _____ I have a very active sex life, but I don't really enjoy it that much.
35. _____ I am scared of the opposite sex.
36. _____ After having a sexual encounter, I feel empty or lonely
37. _____ I am embarrassed about my body and would rather that no one would see me.
38. _____ People get angry with me when I don't do what I said I would do.
39. _____ I have been accused of lying by others.
40. _____ Sometimes I cheat on my taxes.
41. _____ I feel that the government doesn't deserve to have my hard-earned taxes.
42. _____ When I commit to one thing, it usually means missing out on something else.
43. _____ I prefer to have several men/women partners but not get too close to any of them.
44. _____ Commitment means loss of choices, so I prefer not to commit.
45. _____ I often feel smothered in relationships.
46. _____ I react strongly to rules and regulations.
47. _____ I've found that in life you just can't trust most people.
48. _____ It's hard for me to ask for what I want in relationships.
49. _____ I hate when people try to tell me what to do.
50. _____ My spouse or significant relationship always puts me down verbally.

51. I just never seem to have enough (0 to 5 for each of these that apply to you):

    _____ time

    _____ money

    _____ sex

    _____ love

52. My most frequent arguments with my spouse/partner are about (0 to 5 for each of these that apply):

    _____ time

    _____ money

    _____ sex

53. My most frequent arguments with bosses, teachers, or co-workers are about (0-5 for each that apply):

    _____ time

    _____ money

    _____ recognition

54. My most frequent arguments with my children and/or parents are about (0-5 for each that apply):

    _____ time

    _____ money

    _____ recognition

Chapter 10
Conscious Communication Questionnaire

Principles of Conscious Communication in Conscious Community

The purpose of conscious communication is to promote healthy community and to reduce gossip, unconscious chatter and destructive family patterns of triangulation. Check those items that apply.

✔
- ❏ A. I have shame about and try to keep certain aspects of my life hidden:
  - ❏ 1. Abuse
  - ❏ 2. Addictions
  - ❏ 3. Cheating or lies
  - ❏ 4. Sexual practices

- ❏ B. I gossip:
  - ❏ 1. I share with others the experiences of a third person who is not present.
  - ❏ 2. I talk about others in destructive or judgmental ways.
  - ❏ 3. I assume or speculate about a person instead of asking directly for clarification
  - ❏ 4. I indulge unconscious chatter to avoid feelings or fill empty space in a relationship
  - ❏ 5. I often find silence with others unbearable.

- ❏ C. I listen to gossip:
  - ❏ 1. I am often not very discriminating in what I listen to when others are speaking.
  - ❏ 2. I often am "triangulated" or caught in the middle between two people.
  - ❏ 3. I could never say, "I am uncomfortable hearing what you are sharing. Please stop."

Check any of the healthy communication patterns that you utilize or commit to begin using:
- ❏ Ask yourself, "Is my intention to shame, embarrass or make the other person wrong?"
- ❏ If someone is gossiping, direct them to speak directly with the person being spoken about.

❏ Ask yourself, "Is my intention to evoke sympathy (a victim ploy) for my own point of view?"

❏ Tolerate, or even appreciate, periods of silence when I am with others.

❏ Ask yourself, "Is my intention to gossip, triangulate or gather evidence about someone else?"

❏ Focus on talk about the present moment rather than talking about the past or the future.

❏ Allow yourself to reserve certain information about yourself or your relationships as private without any shame motivation.

❏ Honor a person's request when they state clearly that they want something to remain private.

❏ To keep confidentiality when there is a moral obligation not to disclose information you know.

❏ If you are not sure whether you can share something, ask the person who is the source.

❏ Other

_____

❏ Other

_____

Your Project: Select three behaviors from the list above to commit to honoring, the three that will be the most difficult to stick to. Ask your friends for support in following through on your commitment.

1. _____

_____

2. _____

_____

3. _____

_____

Epilogue
The Never-ending Pilgrimage:
Pulling the Threads Together

The Garden

I have been wondering why I have been procrastinating on the completion of this book. Today I began to see that the reason is that my life is not over and so it is difficult to put the final lessons in here. However, today is Easter Sunday and I spent the day playing in my garden and learning from Nature. My plants teach me many lessons for which I am ever grateful. So I am now going to share those with you, the readers, and that will have to do for now.

One time one of my great Gurus, Karunamayi, came to our home to do a spiritual retreat. She took my hand and lead me out to my garden which was filled with six-foot tall Dahlias. Amma motioned for us to sit down in the middle of the garden. As we looked up, it felt like we were in a forest of flowers, surrounded by beauty and the smells of Nature. Her teaching to me that day was that all the lessons we need are in Nature and we must continue to be open to being a student so that we may continue to learn these lessons. It was a magical time with her there which I have never forgotten.

Today as I was experiencing Nature and the Holiness of Easter, it felt like Spirit had many messages for me. I have these beautiful Phlox plants in my garden which have been there for years. They are very dependable and I can always count on them to return. Just like night follows day, spring follows winter, and when spring begins the phlox come back. But last year for the first time they had a disease, some kind of a fungus that was very difficult to get rid of. They were the only plants to have this fungus. So I sat before them today and asked them what they needed and why they had been so unhealthy last year. The message I received was that they were "root bound," that they felt extremely confined and held back from expanding. The message was that they couldn't grow as strong as they were truly capable of and this holding back caused their usually disease-resistant nature to be thwarted. WOW! That was a profound message and certainly applicable to life in many ways.

I thought of so many of our students over the years who had come to our Institute for exactly that reason; they needed to grow, to expand and to release the chains that were binding them. So, what was holding back these plants? Then I realized that I had put a weed protector over the garden, many years ago so that I could plant the flowers in little holes and never have to weed. Now I realized that their protection was actually choking them! Another interesting idea is how many times do we try to keep ourselves safe from outside interference only to discover that we are being driven by fears that actually stifle our own growth? This was one of the lessons being taught by these plants.

I also realized that I had taken these beautiful plants for granted and never given them the time or attention I give to my other, more delicate plants. This is very similar to what happens in families where the good child often doesn't get his/her needs met because the parents are too busy taking care of the child with problems. So I sat down with each one of the developing phlox plants and asked what was needed. They let me know that they needed the weed cloth to be cut so that their roots had more room to expand and grow. I began noticing that in certain places, the Phlox liked to send up new shoots so that each year it could be bigger and produce more fragrant flowers. Then the message was clear that they needed some new rich organic soil with just a bit of fertilizer. As I engaged in this process, I felt so connected with Spirit, with myself and with Mother Earth. The Divine Mother, Amma, as we call her, was here inside and all around. This is the feeling of Oneness that everyone longs for and reaches occasionally. The sun was shinning inside and out. The birds were singing and so was my heart. My dogs were playing quietly with a stick and it became quite clear to me at this moment, that this is fulfillment. This garden is truly the Garden of Eden.

Many people, as we've spoken about previously in this book, are searching for something. And as I reflect back on my life, I spent the first thirty years searching, longing and desiring. During the second thirty years I learned how to see life as a learning experience. I've learned and taught how to get very clear on what you want, release the unworthiness and begin attracting what you desire. In our early years we often set education as a goal in order to attain lifestyle comforts such as a soulmate, home, children and some amount of material wealth. And while all these things have helped me to relax and remember what my Guru in India taught me: to trust implicitly that all my needs were always being met, yet none of them, in and of themselves would truly satisfy me. There is a huge difference between being happy and being fulfilled. There is no amount of money, no amount of material possessions and no amount of worldly success that can satisfy the hunger of Spirit. Whatever leads us to Oneness and connection to Spirit is the activity for that day or that moment in time.

Nurturing, Nourishment and Attention

As I communicated with Nature on Easter Sunday, I realized how every plant was different, just like people. Some plants, like Dahlias, need a considerable amount of nurturing, protection from predators and a source of nutrients along with the sunshine and water. As they begin to grow, they really thrive and need less and less care. However, what I have learned from Peonies is that the less care they receive, the better they do. One year, I fertilized the peonies and it burnt up all the flowers. Not one of them bloomed. All the flower buds were brown and just shriveled up and dropped off!

I have experienced this same lesson over the years with the thousands of students that I have been blessed to train. Some of them come and are very needy at the beginning. Their egos want me to notice them, to praise them and to somehow make them special or different than the others. Of course I am happy to do that, since they are still tender young shoots and they need to be cultivated and fed. As they begin to grow and become more confident, they need less and less "special attention." Some of them really thrive on the nourishment that they receive. Then they can go out and give to others, as I have given to them. There are always, however, some peonies who really don't want or need too much attention. In fact they would feel smothered by the amount of attention that some of the others need. So I give these "peonies" their own space and just watch them grow and flower. At some point in their early lives, they have probably let their needs show and were burnt.

Jealousy, Unworthiness and Ego

The day that I sat with Amma among the giant Dahlia plants, she asked me to notice the honey bees flying from flower to flower. She said they are here to teach us about jealousy. They are not jealous of each other, they do not compare who got the most honey that day. The bees just go about and fulfill what Nature has set for them to do. They are fulfilled by being one with spirit every moment of the day. They have no ego and so they can just be. I noticed the same thing with each different type of flower plant. They don't say, "Your flowers are bigger than mine, you have so many more blossoms than I do or you bloom all summer while I only bloom in the spring!" In Nature everything instinctively knows its own individual nature and sets about fulfilling it. We as humans seem to have to discover what our purpose in life is. The sooner in our life process we can discover this, the more of our life we can spend in the state of Bliss and fulfillment.

I have known since high school that I am here to help others which lead me to psychology, my own self discovery process, traveling to India and finally to teaching spiritual healing work. So as I look back, I see that as humans, our nature is very complex. I am so clear that there are layers upon layers of purposes and relationships to be discovered in each and every one of us. No one ever gives us a clear map with directions to follow. That is why self-discovery is so important. As you can see from my own self-discovery process, it takes many twists and turns to discover your past lives, your unfinished relationships and even the karmic lessons that you have been brought here to learn.

I hope that from reading this book you will be inspired to make your life into fulfilling your Soul's purpose, whatever that may be. I pray that each moment brings peace and joy into your heart. Discover what feeds your soul. Ask yourself in each situation, "Is this in my highest good?"

Our Purpose in this Life on this Planet: Spiritual Yearning

It is so important to become and stay conscious of our purpose here on this planet. And it is so easy to become unconscious or distracted. It never ceases to amaze me that when we are awake, we can so easily put the connections together.

I have always thought that my spiritual journey began when I asked my parents to let me go to temple because of that longing I had inside. But now I remember that it began even earlier. When I was six, we lived in the city of Chicago. One time we were driving through Lincoln Park and I saw some people riding horses. I got very excited and told my mother I wanted to ride a horse. She pretty much dismissed the idea, thinking it was silly since we didn't live on a farm or anywhere near any horses.

Day after day, that longing grew and grew inside of me. I kept reminding her until she finally found the Ambassador Stables which was located right within Lincoln Park. As a six-year-old, I ended up finding a wonderful 75 year old man to be my horseback riding instructor at the stables. He and I immediately connected and "recognized" each other. He told me to call him "Pops" and I instantly became his favorite student. He was so familiar to me even when I was only six, that I now know that we definitely had a past life together. The life was as Natives riding horses through the mountains and onto the beaches and he was my father in that life.

I felt totally naturally high on horseback and loved to have the horse run fast through the trees to feel the wind in my face. It's one of my very first memories of feeling free and very connected to the earth.

I now know that this connection to the earth, and this longing to return to the earth came from Native past lives, including several with Pops and others. As a child I always wanted to go to camp so I could be out in the woods. My parents never quite understood this part of me since they were completely city people. The first thing I wanted to learn at camp was archery or how to use a bow and arrow. This all felt very natural to me. Sitting around a campfire singing songs and sharing stories was all part of coming home and discovering my past. I also loved to fish and they would take us out in boats to catch trout. I could sit all day fishing and just being there in the boat. I never minded baiting my own hook or taking the fish off the lines when some were caught. Many of the other kids hated touching the fish, were restless in the boats and in general were "homesick" at camp. They were afraid of the woods, hated the bugs and couldn't wait for their two weeks to be over. I kept begging my parents to let me stay all summer. To me camp was where I felt most at home. Now that I have discovered my true nature, it all makes a lot more sense to me.

During those years when I was riding horses and fishing, my mother would say to her friends and to family members, "I don't know where we got this child from. No one in our family has ever liked these things. Someone must have taken the wrong baby from the hospital!" She always was indicating how different I was from everyone else in our family, so I was ever grateful for my discovery of horses; riding became the love of my life during my childhood and even into my teens.

When I was a very small child I used to go with my father and his father to *shul* (temple). It was very orthodox and the men and women were separated. The men would all *daven* (pray in a bowing or rocking movement) repeating in Hebrew all the biblical prayers. I loved to go with my dad and grandfather and I would sit on the woman's side often with an aunt or with my grandmother. Even though I didn't understand the words, it felt very holy and safe to me to be there.

A few years later, I did experience that longing and did not connect it with the fact that my grandfather had died and my grandmother moved to New York. There was no more going to Orthodox shul since my mother wanted desperately to assimilate into modern American culture and wanted my father to do the same. They eventually moved to a reformed Jewish temple that I experienced as "watered down" with no mystical experiences at all. As a child I could see that my mother attended mostly for the social interaction it provided her and the sense of belonging in her community. My father was always very spiritual and taught me as much as he could.

After I rejected all organized religion, I went to India to have a direct spiritual experience and I hardly ever looked back. I learned the traditions of the mystics there and knew that was my path.

Recently, in my life with David, I have discovered him to be a wildly curious human being and very excited about learning, growing and serving. He is highly intelligent and soaks up all the psychology and spirituality he can. One day I happened to go searching for our local newspaper. I needed a handyman. I never read this paper since it was very limited in news. However, I happened to open up to a big beautiful picture of an Orthodox Rabbi and a big Menorah! I was quite surprised since our community has no temple. I read the article which said this learned Rabbi had moved here and was teaching Kaballah classes. I had always been interested in Kaballah since it was known to be the mystical part of the Jewish religion. I remember as a young person asking my father about it and he said that it wasn't allowed to be taught except to Rabbis.

Now here it would be offered by this beautiful Hasidic rabbi right here in our own community. I immediately called him up and we connected. David was excited to go with me and that began the full circle of returning to my roots. We attended every week and began to learn in a Judaic context all the things I had learned over the past thirty years through spirituality and hypnotherapy. The Kaballah verified all the work we had been doing in past lives and what we called Karmic Therapy. It explained all about the Soul in much more detail than we had ever imagined. We discovered this to be the richest teaching in spirituality so far. And it validated the work we had been doing and added so much more depth to it.

I am ever so grateful now to have a personal relationship with my rabbi and his wife and children. I notice that, unlike my parents, I am very uninterested in the social activities of the community because our healing community satisfies those needs for me. But I feel very grateful to have such a learned Rabbi in my life.

When David and I learned about how to manifest what we wanted in life, our journey became even more amazing. The past lives seemed to all come together as we became more aware of what we were drawing to us. I became more and more aware of the different threads flowing through my life like different colored ribbons. Each one was flowing through the breeze and as I took hold of it the colors became brighter.

Learning How to Manifest Our Dreams

Earlier I related the stories about how David and I came to live in the beautiful retreat where we have done our healing and teaching work. My living on this land before, riding horses to travel, hunting with bow and arrows, and fishing from the plentiful waters around the Pacific Northwest helped me to understand many of my lifelong interests (drives) such as horseback riding and fishing, drumming, and my strong connection with the sea.

It is now nearly twenty years later and we have indeed been living here on this land where we developed the retreat and healing center. Literally thousands of people have come here for classes, healing, meditation and spiritual connection. The Native American thread has been amazing to watch as it has continued to weave through our lives. In our first years of teaching I would bring a Native American tape to play so that we could sing and chant and drum together. We had no idea what we were singing, but it brought us all together in a very deep way.

Since that time, we have attracted many Natives, shamans and spiritual teachers to us. They have all brought their special gifts. Some taught us their cultures which we have incorporated into our teachings; some brought us behavior and boundary violations that were inconsistent with our spiritual beliefs. One of the biggest lessons was learning to discern the teachings consistent with our own integrity. We had to sift through many different sets of boundaries in order to discover what karmic lessons needed to be learned from each person who presented himself to us. These were sometimes painful lessons but more often they were joyful.

We have been blessed to have wonderful Natives come and build a sweat lodge on our property. They also come whenever we call to lead the sweat lodge ceremony for our students. They tell us that we feel like family to them and we feel the same about them. Each time I drum in the Native circles and participate in the sweat lodge, I know for sure that my past lives are coming together with my current life. And that another part of my dream is being fulfilled. Sitting in the sweat lodge with groups of our students, I again re-experience how ancient our soul connections are. I experience being one with every part of nature like the earth, the trees, the water and the sky.

I am so clear that our souls attract the people who have previously been in our soul-groups. One of the most important teachings I have gotten is that our soul groups have been together many times before in order to grow as community, to learn our tribal lessons and to learn to give and receive love.

Longing for Belonging

As long as you have a spiritual practice that helps you to feel the oneness. Whenever our mind is totally quiet, then all you hear is the name of God. God always hears you. Why me? Because you sincerely asked for God. Oneness with God. Sincerely ask. As you become one with God, the awareness that god is in our hearts…clearing out all the junk, negative self-messages, then all that is left is The oneness. We need to let it all go. God is not a specific person God is the energy of love that we feel.

Making Your Dreams Come True

What are your dreams? What is it that you want to make sure you do before you leave this planet? A lot of people answer this question by saying they want to travel and see the world. I was certainly able to do that in my younger years when I traveled on ships and followed my dream to go to India. However, David and I became clear that we wanted to travel as a way to serve others and to bring healing to other places in the world. We also knew that by doing this type of service, we would learn from others and also attract more karmic lessons for ourselves. So we meditated on this and asked Spirit to send us to three countries where we could serve humanity in some way. We made our request very clear and remained open as to what the Universe would bring to us. We meditated on this goal for several months.

Kuwait

One day we got a phone call from a man saying that the Amiri Diwan, the government of Kuwait, was inviting us to come and teach our courses in their country. We were stunned, as we had never thought of Kuwait as being a place that would be open to our work. When we did our manifestation process we were thinking of some European countries that were more Westernized. However, they said that they had been searching for training for their psychologists following the first Gulf War. These professionals needed to treat all the PTSD that had developed since Saddam's Iraqi army had invaded their country, raped their women and tortured their men.

As we traveled there, first class, we had no idea what to expect and wondered what our karmic lessons would be. Getting off the plane was quite a shock. It was definitely one of the most "foreign" countries we had ever seen. The men were all dressed in long white robes which we later learned were called dishdashas. They had headdresses which all seemed very strange especially since it was so hot there. The women all had long black dresses and many had their faces covered. My first thought was how in the world we were going to teach them our very Westernized approach to therapy.

We were treated like royalty, ushered through customs in two minutes and driven in a limo to one of the most luxurious hotels I'd ever seen. The people were very friendly and were most interested in getting to know us. We still weren't quite aware of why we had been invited there until our main driver began telling us of all the atrocities that had been committed, for no reason and without any warning. in his country by the Iraqi army. Suddenly it became clear that these peace-loving people had been severely traumatized and had no methods for dealing with the results of sudden trauma.

The Kuwaitis previously didn't even have a mental health system in place because they had no need for it. Now they were discovering so much depression, suicidal ideation, nightmares and all the many symptoms of Posttraumatic Stress Disorder. They had done the research to discover how successful hypnotherapy was for treating PTSD. Then they interviewed a wide range of American students and found that our school had the most positive feedback from previous students of all the other schools they had surveyed. That was quite a compliment to us, as we had been wondering how and why they invited us to their country to teach.

Our classes there were amazing as each person shared the stories of how their families had been brutalized for no reason. They felt so betrayed because many of the Kuwaiti people were married to Iraqis. They said their tribes had been connected for centuries and suddenly they had been attacked by their neighbors for no reason at all.

As we began doing the hypnotherapy sessions, we uncovered many women and young girls that had been raped and brutalized by Saddam's army. The men were beaten and terrorized and many of them shot in front of their family members. It soon became clear that the emotional release work that we do was very appropriate for them. Every session was so amazing as they used the techniques to release their anger, fear and shame. The healing was happening right before our eyes. One of the most healing experiences was hugging. The men were not allowed to hug in public or to hug any women. But they became more and more comfortable hugging each other and learning to comfort each other.

They invited us back again to complete the hypnotherapy training. Our spiritual calling to heal the healers and teach the teachers became even more clear to us. We felt amazed at how the Universe brought us to these people half-way around the world so that we could learn from them as much or more than they had learned from us. We learned that no matter how different people look on the outside, we humans are all so similar on the inside. The Kuwaiti people will always have a place in our hearts, regardless of the politics of governments.

One of our classes of psychotherapists in Kuwait, 1995

Taiwan

The second country to which we were invited was Taiwan, and it happened practically as we stepped off the plane returning home from Kuwait. A woman from Taiwan showed up in our very next class, in San Francisco. She let us know that she had been sent to our training from a university in Taipei to find the best hypnotherapy instructor to bring back to her country. We were amazed at how the manifestation principles work so quickly when our vision is clear. We spent several conversations during that training talking with her about what the university wanted and how we could work together to accomplish their mission as well as ours. We left for Taiwan several months later.

The people from Taiwan were very receptive to us and had state-of-the-art technology in place for the purposes of translation. They were dedicated students and had practically memorized the material even before we arrived. We had a huge class of over fifty people all eagerly awaiting our arrival. Again we wondered what the bigger picture was of why we had attracted these people to invite us to train in their country. They didn't have any apparent invasions from another country as we had encountered in Kuwait. It soon became apparent that there were several issues that needed to be addressed. The obvious one was that they were living in the shadow and under the constant threat of communist China. Again, like Kuwait, the people from mainland China were their own family members, uncles, cousins, sisters and brothers and even parents. And yet, the communist government of China had succeeded in turning these peace loving people into enemies. The theme of helping oppressed people to heal and reclaim their power became more and more clear each and every day that we were there.

Once the training began another very interesting theme became clear to us through our first demonstration session.

I worked with a young woman utilizing the Heart-Centered Hypnotherapy model. She volunteered to be subject in a demonstration session in a professional training setting. At first, she had a big smile on her face and she was about seven or eight months pregnant. She related that she had been very happy during her pregnancy until she had amniocentesis, which told her she was going to have a girl baby. She then began to feel a big pain in her solar plexus area, which had not gone away for two months.

As we talked, the feelings connected with this somatic pain narrowed down to fear and shame. We began hypnotherapy with the induction and then regressed to when she first got the news that she was going to have a girl baby. She began to cry when she realized that she was afraid to tell her husband and her family that it was a girl.

I then used an age regression to take her back to the source of these feelings. She first went back to one day when she was four years old and her mother was very angry at her for no reason at all. Her mother was looking at her with disgust and hatred and then began beating her. She was screaming and crying. I had her sit up, still in the trance state, and yell into a pillow so that she could release the feelings from her body. I asked her to express her anger by hitting a pillow on the bed. She was able to do that, reluctantly. When her feelings subsided, I laid her down to do another age regression.

I tapped on her forehead, taking her back to the source of all this fear and shame. Suddenly she was crying again and she was back in the womb. She intuitively felt that she was not wanted and that she would bring shame to her family. As she began to move through the birth canal, she had more and more shame as well as an intense amount of fear. She wanted to turn back, but realized that was not possible.

When she came out, she could instantly feel her mother's shame and disappointment. She was crying and saying, "I'll be very, very good. You won't be sorry that you had me. Please try to love me. I'll do everything that I can to make things okay." By that time, everyone in the room was weeping, even the men. It was as though all the participants could feel her intense pain and desire just to be loved and wanted. They felt her pain which also tapped into much of their own pain. Many of the women had similar experiences in their own childhood.

At this point, she began to express a lot of resentment. She was saying things like, "Why did you have me if you didn't want me? It wasn't my fault." I could hear the anger coming up in her voice. I sat her up, handed her a rubber hose and asked her to release the anger from her body by hitting down on the chair with the hose. She sat there holding it, shaking with anger, but fearful to let it out. "You're supposed to respect your parents, not get angry at them," she said.

"You are not hitting them," I responded, "just releasing the anger from your body so that you don't have that pain anymore. By releasing the resentments you have held inside for all these years, you will be able to love your parents more." Suddenly she began wailing away with the hose. She was crying and yelling, "How could you not love your own baby? You produced me, why didn't you love me? It was you that made me a girl anyway, it wasn't my doing."

When she had completed, I laid her back down and handed her a fluffy teddy bear. I asked her to let this represent her inner child who had just been born and to become the loving, nurturing parent who was so glad that she was born. She really connected with the "little child", caressing her and telling her all the positive things that she needed to hear. "I'm so glad you were born a little girl. Girls are very important. They have been given the magic gift of being able to give birth to babies. Without females, no one would have life. God doesn't make mistakes and God made you a girl."

As she hugged the inner child and repeated the affirmations that I was giving her, it felt like everyone in the room was bonded together. I then asked her to hold her inner child with one arm, and to bring her other hand to her girl baby inside, connecting with her. She immediately began to cry tears of joy, feeling so connected with her unborn child. She was now giving her the same affirmations that she had given her own inner child.

I also worked with the woman's twenty-five year old younger sister. She was a counselor taking the hypnotherapy training in Taiwan. She also had a smile on her face even though you could feel her pain just below the surface. She wanted to work on the feelings that came up when she was present for her sister's session. Her feelings of sadness were very strong and she did not know what they were about. We began working with her sadness, and almost immediately upon entering the trance state she began to cry what seemed to be endless tears.

I could feel her deep grief and I expressed that to her. I gave her permission to just let the grief come out. She didn't know what it was about and I told her that was okay. After about fifteen minutes of expressing that deep grief, I tapped her forehead and asked her to go back to the source of it. She was quiet for a few minutes and I asked her what was happening. She said it was very dark and warm and her head was hurting. These are very common signs of being in the womb and going through the birth canal. I asked her where she was and she said it felt like she was very, very little. She said she felt like she was inside of her mother. She began to cry and move around a lot, and her toes were moving as if she wanted to push. I put a pillow up against her toes and told her to push, which she did. I also pushed slightly on her head. This helps to give the infant the experience of moving out of the canal. After much struggle and intense crying, she was finally still and quiet.

She then began shaking and saying she was cold. This is a common experience for babies born in hospitals when they are laid on a cold metal table for some time until they can be washed off. But she was not in a hospital. This was a home-birth about twenty-five years ago in China. I couldn't quite figure out what was happening and so I asked her again, "What is happening now?" Suddenly she screamed out, "My father is trying to kill me. He has put me outside in the freezing night cold without a blanket." By now she was violently shivering and shaking. I put several blankets on her, but nothing seemed to help. Her experience of freezing was a body memory and had nothing to do with the actual temperature in the room. Suddenly she shouted out, "He's trying to kill me because I'm a girl!" Everyone present felt like we had been stabbed in the heart. Her pain and grief was so intense, we realized that during this whole session she had been grieving about the loss of herself!

I asked her to yell, but she was not yet in touch with her anger; the grief and sadness were just too overwhelming. Suddenly, she was quiet and a faint smile came over her face. She looked serene and peaceful and the shaking subsided. I asked her gently what was happening. She said her grandmother had come to the house and found her out in the cold. The grandmother instinctively knew that the father, in his deep cultural shame about having a fourth girl child, had put her out there to die. She picked her granddaughter up and quickly brought her back to the grandmother's home. She loved her and fed her and was determined to keep her granddaughter and raise her.

We used the grandmother's love as an anchor that she held in her hand over her Heart Center. This anchor helped to heal the inner child as we gave her the teddy bear and asked her to become the loving, nurturing parent for the infant baby. We gave her many of the same affirmations that we had given to her sister, but they had their own personal meaning to her. While we were completing the healing part of the session, we could feel her relaxing and melting into a place of Heart-Centered, unconditional love for herself. She said it was the first time she ever connected with herself inside. She liked that feeling and in that moment we knew that true healing had taken place.

The main issue that was coming up for her was gender shame. She stated that she had been in therapy for over five years and had never really gotten down to the core of her problem. She now realized that she could never have an on-going relationship with a man or a female friend because she always created some disagreement which caused them to go away or abandon her. Suddenly all her relationships made sense to her. She reported that her deep feelings of depression had lifted now that she had uncovered the family secret. There was a lot of family shame around her female existence which up until now had never been acknowledged or expressed. She felt very relieved to be able to discuss this with her sister and get the support from her that she needed.

One of the most powerfully healing parts of this session was the reaction of the rest of the class members. They all were wiping the tears from their eyes as their own cultural shame and grief emerged. During our group sharing session, many of them admitted that in their country male children were much more highly valued than females. During the communist domination, couples were only allowed to have one or two children. It was during those years that many female babies were killed so that they could still have the chance to have a baby boy. From the demonstration sessions we had done, one of the deepest cultural issues in Taiwan, emerged almost immediately. This human experience brought us all closer as we shared the pain of gender shame and the effect it actually had on these two beautiful young sisters.

While in Taiwan we trained a young male psychiatrist named Dana, who became very good friends with us. He arranged to show us around his country during our free time. He knew we felt very connected to Native

Americans and he wanted to introduce us to the Taiwanese indigenous people. Dana drove us up into the mountains to their reservation and we were in awe. They looked exactly like Native Americans except that they spoke Chinese. Their artwork and crafts were very similar to Native Americans, such as their pottery, jewelry, their drums and even their buckskin regalia. We spent several days speaking with them and finally learned that there used to be a land bridge that connected the two continents. Native peoples migrated from Asia across the land bridge in the Bering Sea and came down through Canada into the United States and down into Central America. Now I knew why we had been brought to Taiwan. By meeting these people we got the lesson that we are all connected! I know those words sound trite; however, they took on a whole new meaning to me at this moment. This longing for belonging suddenly made sense to me. My whole life I have been searching for connection and to discover who I am, who we all are. I have learned hypnotherapy so that I could discover my past lives. I have traveled all over the world and visited so many different cultures, always searching for that human connection. And here it is in Taiwan, brought to me by one of my students who has become one of my greatest teachers simply by introducing me to some of his friends.

One of our classes of psychotherapists in Taiwan, 1996

South Africa

We soon began to hear from one of our trainers that a woman from South Africa had come to our class in an effort to bring our hypnotherapy training to South Africa. We were very excited as I had always wanted to travel to Africa. I remembered that when I got married one of our family friends asked me, "What is your wildest dream that you would like to fulfill before you die?" and I replied, "To go to Africa." Again we were amazed at how our vision had manifested!

South Africa was only a couple of years post-apartheid, and needed training in treating PTSD. When we first arrived in Johannesburg, it did not appear to be as foreign as either Kuwait or Taiwan. The people spoke English but with a very heavy British accent. However, as we saw more and met more people, we began to really learn about the cultural differences. We learned about the white Afrikaaners who had similar values to the White Southerners in America during the first half of the 20th century. We were invited to take trips into some of the villages where black people lived and still farmed. We saw their children walking to school for hours through the mountains. We saw them herding sheep and goats and carrying heavy buckets of milk and water to their families.

Our real education, however, came through our students in the trainings. We insisted that our classes be integrated, and they were. In the regressions, we became aware of how the power structure of the country had totally shifted since the end of apartheid. The white power structure had now been largely transferred to the blacks. Government officials were mostly black and many whites, being in the minority, were feeling extremely vulnerable. Many hypnotherapy sessions in our training courses were about this power struggle and all the violence that was so prevalent in South Africa. Many whites felt terrorized by carjackings, robberies and the violence in the streets. Many blacks were reliving the recent past of being terrorized by the whites during apartheid.

Our techniques worked very well to help people express their feelings in healthy ways, to reclaim their self-esteem and release their shame. We were continually humbled by the healings that took place in our classes. One day we came into our advanced program to find a big argument taking place between the races. We saw that all the people from South Africa were victimized by the apartheid system, but on this day, they continued to blame and shame each other. We were just about to do a process to help folks release their underlying shame. So we felt it was no accident that this subject was up in a big way for all of them.

One of the white Afrikaaner farmers (let's call him Fred) was very upset because he had just learned that three of his long time friends and their families had been shot in cold blood by some blacks who were trying to take over their farmland as their own. As Fred did the release process, he was able to release some of the shame he carried over the violence he had participated in during the time when the whites were in power. Each member of the class was given a chance to release their own guilt and shame. It was very powerful and we all had tears in our eyes as we listened to the confessions of all of the races.

The last day of this training was one of the most healing and amazing memories that David and I have from our work in South Africa. A very quiet Black woman sat in the circle on Sunday morning and told us of her dream the night before. She said that she saw herself washing the feet of Fred, the Afrikaaner farmer. We said nothing, but David and I looked at each other smiling. We had a surprise process planned for their closing. It was, indeed a foot washing experience. We told people to get into groups of three without talking. As I looked around to see who had paired up together, I noticed that a few people had still not come into the room yet. Fred was one of them. At the last minute he appeared at the door and I told him to join any group that had room for him. The only place available was at the feet of the quiet black woman who had had the vision. He looked at me and I shrugged my shoulders as if to say, "there is only one place left for you." He took it and tears began to flow from my eyes. As he began to wash her feet, several people began to cry as we all felt the healing that was taking place right then and there. And then we asked the group to switch places so that those at the feet were sitting in the chair and those in the chair, were at the feet. Now the black woman was at Fred's feet, just as it had been in her dream, and she began to wash. She had tears streaming down her cheeks, as many of us did also. I felt like I was sitting in the middle of my dream come true. No one could have planned a more powerful healing experience if they had planned it for a year! All the work I had persevered during my lifetime in working with traumatized people such as the civil rights work in Mississippi during the sixties, in the women's movement during the seventies, and children who had been sexually abused in the eighties were all coalescing in this moment in Africa.

I began to realize that all humans experience suffering and at times it is our suffering that brings us together. That is what the longing for belonging has continued to teach me. In all the different cultures and countries, that is the one thread that ties all humans together. The strong desire to feel connected to other human beings. The strong desire to share our pain, our joy, our tears, our grief, our joy and our laughter. Our human suffering is bearable as long as it is witnessed, shared and accepted by others. It is the suffering together that makes our soldiers so bonded with their brothers in war. This is the only thing that makes war bearable at all.

And along with the deep suffering comes the deep longing for spiritual meaning in our lives. The longing for a deep heart centered connection with the Creator, with God or goddess, with Jesus or Moses or Allah or whatever name we use to bring that feeling of Oneness to ourselves. Every addict knows this longing and for years most people numb the pain of suffering and loneliness with food, sex, tobacco, alcohol, drugs or whatever else they can find. But once we stop numbing the pain, we can use the longing as a rocket launcher to take us to our highest goals.

One of our training groups in South Africa

The Pilgrimage of Transformation is never-ending:
We "end" where we started, but wiser.

Diane and David drumming at the sweat lodge

Notes

[1] Jelaluddin Rumi. (1995). "Love Dogs." In *The Essential Rumi*, translated by
Coleman Barks, pp. 155-156. San Francisco, CA: HarperSanFrancisco.

[2] Rabbi Menachem M. Schneerson, the Lubavitcher Rebbe, in a talk delivered on
February 12, 1979, translated by Naftali Silberberg. Available online at
http://www.chabad.org/therebbe/article_cdo/aid/480391/jewish/Searching-for-
G-d.htm.

[3] Emmet Fox. (1934). *The Sermon on the Mount: The Key to Success in Life*, 34-
35. San Francisco, CA: HarperSanFrancisco.

[4] The name for this concept was provided by William Emerson many years later.

[5] Isaac Landman, "Souls, Transmigration of" (*gilgul hanefish*).

[6] S. Ansky, *The Dybbuk*, pp. 71-72, 78-79.

[7] *Ibid.*, pp. 81, 101.

[8] Matthew 16:13-14

[9] Mathew 17:9-13

[10] Mathew 11:7, 10-11, 14-15

[11] Luke 1:17

[12] Pearsall, Schwartz, & Russek, Apr/May 2005.

[13] For example, see Fiore, 1987; Modi, 1997; Baldwin, 1992.

[14] Ham & Klimo, 2000.

[15] Chiron et al., 1997.

[16] Brewin, 2003.

[17] Gruzelier, 2006.

[18] Piontelli, 1992.

[19] Birnholz, 1981.

[20] Roffwarg, Muzio, & Dement, 1966.

[21] Anand & Hickey, 1987.

[22] Satt, 1984. Also Panneton, 1985.

[23] DeCasper & Spence, 1982. Also Woodward, 1992.

[24] Hepper, 1988 and 1991.

[25] van der Kolk, 1996.

[26] Pert, 1987. Also Pert, Ruff, Weber, & Herkenham, 1985.

[27] Verny & Weintraub, 2002, p. 159.

[28] Feldmar, 1979.

[29] Emerson, 1996.

[30] Bustan & Coker, Mar 1994.

[31] Allen, Lewinsohn, & Seeley, 1998.

[32] Downey & Coyne, 1990.

[33] Cantor-Graae, et al., 1994; Eagles, et al., 1990; Kinney, et al., 1994; Lewis &
Murray, 1987; O'Callaghan, et al., 1990; Parnas, et al., 1982.

[34] Woerner, Pollack, & Klein, 1973.

[35] Szatmari, Reitsma-Street, & Offord, 1986.

[36] Kinney, Yurgelun-Todd, Tohen, & Tramer, 1998.

[37] Bolon & St. Omer, 1992.
[38] DiPietro, Novak, Costigan, Atella, & Reusing, May 2006.
[39] Van den Bergh & Marcoen, July 2004.
[40] Ellis, Peckham, Ames, & Burke, 1988. See also Dörner, 1991.
[41] Bremner, Krystal, Charney, & Southwick, 1996.
[42] Wilson & McNaughton, 1998.
[43] Verny & Weintraub, 2002, p. 167.
[44] Bauer & Wewerka, 1995.
[45] Bohus, et al., 1978.
[46] Verny & Weintraub, 2002.
[47] Bowman, 1996.
[48] Bowman, 1996.
[49] Bowman, 1996.
[50] Facchinetti, Storchi, Petraglia, Garuti, & Genazzani, 1987.
[51] Anand & Hickey, 1987.
[52] Bieniarz, et al, 1968; Goodlin, 1979; Humphrey, et al, 1973.
[53] Grof, 1985.
[54] Feher, 1981, p. 188.
[55] Connor, 1977.
[56] Jung, 1959, p. 119.
[57] Boklage, 1995.
[58] Eugster & Vingerhoets, 1999.
[59] Bustan & Coker, 1994.
[60] Ferenczi, 1929.
[61] Salk, et al., 1985.
[62] Mednick, 1971.
[63] Lagercrantz & Slotkin, 1986.
[64] Flanagan, 1963; Guttmacher, 1956; Rodale, 1968.
[65] Spitz, 1962.
[66] Bovard, 1958; Weininger, 1954.
[67] Rice, 1977.
[68] Werner, 1989.
[69] Ritzman, 1984.
[70] Banner, 1969; Gemmette, 1982; Ritzman, 1988.
[71] Modlin, 1991.
[72] Grotberg, 1970.
[73] De Sousa, 1974.
[74] Janov, 1974b; Taylor, 1969; Wilcox & Nasrallah, 1987.
[75] Janov, 1974a; Roedding, 1991.
[76] Allen, 1987.
[77] Randolph, 1977.
[78] Van Zyl, 1977.
[79] Rosenthal, 1966; Torrey, 1977; Batchelor, et al., 1991.

[80] Bakan & Peterson, 1994.
[81] Hull, 1984 and 1986.
[82] Koelling, 1984.
[83] Verny, 1977.
[84] Mednick, 1971; Chamberlain, 1995.
[85] Zimberoff & Hartman, 1998.
[86] Givens, 1987.
[87] Feher, 1981.
[88] Barnett, 1987.
[89] Emerson, 1993.
[90] Ademec & Stark-Ademec, 1987.
[91] O'Keefe & Nadel, 1978.
[92] Etheridge, 1993, p. 41.
[93] Erikson, 1979, p. 60.
[94] Edinger, 1972, p. 5.
[95] Watkins, 1978.
[96] Watkins, 1993.
[97] Jung, 1959, p. 122.
[98] Jung, 1964, p. 161.
[99] Maslow, 1943, 1954, 1968, and 1971.
[100] Case, 1947, pp. 154-199.
[101] Erickson, 1950, p. 269.
[102] Levitan, 1985.
[103] Institute of Heartmath.
[104] Reich (1949); Lowen, 1967 and 1976.
[105] Affleck & Tennen, 1996; Silver, et al., 1983; Thompson, 1985.
[106] Nagy, 1991, p. 57.
[107] Plato, *The Phaedo*, quoted in Edinger, 1985, pp. 169-170.
[108] James & Goulding, 1998, p. 17.
[109] Rossi & Cheek, 1988.
[110] Hartman & Zimberoff, 2003, p. 116.
[111] Reich, 1949.
[112] Rothschild, 1998.
[113] Rothschild, 1998.
[114] Assagioli, 1971 and 1976.
[115] Moreno, 1946.
[116] Dayton, 1994.
[117] Piaget, 1947.
[118] A full explanation of this process can be found in Zimberoff, *Breaking Free from the Victim Trap* (2004 edition) on page 136.
[119] Reich, 1949.
[120] Janov, 1996, p. 230.
[121] Janov, 1996, pp. 225-228.

[122] Grof, 1985, pp. 387-390.

[123] Gellhorn & Keily, 1972; Hugdahl, 1996.

[124] Newberg & d'Aquili, 1994 and 2000.

[125] Childs-Gowell, 1992.

[126] The conceptualizations of the Victim Trap, with Victim, Rescuer, and Persecutor roles, derives from Eric Berne. In his seminal book *Games People Play*, Berne first elucidated his conceptualization of interactional roles between people as "Games." While he identified many different Games, one included the roles of "victim," "persecutor" and "rescuer." It was the Alcoholic Game (pages 73-81). He clearly describes with many examples how people in relationship with each other can shift from one role to another — from persecutor to rescuer, for example, and back again. I have adapted this conceptualization to explain a wide variety of dysfunctional codependent relationships.

    The graphical representation of it as a triangle was first proposed by Stephen Karpman (1968), calling it the "drama triangle." Ruppert & Ziff (1994) refer to the "Persecutor/ Rescuer/ Victim Triangle."

[127] Jung, 1959, pp. 125-127.

[128] Walsh & Vaughan, 1993, p. 112.

[129] Jung, 1959, p. 127.

[130] Jung, 1966, p.108.

[131] Metzner, 1998, p. 70.

References

Ademec, R. E., & Stark-Ademec, C. (1987). Behavioral inhibition and anxiety. In J. S. Reznick (Ed.), *Perspectives on Behavioral Inhibition*, 93-124. Chicago, IL: University of Chicago Press.

Affleck, G., & Tennen, H. (1996). Construing benefits from adversity: Adaptational significance and dispositional underpinnings. *Journal of Personality*, 64, 899-922.

Allen, B. P. (Summer 1987). Youth suicide. *Adolescence*, 22(86), 271-290.

Allen, N. B., Lewinsohn, P. M., & Seeley, J. R. (1998). Prenatal and perinatal influences on risk for psychopathology in childhood and adolescence. *Development and Psychopathology*, 10(3), 513-529.

Anand, K. J. S., & Hickey, P. R. (November 19, 1987). Pain and its effects in the human neonate and fetus. *New England Journal of Medicine*, 317(21), 1321-1329.

Ansky, S. (pseudonym for Solomon Judah Rapoport). (1926). *The Dybbuk*, trans. H. Alsberg and W. Katzin. New York: Boni & Liveright.

Assagioli, R. (1971). *The Act of Will*. Baltimore, MD: Penguin Books.

Assagioli, R. (1976). *Psychosynthesis*. New York: Penguin Books.

Bakan, P., & Peterson, K. (Winter 1994). Pregnancy and birth complications: A risk factor for schizotypy. *Journal of Personality Disorders*, 8(4), 299-306.

Baldwin, W. J. (1992). *Spirit Releasement Therapy: A Technique Manual*. Terra Alta, WV: Headline Books, Inc.

Banner, R. H. (1969). Anxiety, personality and birth delivery. Dissertation Abstracts International (Colorado State University). 29(10-B), 3906.

Barnett, E. A. (Spring 1987). The role of prenatal trauma in the development of the negative birth experience. *Pre- & Peri-Natal Psychology Journal*, 1(3), 191-207.

Batchelor, E. S., Jr., Dean, R. S., Gray, J. W., & Wenck, S. (1991). Classification rates and relative risk factors for perinatal events predicting emotional/behavioral disorders in children. *Pre- and Perinatal Psychology Journal,* 5(4), 327-346.

Bauer, P. J., & Wewerka, S. S. (1995). One- to two-year-olds' recall of events: The more expressed, the more impressed. *Journal of Experimental Child Psychology*, 59, 475-496.

Berne, E. (1964). *Games People Play: The Psychology of Human Relationships*. New York: Ballantine.

Bieniarz, J., Maqueda, E., Hashimoto, T., et al. (1968). Iotocaval compression by the uterus in late human pregnancy, 2, in Arteriographic Study, *American Journal of Obstetrics and Gynecology*, 100, 203-217.

Birnholz, J. C. (1981). The development of human fetal eye movement patterns. *Science*, 130, 679-681.

Bohus, B., et al. (1978). Oxytocin, vasopressin and memory: Opposite effects on consolidation and retrieval processes. *Brain Research*, 157, 414-417.

Boklage, C. E. (1995). Frequency and survival probability of natural twin conceptions. In L. G. Keith, E. Papiernil, D. M. Keith, & B. Luke (Eds.), *Multiple Pregnancy: Epidemiology, Gestation and Perinatal Outcome*. New York: Parthenon.

Bolon, B., & St. Omer, V. (1992). Biochemical correlates for behavioral deficits induced by Secalonic Acid D in developing mice. *Neuroscience and Biobehavioral Review*, 16, 171-175.

Bovard, E. (1958). The effects of early handling on viability of the albino rat. *Psychological Review*, 69(5), 257-269.

Bowman, E. S. (1996). Delayed memories of child abuse. Part I: An overview of research finding on forgetting, remembering, and corroborating trauma. *Dissociation*, 9, 221-231.

Bremner, J. D., Krystal, J. H., Charney, D. S., & Southwick, S. (1996). Neural mechanisms in dissociative amnesia for childhood abuse: Relevance to the current controversy surrounding the 'false memory syndrome.' *American Journal of Psychiatry*, 153, 7.

Brewin, C. (2003). *Posttraumatic Stress Disorder: Malady or Myth?* New Haven: Yale University Press.

Bustan, M. N., & Coker, A. L. (Mar 1994). Maternal attitude toward pregnancy and the risk of neonatal death. *American Journal of Public Health*, 84(3), 411-414.

Cantor-Graae, E., McNeil, T. F., Sjostrom, K., Nordstrom, L. G., & Rosenlund, T. (1994). Obstetric complications and their relationship to other etiological risk factors in schizophrenia. *Journal of Nervous and Mental Disorders*, 182(11), 645-650.

Case, P. F. (1947). *The Tarot: A Key to the Wisdom of the Ages*. New York: Macoy Publishing.

Chamberlain, D. B. (Winter 1995). What babies are teaching us about violence. *Pre- and Perinatal Psychology Journal*, 10(2), 57-74.

Childs-Gowell, E. (1992). *Good Grief Rituals: Tools for Healing*. Station Hill Press.

Chiron, C., Jambaque, I., Nabbout, R., Lounes, R., Syrota, A., & Dulac, O. (1997). The right brain is dominant in human infants. *Brain*, 120, 1057-1065.

Connor, L. (1977). Cesarean birth. *Birth and the Family Journal*, 4(3), 106-115.

Dayton, T. (1994). *The Drama Within: Psychodrama and Experiential Therapy*. Deerfield Beach, FL: Health Communications.

DeCasper, A., & Spence, M. (1982). Prenatal maternal speech influences human newborn's auditory preferences. *Infant Behavior and Development*, 9, 133-150.

De Sousa, A. (Jan. 1974). Causes of behaviour problems in children. *Child Psychiatry Quarterly*, 7(1), 3-8.

DiPietro, J. A., Novak, M. F. S. X., Costigan, K. A., Atella, L. D., & Reusing, S. P. (May 2006). Maternal psychological distress during pregnancy in relation to child development at age two. *Child Development*, 77(3), 573-587.

Dörner, G. (1991). Hormone-dependent brain development and behavior. *International Journal of Prenatal and Perinatal Studies*, 3(3/4), 183-189.

Downey, G., & Coyne, J. C. (1990). Children of depressed parents: An integrative review. *Psychological Bulletin*, 108, 50-76.

Eagles, J. M., Gibson, I., Bremner, M. H., Clunie, F., Ebmeier, K. P., & Smith, N. C. (1990). Obstetrical complications in DSM-III schizophrenics and their siblings. *Lancet*, 335, 1139-1141.

Edinger, E. F. (1972). *Ego and Archetype: Individuation and the Religious Function of the Psyche*. Boston: Shambhala Publications.

Ellis, L., Peckham, W., Ames, M. A., & Burke, D. (1988). Sexual orientation of human offspring may be altered by severe maternal stress during pregnancy. *Journal of Sex Research*, 25(1), 152-157.

Emerson, W. (1993). *Treating Birth Trauma During Infancy: Dynamic Outcomes*. Petaluma, CA: Emerson Training Seminars.

Emerson, W. (1996). The vulnerable prenate. *Pre- and Perinatal Psychology Journal*, 10(3), 12-130.

Erikson, E. H. (1950). *Childhood and Society*. New York: W.W. Norton.

Erikson, E. H. (1979). Reflections on Dr. Borg's life cycle. In D. D. Van Tassel (Ed.), *Aging, Death, and the Completion of Being*, 29-67. Philadelphia, PA: University of Pennsylvania Press.

Ethridge, C. (1993). Treating psychological problems through prenatal recall. *Regression Therapy: A Handbook for Professionals, Vol. 2: Special Instances of Altered State Work*, 43-55. Crest Park, CA: Deep Forest Press.

Eugster, A., & Vingerhoets, A. J. (Mar 1999). Psychological aspects of in vitro fertilization: a review. *Social Science & Medicine*, 48(5), 575-589.

Facchinetti, E., Storchi, A. R., Petraglia, F., Garuti, G., & Genazzani, A. R. (1987). Ontogeny of pituitary B-endorphin and related peptides in the human embryo and fetus. *American Journal of Obstetrics and Gynecology*, 156(3), 735-739.

Feher, L. (1981). *The Psychology of Birth: Roots of Human Personality*. New York: Continuum.

Feldmar, A. (1979). The embryology of consciousness: What is a normal pregnancy? In D. Mall & W. Watts (Eds.), *The Psychological Aspects of Abortion*, 15-24. University Publications of America.

Ferenczi, S. (1929). The unwelcome child and his death drive. In J. Borossa (Ed.), *Selected Writings*, 269-274. Harmondsworth Penguin, 1999.

Fiore, E. (1987). *The Unquiet Dead*. New York: Doubleday.

Flanagan, G. (1963). *First Nine Months of Life*. London: Heineman.

Gellhorn, E., & Keily, W. F. (1972). Mystical states of consciousness: Neurophysiological and clinical aspects. *Journal of Nervous and Mental Disease*, 154, 399-405.

Gemmette, E. V. (June 1982). Anxiety associated with birth trauma. *Psychological Reports*, 50(3, Pt 1), 942.

Givens, A. (Spring 1987). The Alice Givens approach to prenatal and birth therapy. *Pre- & Peri-Natal Psychology Journal*, 1(3), 223-229.

Goodlin, R. J. (1979). Aortocaval compression during cesarean section: A cause of newborn depression. *Obstetrics and Gynecology*, 37, 702-705.

Grof, S. (1985). *Beyond the Brain: Birth, Death, and Transcendence in Psychotherapy*. Albany, NY: State University of New York Press.

Grotberg, E. H. (June 1970). Neurological aspects of learning disabilities: A case for the disadvantaged. *Journal of Learning Disabilities*, 3(6), 321-327.

Gruzelier, J. H. (2006). Frontal functions, connectivity and neural efficiency underpinning hypnosis and hypnotic susceptibility. *Contemporary Hypnosis*, 23(1), 15-32.

Guttmacher, A. F. (1956). *Pregnancy and Birth*. New York: Signet.

Ham, J. T., & Klimo, J. (2000). Fetal awareness of maternal emotional states during pregnancy. *Journal of Prenatal and Perinatal Psychology and Health*, 15(2), 118-145.

Hartman, D., & Zimberoff, D. (2003). Hypnotic trance in Heart-Centered therapies. *Journal of Heart-Centered Therapies*, 6(1), 105-122.

Hepper, P. G. (1988). Foetal 'soap' addiction. *Lancet*, ii, 1347-1348.

Hepper, P. G. (1991). An examination of fetal learning before and after birth. *Irish Journal of Psychology*, 12, 95-107.

Hugdahl, K. (1996). Cognitive influences on human autonomic nervous system function. *Current Opinion on Neurobiology*, 6, 252-258.

Hull, W. F. (January 1984). Prenatal oxygen deprivation, the source of birth trauma. *Medical Hypnoanalysis Journal*, 5(1), 7-16.

Hull, W. F. (Winter 1986). Psychological treatment of birth trauma with age regression and its relationship to chemical dependency. *Pre- & Peri-Natal Psychology Journal*, 1(2), 111-134.

Humphrey, M., Hounslow, P., Morgan, S., & Wood, C. (1973). The influence of maternal posture at birth on the fetus. *Journal of Obstetrics and Gynecology for the British Commonwealth*, 80, 1075-1080.

Institute of HeartMath. See archives of supporting documentation at the website http://www.heartmath.com.

Jacobson, B., Eklund, G., Hamberger, L., Linnarsson, D., et al. (October 1987). Perinatal origin of adult self-destructive behavior. *Acta Psychiatrica Scandinavica*, 76(4), 364-371.

James, M., & Goulding, M. (1998). Self-reparenting and redecision. *Transactional Analysis Journal*, 28(1), 16-19.

Janov, A. (Winter 1974a). Further implications of "levels of consciousness": On suicide. *Journal of Primal Therapy*, 1(3), 197-200.

Janov, A. (Spring 1974b). On psychosis. *Journal of Primal Therapy*, 1(4), 331-341.

Janov, A. (1996). *Why You Get Sick, How You Get Well*. West Hollywood, CA: Dove Books.

Jung, C. G. (1959). *The Archetypes and the Collective Unconscious.* Princeton, NJ: Princeton University Press.

Jung, C. G. (1964). *Man and His Symbols.* Garden City, NY: Doubleday.

Jung, C. G. (1966). *The Practice of Psychotherapy.* Princeton, NJ: Princeton University Press.

Karpman, S. B. (1968). Fairy tales and script drama analysis. *Transactional Analysis Bulletin*, 7, 39-43.

Kinney, D. K., Levy, D. L., Yurgelun-Todd, D. A., Medoff, D., Lajonchere, C. M., & Radford-Paregol, M. (1994). Season of birth and obstetrical complications in schizophrenics. *Journal of Psychiatric Research*, 28(6), 499-509.

Kinney, D. K., Yurgelun-Todd, D. A., Tohen, M., & Tramer, S. (September 1, 1998). Pre- and perinatal complications and risk for bipolar disorder: A retrospective study. *Journal of Affective Disorders*, 50(2-3), 117-124.

Koelling, L. H. (January 1984). Birth trauma and psychosomatic illness in children and adolescents. *Medical Hypnoanalysis*, 5(1), 34-41.

Lagercrantz, H., & Slotkin, T. (1986). The stress of being born. *Scientific American*, 254, 100.

Landman, I. (1942). "Souls, Transmigration of" (gilgul hanefish). *Universal Jewish Encyclopedia.*

Levitan, A. A. (1985). Hypnotic death rehearsal. *American Journal of Clinical Hypnosis*, 27(4), 211-215.

Lewis, S. W., & Murray, R. M. (1987). Obstetric complications, neuro-developmental deviance and risk of schizophrenia. *Journal of Psychiatric Research*, 21, 413-421.

Lowen, A. (1967). *The Betrayal of the Body.* New York: Macmillan.

Lowen, A. (1976). *Bioenergetics.* New York: Penguin Books.

Maslow, A. (1943). A theory of human motivation. *Psychological Review*, 50, 370-396.

Maslow, A. H. (1954). *Motivation and Personality.* New York: Harper & Row.

Maslow, A. (1968). *Toward a Psychology of Being*, second edition. Princeton, NJ: Van Nostrand.

Maslow, A. (1971). *The Farther Reaches of Human Nature.* New York: Viking.

Mednick, S. A. (1971). Birth defects and schizophrenia. *Psychology Today*, 4, 49.

Metzner, R. (1998). *The Unfolding Self: Varieties of Transformational Experience.* Novato, CA: Origin Press.

Modi, S. (1997). *Remarkable Healings: A Psychiatrist Discovers Unsuspected Roots of Mental and Physical Illness.* Charlottesville, VA: Hampton Roads Publishing Company.

Modlin, C. T. (June 1991). The origin and treatment of conduct and antisocial personality disorder. *Medical Hypnoanalysis Journal*, 6(2), 69-76.

Moreno, J. L. (1946). *Psychodrama: Volume One.* Beacon, NY: Beacon House.

Nagy, M. (1991). The *lumen naturae*: Soul of the psychotherapeutic relationship. In K. Gibson, D. Lathrop, & E. M. Stern (Eds.), *Carl Jung and Soul Psychology*, 55-61. Binghamton, NY: Harrington Park Press.

Newberg, A. B., & d'Aquili, E. G. (1994). The near death experience as archetype: A model for 'prepared' neurocognitive processes. *Anthropology of Consciousness*, 5, 1-15.

Newberg, A. B., & d'Aquili, E. G. (2000). The neuropsychology of religious and spiritual experience. In J. Andresen & R. K. C. Forman (Eds.), *Cognitive Models and Spiritual Maps: Interdisciplinary Explorations of Religious Experience*, 251-266. Charlottesville, VA: Imprint Academic.

O'Callaghan, E., Larkin, C., & Waddington, J. L. (1990). Obstetric complications in schizophrenia and the validity of maternal recall. *Psychological Medicine*, 20, 89-94.

O'Keefe, J., & Nadel, L. (1978). *The Hippocampus as a Cognitive Map*. Oxford: Clarendon Press.

Panneton, R. K. (1985). Prenatal Auditory Experience with Melodies: Effect on Post-Natal Auditory Preferences in Human Newborns. Dissertation, University of North Carolina, Greensboro.

Parnas, J., Schulsinger, F., Teasdale, T. W., Schulsinger, H., Feldman, P. M., & Mednick, S. A. (1982). Perinatal complications and clinical outcome within the schizophrenia spectrum. *British Journal of Psychiatry*, 140, 416-420.

Pearsall, P., Schwartz, G. E., & Russek, L. G. (Apr/May 2005). Organ transplants and cellular memories. *Nexus Magazine*, 12(3). Available online http://www.nexusmagazine.com/articles/CellularMemories.html.

Pert, C. (1987). Neuropeptides, the emotions and bodymind. In J. Spong (Ed.), *Proceedings of the Symposium on Consciousness and Survival*, 79-89. Institute of Noetic Sciences.

Pert, C., Ruff, M., Weber, R. J., & Herkenham, M. (1985). Neuropeptides and their receptors: A psychosomatic network. *Journal of Immunology*, 135(2), Supplement, 820-826.

Piaget, J. (1947, in English 1950). *The Psychology of Intelligence*. London: Routledge & Kegan Paul.

Piontelli, A. (1992). *From Fetus to Child*. London: Routledge.

Randolph, B. M. (Jan-Mar 1977). Birth and its effects on human behavior. *Perspectives in Psychiatric Care*, 15(1), 20-26.

Reich, W. (1949). *Character Analysis*. New York: Noonday Press.

Rice, R. (1977). Neurophysiological development in premature infants following stimulation. *Developmental Psychology*, 13(1), 69-76.

Ritzman, T. A. (May 1984). Stress and the birth experience. *Medical Hypnoanalysis*, 5(2), 51-56.

Ritzman, T. A. (Sept 1988). The cause and treatment of anxiety. *Medical Hypnoanalysis Journal*, 3(3), 95-114.

Rodale, J. I. (1968). *Natural Health and Pregnancy*. New York: Pyramid.

Roedding, J. (1991). Birth trauma and suicide: A study of the relationship between near-death experiences at birth and later suicidal behavior. *Pre- and Perinatal Psychology Journal*, 6(2), 145-167.

Rottwarg, H. A., Muzio, J. N., & Dement, W. C. (1966). Ontogenetic development of the human sleep-dream cycle. *Science*, 152, 604-619.

Rosenthal, D. (1966). The offspring of schizophrenic couples. *Journal of Psychiatric Research*, 4, 169-188.

Rossi, E. L., & Cheek, D. (1988). *Mind-Body Therapy: Ideodynamic Healing in Hypnosis.* New York: W. W. Norton.

Rothschild, B. (Feb 1998). Post-traumatic stress disorder: Identification and diagnosis. *The Swiss Journal of Social Work.* Online at http://www.healing-arts.org/index2.htm.

Ruppert, E., & Ziff, J. (July 1994). The mind, body, and soul of violence. *Transactional Analysis Journal*, 24(3), 161-177.

Salk, L., et al. (1985). Relationship of maternal and perinatal conditions to eventual adolescent suicide." *The Lancet*, 1, 624-627.

Satt, B. J. (1984). *An Investigation into the Acoustical Induction of Intrauterine Learning.* Dissertation, California School of Professional Psychology, Los Angeles.

Silver, R. L., Boon, C., & Stones, M. H. (1983). Searching for meaning in misfortune: Making sense of incest. *Journal of Social Issues*, 39, 81-102.

Spitz, R. R. (1962). Hospitalism: An inquiry into the genesis of psychotic conditions in early childhood. *The Psychoanalytic Study of the Child*, Vol. 1. New York: International University Press.

Szatmari, P., Reitsma-Street, M., & Offord, D. R. (1986). Pregnancy and birth complications in antisocial adolescents and their siblings. *Canadian Journal of Psychiatry*, 31, 513-516.

Taylor, M. A. (1969). Sex ratios of newborns associated with prepartum and postpartum schizophrenia. *Science*, 164, 723-724.

Thompson, S. C. (1985). Finding positive meaning in a stressful event and coping. *Basic and Applied Social Psychology*, 6, 279-295.

Torrey, E. F. (1977). Birth weights, perinatal insults, and HLA types: Return to "original din." *Schizophrenia Bulletin*, 3(3), 347-351.

Van den Bergh, B. R. H., & Marcoen, A. (July 2004). High antenatal maternal anxiety is related to ADHD symptoms, externalizing problems, and anxiety in 8- and 9-year-olds. *Child Development*, 75(4), 1085.

van der Kolk, B. A. (1996). The body keeps the score. In B. A. van der Kolk, A. C. McFarlane, & L. Weisaeth (Eds.), *Traumatic Stress: The Effects of Overwhelming Experience on Mind, Body and Society.* New York: The Guilford Press.

Van Zyl, D. A. (Fall 1977). Traumatic birth symbolized in play therapy. *Journal of Primal Therapy*, 4(2), 154-158.

Verny, T. (November 1977). *The Psychic Life of the Unborn.* Fifth World Congress of Psychosomatic Obstetrics and Gynecology, Rome.

Verny, T. R., & Weintraub, P. (2002). *Tomorrow's Baby: The Art and Science of Parenting from Conception through Infancy.* New York: Simon & Schuster.

Walsh, R., & Vaughan, F. (1993). Transpersonal dimensions of development. In R. Walsh & F. Vaughan (Eds.), *Paths Beyond Ego: The Transpersonal Vision*, 109-115. New York: Jeremy P. Tarcher/Putnam.

Watkins, H. H. (Apr 1993). Ego-state therapy: An overview. *American Journal of Clinical Hypnosis*, 35(4), 232-240.

Watkins, J. G. (1978). *The Therapeutic Self.* New York: Human Sciences Press.

Weininger, O. (1954). Physiological damage under stress as a function of early experience. *Science*, 119, 285-286.

Werner, E. (1989). Children of the Garden Island. *Scientific American*, 260, 106-111.

Wilcox, J. A., & Nasrallah, H. A. (1987). Perinatal distress and prognosis of psychotic illness. *Neuropsychobiology*, 17(4), 173-175.

Wilson, M., & McNaughton, B. (August 29, 1998). Memory building. *The Economist*.

Woerner, M. G., Pollack, M. U., & Klein, D. F. (1973). Pregnancy and birth complications in psychiatric patients: A comparison of schizophrenic and personality disorder patients with their siblings. *Acta Psychiatrica Scandinavica*, 49, 712-721.

Woodward, S. C. (1992). *The Transmission of Music into the Human Uterus and the Response to Music of the Human Fetus and Neonate*. Dissertation, University of Capetown, South Africa.

Zimberoff, D. (2004). *Breaking Free from the Victim Trap: Reclaiming Your Personal Power*. Issaquah, WA: Wellness Press.

Zimberoff, D., & Hartman, D. (1998). Insidious trauma caused by prenatal gender prejudice. *Journal of Prenatal and Perinatal Psychology and Health,* 13(1), 45-51.

Index

PERSONAL TRANSFORMATION

Breaking Free from the Victim Trap
Fourth printing 2004: over 30,000 books in print

This book has changed the lives of tens of thousands of readers.

It is written clearly and simply, yet carries a profound message of hope. The damage has been done, but the good news is that each of us can repair that damage.

The Victim Game is a family game taught to children in three ways.

The first is by direct example since one or more of the parents is usually a victim in families where this game is played.

Second, the child is programmed by the parent to be a victim.

Third, the victim behavior is reinforced by the parent until it becomes a permanent part of the child's identity.

The child goes through life then having one victim experience after another and each experience reinforces this person's victim position.

The Victim Game can be stopped and changed, but it takes (1) desire to change; (2) awareness; and (3) intensive therapy to change the subconscious programming.

Now, BREAKING FREE from the VICTIM TRAP
The <u>Audio</u> Program

This CD is a companion experience to the book. It is not an audio reading of the book.

Discounts for quantity purchases.

Track 1
INTRODUCTION to BREAKING FREE from the VICTIM TRAP

1. The Law of Attraction
2. Healing through Relationships
3. Addiction to the Drama
4. Reclaiming Personal Power

Track 2
HEALING *VICTIM* CONSCIOUSNESS HYPNOTHERAPY EXPERIENCE

1. Discovering Your Safe Place
2. Identifying Current **Victim** Patterns
3. Discovering the Source of the **Victim**
4. Releasing the Feelings
5. Nurturing the Inner Child
6. Creating a New Healthy Pattern
7. Empowerment Affirmations

Track 3
HEALING VICTIM CONSCIOUSNESS
Beautiful Butterfly (Bobbi Branch)

Track 4
HEALING *RESCUER* CONSCIOUSNESS HYPNOTHERAPY EXPERIENCE

1. Discovering Your Safe Place
2. Identifying Current **Rescuer** Patterns
3. Discovering the Source of the **Rescuer**
4. Releasing the Feelings
5. Nurturing the Inner Child
6. Creating a New Healthy Pattern
7. Empowerment Affirmations

Track 5
HEALING RESCUER CONSCIOUSNESS
Sing Your Own Song (Bobbi Branch)

Track 6
HEALING *PERSECUTOR* CONSCIOUSNESS HYPNOTHERAPY EXPERIENCE

1. Discovering Your Safe Place
2. Identifying Current **Persecutor** Patterns
3. Discovering the Source of the **Persecutor**
4. Releasing the Feelings
5. Nurturing the Inner Child
6. Creating a New Healthy Pattern
7. Empowerment Affirmations

THE WELLNESS INSTITUTE

Collecting Lessons: A Fable

By David Hartman

The stories in this book combine the primeval earth wisdom of indigenous peoples with cutting edge neuroscience and perennial spiritual wisdom.

With these stories, you will have fun and learn ways to progress on your path.

This book offers an intriguing story told by a compelling storyteller. It combines folklore, fairy tales, appreciation for our interdependence with nature, state-of-the-art trauma neuroscience, and ancient wisdom (Buddhist, Kabbalah, Tarot, Sufi, and Perennial Wisdom) in a playful, entertaining format: a fable in the tradition of Carlos Castaneda's recounting of *The Teachings of Don Juan* or Aesop's wisdom tales. The story presents practical life lessons to ease the reader through six stages of spiritual unfoldment. In this book the teachings come directly from power animals, and will inspire the reader to discover steps on their own practical path toward fulfillment. The ideas presented are carefully annotated in extensive endnotes for those who want sources.

PERSONAL TRANSFORMATION

Self-Improvement Audio Programs
by Diane Zimberoff

Audio Programs on CD

1. Codependency
2. Extinguishing Unwanted Behaviors
3. Healing and meditation
4. Prosperity
5. Self-esteem and Parenting
6. Self-hypnosis Program
7. Strengthening the Immune System
8. Visualization & Eliminating Stress

Order these and other audio programs today!

Call our office at 800-326-4418
or
Visit our online store
www.wellness-institute.org

The Chakras Meditation
2 CD set

FIRST CD
Track 1
INTRODUCTION TO MEDITATION
1. Creating Sacred Space
2. Benefits of Chakra Meditation
3. Quieting the Mind
4. Receiving a Spiritual Mantra

Track 2
ACTIVATING LOWER CHAKRAS
1. Connecting with the Earth
2. Power Animal's Message
3. Cleansing the Chakras
4. Release Energetic Drains
5. Connecting with Divine Presence

Track 3
ACTIVATING HIGHER CHAKRAS
1. Cleansing the Higher Chakras
2. Heart Space above the Head
3. Compassion for Humanity
4. Soul Retrieval
5. Aura Expansion & Healing Energy

SECOND CD
Track 1
SOUL RETRIEVAL MEDITATION
1. Discovering Soul-splits in each Chakra
2. Cleansing Soul Fragments
3. Reclaiming Soul Fragments
4. Hearing your Soul's Message
5. Embracing the Symbol in each Chakra
6. Sealing the Soul in each Chakra

Track 2
MIND - BODY - SPIRIT HEALING
1. Pranayama Breathing
2. Discovering the Glands, Hormones and Organs in each Chakra
3. Manifesting Healing in each Chakra
4. Affirmations for Mind-Body Healing
5. Focusing on specific areas for Increased Healing
6. Calling in your Healing Angels

Divine Mother and Power Animal Meditations

Track 1
CALLING IN THE DIVINE MOTHER

1. The Root Chakra - Lakshmi
2. The Sacral Chakra - Shakti
3. The Solar Plexus Chakra - Kali
4. The Heart Chakra - Durga
5. The Throat Chakra - Saraswati
6. The Third Eye Chakra - Parvati
7. The Crown Chakra – Narayani/Ishwari

Track 2
POWER ANIMAL MEDITATION

Discovering the Power Animal
in each Chakra

Finding the individual message
carried by each animal
for your healing
and personal growth

$\mathcal{P}$ersonal $\mathcal{T}$ransformation $\mathcal{I}$ntensive
PTI

Find a PTI near you

www.PTIntensive.com

This is a profoundly healing group process, meeting for five weekend retreats over five months, in a loving environment. Do you long for these changes in your life?

Attract Healthy, Loving, Fulfilling Relationships
Belong to a new healthy, high-powered family • Develop close in-depth friendships instead of "cocktail party superficial phoniness" • Learn healthy support (not competition) • Learn to love yourself so you can love others

Experience Personal Growth and Transformation
Self-awareness • Higher consciousness • Self-discovery

Manifest Your Goals using the full power of your mind:
It's time to stop wanting things to happen in your life and time to start making things happen • Learn to use 100% of your mind to reach your full potential with a new goal-setting process • Discover your unconscious goals • Get clear on what you want • Become a member of a Master Mind Group

Improved Health with Powerful Stress Reduction Tools
Learn messages that your body is telling you • Release body hatred and shame • Relaxation Anchors • Heart-centered meditation • Conscious Breathing

Improved Finances
Prosperity and abundance principles • Master Mind groups • Learn the role of integrity in creating your abundance

Release Self -Defeating Patterns
Procrastination • "Victim, Rescuer, Persecutor" • Fear-based decisions (learn to make clear decisions) • Codependency • Unhealthy relationship patterns

Improved Communication Skills
Learn "The Clearing Process" • Stop "The Blame Game"

Take Full Responsibility for your Life!
Stop sabotaging yourself • Learn accountability and integrity • Release the shame which diminishes your self-esteem • Release self-judgment, self-blame

THE WELLNESS INSTITUTE
800-326-4418

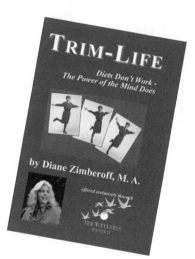

Journal of Heart-Centered Therapies

Selected articles
APPROVED
for
Distance CE credit
(5 hours each)

APPROVALS:

Social Workers
The Wellness Institute is approved as a provider for distance continuing education by The National Association of Social Workers (NASW) to offer 5 hours of credit for each Journal article (provider # 886422919).

Professional Counselors
The Wellness Institute is recognized by the National Board of Certified Counselors to offer continuing education for certified counselors. We adhere to NBCC continuing education guidelines. Provider #5460 (5 hours of credit for each Journal article).

There are test questions and a fee of $50.

For complete details, call 800-326-4418, or go to:
http://www.heartcenteredtherapies.org/Journal/Distance_Learning_CEUs.htm

The Heart-Centered Therapies Association
3716 - 274th Ave SE, Issaquah, WA 98029 ❖ 425-391-9716 ❖ 800-326-4418

Index of Back Issues of the Journal
(all available)

The Heart-Centered Therapies Association
3716 - 274th Avenue SE, Issaquah, WA 98029 USA ❖ 425-391-9716 ❖ 800-326-4418